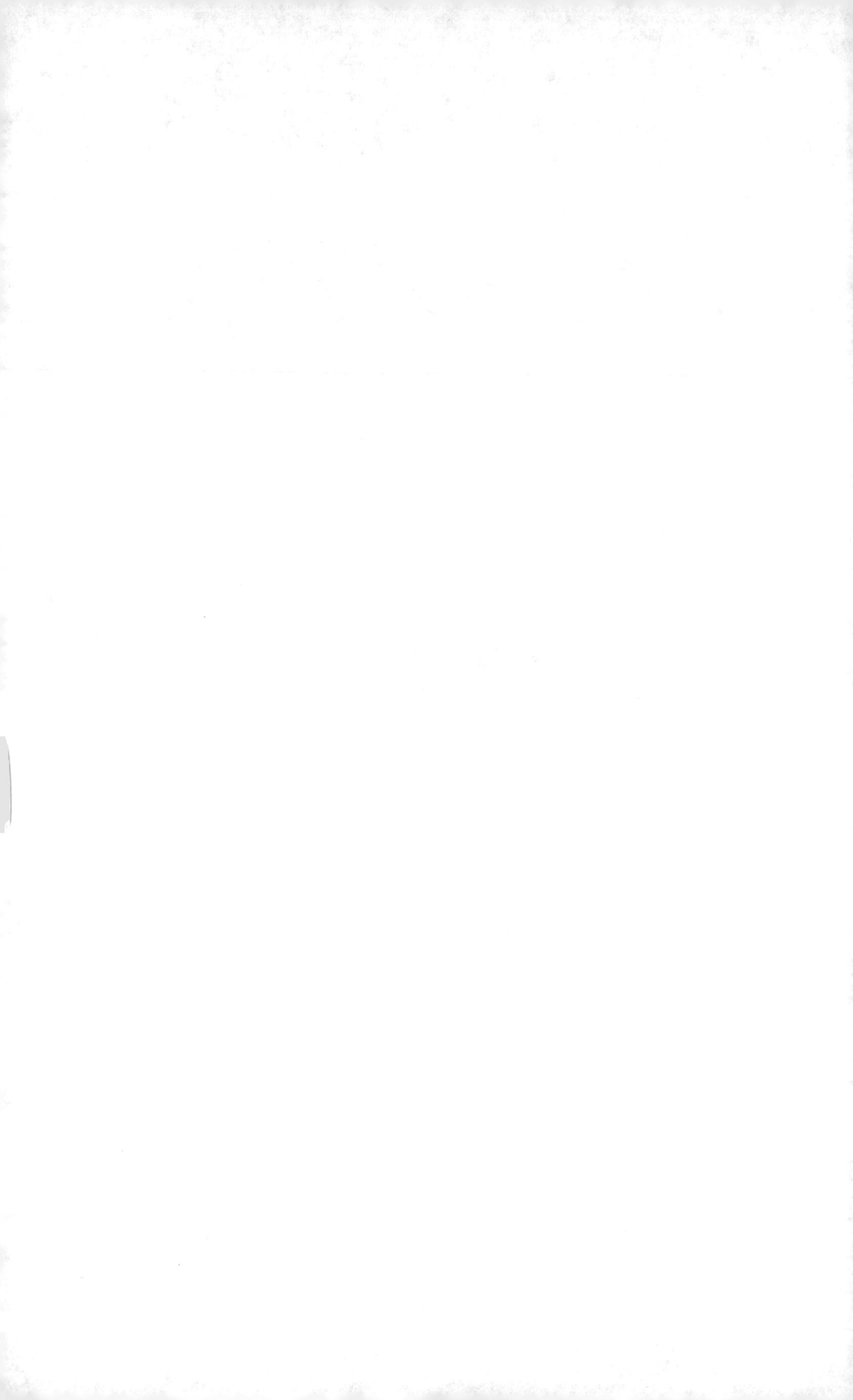

F. X. Blanchet.

TESTIMONIALS.

CHURCH OF ST. CHARLES BORROMEO,
SYDNEY PLACE,
BROOKLYN, August 28, 1874.

Rev. dear Father Müller:

I have carefully read and examined your excellent manuscript, entitled "Familiar Explanations," etc. As far as I can judge, it is a clear, sound, orthodox exposition of Catholic doctrine, in a form of question and answer, which cannot fail to be extremely useful for the right understanding of the truths, commandments, and sacraments of our holy religion. Particularly useful seem to be the parts which explain the True Faith, the True Church, the Infallibility of the Pope, and, well, I should have to mention every chapter, from the beginning to the end. It is another great Godsend for these days of unbelief and corruption.

I am your humble servant in the Sacred Hearts of Jesus and Mary,

FRANCIS J. FREEL, D.D.

(From Rev. A. Konings, C.S.S.R., Professor of Moral Theology and Canon Law.)

Ilchester, Howard Co., Md.
September 12, 1874.

Rev. and dear Father Müller :

I have most carefully read and examined your excellent manuscript, "Familiar Explanation of Christian Doctrine." I took the liberty to make a few alterations. I do not hesitate for a moment to pronounce this work of yours one of the most useful for our time and country. It is written in the true spirit of St. Alphonsus. Its theology is sound and solid; its spirit most devout, and its language simple and popular. I was particularly pleased with those chapters which treat on the Church, Papal Infallibility, Indifference to Religion, Prayer, and Grace. Your book cannot but prove most useful to those who are learning and to those who teach the Christian Doctrine. Its diligent and frequent perusal cannot fail to confirm converts in their faith, and supply Catholics with quite popular and solid arguments to refute the fallacious objections of non-Catholics. I feel confident that both the clergy and laity will hail with delight the publication of a book so well calculated to remedy the two great evils of our time and country—want of faith and true piety.

Congratulating you on having so successfully accomplished one of the most difficult works,

I am your devoted confrere,
A. KONINGS, C.S.S.R.

REV. M. MÜLLER'S (C.SS.R.) SERIES.

FAMILIAR EXPLANATION

OF

CHRISTIAN DOCTRINE

ADAPTED

FOR THE FAMILY AND MORE ADVANCED STUDENTS IN CATHOLIC SCHOOLS AND COLLEGES.

No. III.

POPE BENEDICT XIV. says: "We affirm that the greatest part of the damned are in hell because they did not know those mysteries of faith which Christians must know and believe."—INST. 27, No. 28.

PUBLISHED BY KREUZER BROTHERS,
30 NORTH ST., BALTIMORE, MD.
CATHOLIC PUBLICATION SOCIETY,
9 WARREN STREET, NEW YORK.
FR. PUSTET,
52 BARCLAY ST., NEW YORK. 204 VINE ST., CINCINNATI.
1875.

APPROBATIONS.

Nihil obstat.

JOSEPH HELMPRAECHT, C.SS.R.,

BALTIMORE, MD., 24 SEPT., 1874.

Imprimatur.

✠ J. ROOSEVELT BAYLEY,

ARCHIEP. BALTIMORENSIS.

BALTIMORI, 24 SEPT., 1874.

PREFACE.

ABOUT five months ago, a zealous priest, after speaking of the books that I have published, wrote in his letter as follows :

"Permit me to suggest to you what, in my humble opinion, is badly wanted in our barren religious literature and heretical language: A series of correct and concise Catechisms. I know of nothing more needed, and better calculated to do good. Three numbers would abundantly suffice.

"No. 1. For little children in spelling classes—for adults lamentably uninstructed in what is necessary to know and to believe, in order to save their souls, and who, at the same time, are so slow of intellect that only the simplest and most necessary elements of Catholic faith and practice can be imparted to them—for colored people, and others that cannot read, and especially for that legion of stray sheep in the humbler walks of life, who are picked up and brought to the priest for instruction, confession, and communion on occasions of missions or in Paschal time, and who have neither time, inclination, nor sufficient instruction to read bulky mission books or dry catechisms filled with long technical answers, or to learn much by heart.

"What is necessary for these classes, is not so much that they may be able to *explain*, as that they should *know* what they must believe and do in order to save their souls. Therefore, in *first* catechisms, meant for the uninstructed, not to say stupid, the questions should be longer, and the answers shorter, in order that the child may be instructed in, and, as it were, introduced to, the proper answer, by the very wording of the question, that the feeble memory may not be burdened by a load of words, which it is unable to carry with ease or profit. The true idea of a catechism for the classes of people just mentioned is, that by frequent questions on each point, it wakens the intellects of the uninstructed or the torpid to the matter it is wished to communicate. Hence, not only great care must be taken in framing the questions correctly, but these questions must be multiplied for the entirely uninstructed, especially so as to ask attention to each point that it is desired to teach. To illustrate: It would be a very faulty infants' catechism that would have under one question and answer—'Q. How many Gods are there? A. There is but one God in three Persons, each equal to the other Persons, whom we call the Holy Trinity.'

"No. 2. For the use of Parochial Schools, and of catechumens who have more opportunity or more capacity.

"No. 3. For colleges, academies, high schools, for persons of cultivation, old as well as young, for professional men, etc. This number should especially be plain, popular, comprehensive, and interesting, not so dry and clumsy, nor so full or unsatisfactory, as most books of this class are. Objections, however stupid and threadbare, should be noticed and briefly refuted.

"The object of such a series of catechisms is, clearly and deeply to impress the truths of religion upon the minds of the young. A clear knowledge of these truths will, with the grace of God, gradually gain the affections of youth for the Divine Teacher of our religion, Jesus Christ, our Blessed Lord and Redeemer. In order, however, to reach this great object, it is necessary that in each number should be found, as much as possible, the same order and the same questions and answers for the chief truths of religion, so that these truths, by the additional questions and answers in another number, may be but more clearly explained and more solidly established. This rule, I think, ought to be followed in a series of catechisms, as otherwise confusion might be created in many a child's mind and memory. On the contrary, truths clearly proposed and explained and often repeated in the same words, and in the same order, cannot fail to remain deeply impressed upon mind and memory.

"As we live in a heretical country, the best and most natural order to be followed in preparing a series of catechisms seems to me to be this: God has been the teacher of mankind from the beginning of the world, and by means of His Church, He will, to the end of time, continue to teach men,

"I. What they must believe.

"II. What they must do.

"III. The means of grace which they must use in order to be saved.

"The explanation of the commandments should be such as to be a safe guide of conscience or popular moral theology. In this explanation, therefore, should be stated not only the duties of each commandment, but also the sins which are mortal and which are venial.

"In my humble opinion there are two great truths of our religion to the explanation of which there should be devoted almost as much time and space as to all the rest. These truths are the Divine Mission of the Roman Catholic Church and the Holy Eucharist. To-day, more than ever, these truths should be made plain and impressed upon the minds and hearts of the young—the Divine Mission of the Church, because she is the divinely appointed teacher of mankind—the Holy Eucharist, because it is the centre of our religion, its life, strength, and support.

"The objection that the explanation of these truths at length would make the catechism rather diffuse is scarcely worthy of consideration. What is objectionable in a catechism is not so much diffuseness as obscurity in meaning, or deficiency in clearly explaining the doctrines of our religion. It is true, nothing new can be taught in a catechism, since the truths of our holy religion are always the same. But the manner of proposing and explaining those truths may be new. It certainly admits of improvement in our English literature. Whenever a doctrine is clearly proposed and explained it is easily understood and remembered, and makes a lasting impression. But whenever a doctrine is proposed and explained in a dry and obscure manner, it is apt to create disgust, and leave both mind and heart empty. In rendering not only clear, but distinct, every proposition that should be admitted in a catechism, lies the highest *art* of its composer, as his science is tried by his *including* in a given catechism all that ought to be put into it in view of the persons for whom and objects for which it is prepared, and of excluding all else.

"There are some who think and say that our religion may be taught in a few lessons. Be it so. But, generally speaking, a few lessons in religion will not make practical Catholics, or else we should not see so many of the young fall away from the faith. Had they learned better what the Church and the Holy Eucharist are, many of them, instead of having become bitter enemies of the Church, would have become her most strenuous defenders by word and example. A clear, satisfactory explanation of these two great truths in a catechism is alone sufficient to recommend it both to the clergy and laity.

"Each number should contain an appendix with a brief summary of the chief duties which every Christian must know and observe, on Sundays and week-days, in and out of church, in order to be saved, and with short prayers for morning, night, during the day, at church, for confession, Holy Communion, etc. Thus they would serve for convenient prayer-books in the absence of others. Of course, these books must be small in size, and large of print, so as to serve for pocket use, and not injure the eyes.

"I have been sighing for years for such a series of Catechisms, and cannot conceive how you, in your laudable zeal to profit souls, and to assist your brethren of the clergy, school-brothers, and school-sisters, Sunday-school teachers, and parents, could have overlooked them, or not have felt their necessity yourself.

"What I suggest to you is, undoubtedly, one of the most difficult undertakings. It is a work which, no doubt, will be criticised either in a friendly or in a captious spirit. No attention should be paid to the criticisms of those who are not able or willing to supply an admitted want, but who, from unholy motives, labor to search out trifling faults in excellent and necessary works of this kind, without suggesting anything better and more practical. But by the suggestions of many of those competent, that which is already good becomes perfect. Thus at last a series of Catechisms may be given us, which we can put, *pure* and *simple,* into the hands of children and their instructors, as teaching the doctrines of Catholic faith, without need of supplementary explanations.

"Now, should you—as I scarcely dare anticipate —think seriously on my humble proposals, and furnish us with the above mentioned series of Catechisms, you would thereby certainly earn the undying thanks of thousands, especially of priests, parents, school-brothers, school-sisters, and Sunday-school teachers, more worthy and deserving of consideration than your humble but admiring servant in Christ."

I am not quite certain whether or not the good and zealous priest would object to the publication of his letter. So I suppress his name, deservedly held in veneration, and by no one in higher veneration than by myself. In compliance with his request I have prepared this series of Catechisms, and in preparing it, have been guided by his views, as they perfectly agree with mine on the subject. I am impressed more strongly than ever with a sense of the great difficulty of the task. It has always been a matter of considerable difficulty even to the most learned theologians to write a plain, practical Catechism. I could have wished that some one more competent, and more experienced in writing, had engaged in the difficult undertaking. Hence I am ready to charge myself with presumption for venturing on so difficult a task, which has occupied the pens of the ablest theologians.

I can find for myself no excuse but in the sincerity

with which I have sought principally to benefit that portion of the flock of Jesus Christ which is dearest to His sacred heart—little children.

What has greatly encouraged me to place these Catechisms before the public, is the favorable reports made by those who read them in manuscript, and were competent to judge of their theological accuracy, their earnestness and simplicity of language.

As to the defects of my undertaking—which unquestionably are many—I hope the sincerity of a good will, and the earnest desire of benefiting Catholic youth, will be sufficient to plead my cause with my indulgent and considerate brethren of the clergy and laity. And thus, imperfect as the new production may be, I present it to my brethren of the clergy and laity, hoping that it may meet with sound criticisms, communicated to me either publicly or privately.

I have now only to add that I submit this, and whatever else I have written, to the better judgment of our Bishops, but especially to the Holy See, anxiously desirous to think nothing, to say nothing, to teach nothing but what is approved of by those to whom the sacred deposit of Faith has been committed—those who watch over us and are *to render an account to God for our souls.*

Now, should the Prelates of the Church deem this series of Catechisms well calculated to promote the great cause for which it has been prepared, the writer will believe himself amply rewarded for his labor, and will feel extremely grateful if they encourage their introduction by recommending them to the clergy and laity of their dioceses.

NEW YORK:
Feast of the Immaculate Conception, 1874.
St. Alphonsus' Church, 234 South 5th Ave.

CONTENTS.

PART II.

WHAT WE MUST BELIEVE.

Explanation of the Apostles' Creed.

PART III.

WHAT WE MUST DO.

Explanation of the Commandments.

VIOLATION OF THE COMMANDMENTS.

PART IV.

MEANS OF GRACE.

APPENDIX.

INTRODUCTION.

WHY WE ARE IN THIS WORLD.

Question. Who created you?

ANSWER. God created me.

Q. Out of what did God make you?

A. God made me out of nothing. 2 Mach. vii. 28.

Q. Of what are you composed?

A. Of two parts--a soul and a body.

Q. To whose likeness did God create you?

A. "God created me to his own image and likeness." Gen. i. 26.

Q. Is this likeness in your body or in your soul?

A. It is principally in my soul.

Q. Is your soul then a spirit like to God?

A. It is.

Q. Is your soul one like God?

A. It is.

Q. Will your soul live forever like God?

A. It will.

Q. In what else is your soul like to God?

A. In its love for God.

Q. How does this love make the soul like to God?

A. Because in loving God it loves what is infinitely good and perfect, and so loving, tries to make itself good and perfect like to God.

Q. Does God then love Himself?

A. Yes; because being all wise, He knows Himself, who is all wisdom; and being in Himself infinite perfection must love Himself always, and all His creatures in proportion as they resemble Him.

Q. In the one God there are three distinct persons. Is there anything in the soul like to this?

A. Yes; in the one soul there are three distinct powers.

Q. What are these three powers?

A. The understanding, will, and memory.

Q. Of what use are these three powers to man?

A. By means of them he can learn languages, build churches, palaces, great cities, steamboats, and railroads, write and print books, count days, dates, distances, money, and above all, know and love God.

Q. Can animals do all this?

A. No.

Q. Why can they not?

A. Because they have not rational souls.

Q. What lesson are we to learn from this?

A. That man is not a mere animal, made simply for this world, but that he has a soul made to know, love, and serve God, its Creator, whose image and likeness it is.

Q. What is the plain answer to be made to men who say they have no soul?

A. If they say they have no soul they must consider themselves simply animals, and since they are pleased to be animals they had better go and live with the class of beings to which they belong.

Q. Why did God make us to His own image and likeness?

A. That He might bestow upon us His own happiness in heaven. "I am thy reward exceeding great." Gen. xv. 1.

Q. On what condition will He bestow upon us His own happiness?

A. On condition that we always serve Him on earth. "The Lord thy God shalt thou adore, and him only shalt thou serve." Matt. iv. 10.

Q. How must we serve God?

A. By doing God's will. "Not every one

that saith to me, Lord, Lord, shall enter into the kingdom of heaven : but he that doth the will of my Father who is in heaven, he shall enter into the kingdom of heaven." Matt. vii. 21.

Q. Were all men made to be forever happy with God in heaven ?

A. Yes; all without exception. "God will have all men to be saved, and to come to the knowledge of truth." 1 Tim., ii. 4.

Q. Why are many not saved ?

A. Because instead of serving God they seek only the riches and pleasures of this world.

Q. May we not seek and use the goods of this world ?

A. We may, so far as they help us to serve God.

Q. How must we regard those goods and pleasures which keep us from serving God ?

A. We must neither seek nor use them.

Q. Why ?

A. Because God has said: "What doth it profit a man if he gain the whole world, and suffer the loss of his own soul." Matt. xvi. 26.

Q. How can the goods and pleasures of this world cause us to lose our souls ?

A. By drawing us away from God.

Q. Cannot the riches and pleasures of this world make us happy?

A. No.

Q. Why not?

A. Because the soul was not created for and by them, but by God for Himself. It was not created for time, but for eternity. The riches and pleasures of this world end with this world; and if we set our happiness on them, it must end with them.

Q. But cannot we love those pleasures and God at the same time?

A. We cannot love both, above all things, at the same time. If we make the riches and pleasures of this world the sole object of our lives, we must forget God, our Creator.

Q. Where then are we to seek true happiness?

A. In God alone.

Q. How are we to seek for true happiness only in God?

A. By serving God according to His will.

Q. What do we say of the man who serves God as God wishes to be served?

A. That he is united with God, or that he is a follower of the only true religion.

Q. Who then is a follower of the true religion?

A. He alone who serves God according to God's will.

Q. What will happen to us after death if we have not served God?

A. God will cast us into the everlasting torments of hell. As we have cast Him off, so will He cast us off, and have nothing to do with us.

Q. What then must always be our greatest care?

A. To do the holy will of God.

FAMILIAR EXPLANATION

OF

CHRISTIAN DOCTRINE.

PART I.

LESSON I.

GOD, OUR TEACHER.

Question. Who can teach us how to serve God according to His will?

ANSWER. Either God Himself, or he to whom God has made His will known.

Q. Has God ever spoken to men, and made His will known to them?

A. Yes; very often.

Q. To whom did He speak?

A. To the patriarchs and the prophets.

Q. What do you mean by "patriarchs?"

A. All those holy men who lived before Moses.

Q. Name some of them.

A. Adam, Noah, Abraham, Isaac, Jacob, etc.

Q. What did God say to them?

A. He told them who He was, why He had made them, in what manner they must worship Him, and what they must believe and do to be happy with Him in heaven, and escape the everlasting pains of hell.

Q. What else did God say to those holy men?

A. He commanded them to tell their fellow-men what he had spoken to them.

Q. What do you mean by "prophets?"

A. Men filled with the Spirit of God.

Q. What Spirit was this?

A. The Holy Ghost, the Lord and Life-giver.

Q. Name some of the prophets.

A. Moses, Elias, Isaias, Jeremias, Ezechiel, Daniel, Malachias, etc.

Q. Why are they called prophets?

A. Because they foretold things to come.

Q. How could they know things to come?

A. Because God made them known to them.

Q. What did they foretell?

A. They foretold especially the time of the coming of the Redeemer, the circumstances of His birth, of His life, passion, and death.

Q. What else did the prophets foretell of the Redeemer?

A. His Resurrection and Ascension, and the sending down of the Holy Ghost, the destruction of Jerusalem, the rejection of the Jews, the conversion of the Gentiles, and the founding, spreading, and duration of His Church.

Q. Why was all this foretold by the prophets?

A. That all men might prepare for the coming of the Redeemer, know him by the prophecies, and believe and do all that He would command them.

Q. How were men to know for certain that God had spoken to the patriarchs and prophets?

A. Because God Himself bore witness to the truth of their words by miracles.

Q. What do you mean by a miracle?

A. Miracles are most extraordinary works which cannot be done by mere natural powers, but by the power of God alone; such as the raising of the dead to life, giving sight to the blind, and the like.

Q. If holy men work miracles in confirmation of the truth of their words, must we, then, believe that God has spoken through them?

A. Yes; because God cannot permit a miracle except *in confirmation of the truth*, and therefore, when God speaks, whether it be through man, or in His own divine person, we must listen and obey, simply because it is the voice of God.

Q. Why cannot God permit a miracle in confirmation of error?

A. Because he cannot deceive us.

Q. When did God begin to speak to men?

A. When He first created man.

Q. How long did God continue to speak to men through the patriarchs and prophets?

A. For about four thousand years.

Q. Did God, after that time, speak no more?

A. At the end of that time, He sent His only Son, Jesus Christ, to teach men.

Q. Who is Jesus Christ?

A. Jesus Christ is the son of God, true God and true man in one divine person.

Q. In what condition was mankind when the Redeemer came?

A. The grossest darkness of the understanding, and the most lamentable depravity of the will prevailed almost over the entire world.

Q. What was the consequence of this darkness and depravity?

A. All mankind, with the exception of the Jews, having lost the knowledge of God, worshipped creatures, even the very demons, as gods, and the most shameful vices were praised as virtues.

Q. Why did not the Jews also worship false gods?

A. Because the Jews or Israelites were a people chosen by God from the corrupt mass of mankind, and watched over with special care.

Q. Why did God choose the Jews for his people, and watch over them with special care?

A. Because, notwithstanding their sins, God took pity on men, and wished that through the Jews all those laws and truths which he had made known to mankind should be preserved, and that through them salvation might come to the whole world.

Q. For what other reason did God choose the Jews for his people?

A. God also wished that from them at last should be born one holy enough to be the mother of the Redeemer.

Q. What remedy did Jesus Christ apply to heal those universal evils of the understanding?

A. He enlightened men by His divine doctrine and example.

Q. What remedy did our blessed Redeemer apply to heal the great evils of the will ?

A. He gave us the sacraments and prayer as means to obtain those graces which He merited for us by His life and death, whereby we would be enabled to believe and practise what he had taught us.

LESSON II.

GOD, OUR TEACHER BY HIS CHURCH.

Q. What did Jesus Christ do in order that all men, even to the end of the world, might learn His holy Doctrine, and have the means of grace by which alone they could be saved?

A. He established a well-organized society of those who believed in Him and professed His whole Doctrine.

Q. What did Jesus Christ call this society ?

A. He called it His Church.

Q. Who were the first members of that society?

A. The Immaculate Virgin Mary, the twelve Apostles, the seventy-two disciples, and some other followers of Jesus Christ.

Q. How did Jesus Christ organize His society ?

A. From among His followers He chose

twelve men to be the witnesses and teachers of His Doctrine and works.

Q. What were those twelve men called?

A. Apostles.

Q. Where were the Apostles to be the witnesses of Christ's doctrine and works?

A. "In Jerusalem, in all Judea and Samaria, and even to the uttermost part of the earth." Acts i. 8.

Q. What did Jesus Christ give the Apostles to understand when He said to them that they would be witnesses unto Him all over the world?

A. That He had chosen them in order that, after His ascension into heaven, they should preach to all nations what they had seen and heard from Him.

Q. How did He prepare the Apostles for so difficult and important an office?

A. He first instructed them publicly and privately, for three years and a half, and during forty days after His Resurrection, in all the doctrines which they should make known to all nations, and then sent to them the Holy Ghost to enlighten and strengthen them in their office.

Q. What else did He do?

A. He gave His Apostles those very powers which He Himself exercised on earth.

Q. What were those powers?

A. His power as Teacher, as Priest, and as Ruler or King of an everlasting kingdom.

Q. When did Jesus Christ bestow His powers upon His Apostles?

A. When He said to them: "All power is given to me in heaven and on earth." Matt. xxviii. 18. "As the Father hath sent me, I also send you." John xx. 21.

Q. What were the Apostles' powers as Teachers?

A. Power to spread abroad, explain, and preserve uncorrupted the holy doctrines of Jesus Christ, and to condemn all false teaching.

Q. In what words did Jesus Christ bestow this power upon the Apostles?

A. In these words: "Go and teach all nations, preach the Gospel to every creature." Matt. xxviii. 18.

Q. What were the Apostles' powers as Priests?

A. Power to offer sacrifice, and administer the sacraments of Christ.

Q. In what words did He bestow this power upon them?

A. In these words: "Do this that I have done, that is, sacrifice this in remembrance of me." Luke xxii. 19. "Go, baptize mankind in the name of the Father, and of the Son, and of the Holy Ghost." Matt. xxviii. 19. "Whose-soever sins you forgive, they are forgiven them." John xx. 21.

Q. What were the Apostles' powers as Rulers?

A. Power to govern the Church, make laws for the people, and enforce those laws.

Q. In what words did He bestow this power upon them?

A. In these words: "Teach mankind to observe all things whatsoever I have commanded you." Matt. xxviii. 18. "I give thee the keys of the kingdom of heaven; whatsoever thou shalt bind on earth shall be bound in heaven, and whatsoever thou shalt loose on earth shall be loosed in heaven." Matt. xvi. 19.

Q. Were these powers of Teacher, Priest, and Ruler given to all men alike, who believed in Jesus Christ?

A. No; to the Apostles only and their successors.

Q. When, then, our Lord bestowed on His Apostles His own powers of teaching, administering the sacraments, and governing the Church, did He at the same time command all men to hear and obey them?

A. He did, in these words: "Whosoever will not believe, shall be condemned;" and, "He who heareth you heareth me;" and, "He who will not hear the Church, let him be as the heathen and publican." Matt. xviii. 17.

Q. What do we learn from all this?

A. That the Church of Jesus Christ was made up of two classes of men: of teachers and hearers; of priests and people; of rulers and subjects; so that we are bound to believe what the Church teaches, receive her sacraments, and obey her laws.

LESSON III.

ST. PETER THE HEAD OF CHRIST'S CHURCH.

Q. Were the Apostles to exercise their powers as they pleased?

A. They were only to exercise their powers under the supreme authority of St. Peter.

Q. Why?

A. Because Jesus Christ appointed St. Peter to be His Representative on earth, and the visible Head of His whole Church.

Q. But is not Christ Himself the Head of the Church ?

A. Christ is the invisible Head, but Peter is the visible Head of the Church.

Q. Was it necessary that the Church of Christ should have a Visible Head as well as the Invisible One ?

A. Yes; because the entire community of pastors and the faithful are the visible body of the Church of Christ, and a visible body or society must also have a visible head.

Q. Why ?

A. Because the principle of supreme authority is a *fundamental* principle of reason and experience.

Q. What do you mean by this ?

A. I mean that reason and experience teach us that there can be no order, no law, no civilization without supreme authority; in other words, supreme authority is the foundation of order and law.

Q. Can we see the necessity of such authority whithersoever we turn ?

A. We can.

Q. Give some examples ?

A. Every ship or steamboat must have its captain. Every railroad engine must have its engineer. In every society we find a president. In every government there must be a president or a monarch.

Q. Do we find the principle of authority in practice even amongst the savages?

A. Yes; and even amongst brute beasts, even among the tiny insects. We find, for instance, that the ants and the bees have their queen or supreme ruler.

Q. What follows from this?

A. That the same God who observes such wonderful order in the most simple works of nature; the same God who planted in our reason the principle of order and authority, must necessarily observe this order in the greatest of His works—in the establishment of His Church.

Q. How do we know that Christ has established this principle of supreme authority in His Church?

A. We know it from the fact that He gave greater powers to St. Peter than to the rest of the Apostles.

Q. How do we know this?

A. From the words of Christ Himself, who said to Peter: "I say to thee, thou art Peter, and upon this rock I will build my Church;

and the gates of hell shall not prevail against it." Matt. xvi. 18.

Q. What did our Lord understand by this "rock?"

A. St. Peter himself.

Q. Why so?

A. Because Christ called him Cephas, which is a Syriac word, and means a rock.

Q. What else did our Lord say to St. Peter on this occasion?

A. "I will give to thee the keys of the kingdom of heaven; and whatsoever thou shalt bind upon earth it shall be bound also in heaven; and whatsoever thou shalt loose upon earth it shall be loosed also in heaven." V. 19.

Q. But did not Jesus Christ say the same to the rest of the Apostles?

A. He addressed those words to all the Apostles in common, but He addressed them to St. Peter in particular, saying: "I say to THEE, thou art Peter," etc.

Q. Why did He say so?

A. To show clearly that He wished to bestow on St. Peter some especial power.

Q. Did our Lord make this more clear on some other occasion?

A. Yes; when He said to St. Peter: "Feed my lambs, feed my sheep." John xxi. 15–17.

Q. What did He mean by lambs?

A. The faithful.

Q. What did He mean by sheep?

A. The pastors.

Q. Why did Jesus Christ speak thus?

A. To show that just as sheep feed the lambs, so also pastors feed the souls of the faithful.

Q. What follows from this?

A. That Christ intrusted to Peter both the pastors and the faithful.

Q. Did the Apostles themselves recognize Peter's supremacy?

A. They did.

Q. Who called together the disciples, and presided over the council which they held in Jerusalem to elect a new Apostle in the place of Judas?

A. St. Peter.

Q. Might this new Apostle have been chosen by St. Peter himself?

A. Yes; undoubtedly.

Q. Who says so?

A. St. John Chrysostom, who lived in the fifth century.

Q. Who first preached Jesus crucified, and converted by his sermon three thousand persons?

A. St. Peter.

Q. Who first declared that the Gentiles were to be admitted to Baptism, according to a divine revelation which he had received on that subject ?

A. St. Peter.

Q. Who first decided in an assembly of the Apostles at Jerusalem that Christians were no longer to be subjected to the Jewish law of circumcision ?

A. St. Peter.

Q. What are we to learn from this ?

A. That St. Peter was the Head of the Church of Jesus Christ.

Q. Why ?

A. Because he exercised the office of supreme Head of the Church on all those occasions.

Q. When the evangelists give the names of the Apostles whom do they always name first ?

A. St. Peter.

Q. What are the words of St. Matthew, x. 2 ?

A. "The names of the twelve apostles: The first Simon, who is called Peter."

Q. Might it not be said that St. Peter was always named the first either because he was the eldest or because he had been called to the apostleship before the rest ?

A. No; because St. Andrew was both older

than Peter and had become a disciple of Christ before him.

Q. What follows from this ?

A. That the rest of the Apostles acknowledged Peter as the Head of the Church.

Q. What Father of the Church writes: "It was not St. Andrew that was appointed head; it was St. Peter" ?

A. St. Ambrose, who lived in the fourth century. C. 12, in 2 Corinth.

Q. What Father uses this expression: "Behold the Apostle St. Peter, in whom power shines with so much brightness" ?

A. St. Augustine, who lived in the fourth century. 2 Lib. de Bapt.

Q. And who writes: "St. Peter was made the chief of Apostles in order that unity should be preserved in the Church" ?

A. St. Optatus, who lived in the fourth century. 2 Lib. adv. Parmen.

Q. And who again wrote as follows: "It is known in all ages that Peter was the Prince and the Head of the Apostles, the foundation-stone of the Catholic Church. This is a fact which no one doubts" ?

A. The Fathers of the General Council of Ephesus, A.D. 431.

Q. What doctrine do we learn from the writings of those Fathers of the Church?

A. That they and the faithful of all ages acknowledged Peter as the Head of the Church of Christ.

Q. Was it Christ's will that this office of head should be continued from St. Peter to his successors to the end of the world?

A. It was.

Q. Why?

A. Because Christ founded His Church to last to the end of time.

Q. Who has always been acknowledged as the visible Head of the Church of Christ after the death of St. Peter?

A. The Pope or Bishop of Rome.

Q. Why do you say that the Popes or Bishops of Rome are the successors of St. Peter?

A. Because St. Peter established his See at Rome, and died there.

Q. How do you answer those who say that St. Peter never went to Rome?

A. I would ask them these three questions:

1. If St. Peter did not suffer martyrdom at Rome, under the Emperor Nero, where did he die?

2. If St. Peter did not die at Rome, from

what place, and at what time were his remains carried thither?

3. Did not the Fathers of the Church who lived in the first ages of Christendom, know better who was the first Bishop of Rome than the Protestants of our day can know?

Q. What does St. Augustine say about Peter being at Rome?

A. "After Peter came Linus, and Clement followed after Linus." Epist. ad Generos.

Q. What other Father writes: "St. Peter was the first who occupied the See of Rome, after him came Linus, and after Linus came Clement"?

A. St. Optatus. 2 Lib. adv. Parmen.

Q. And who tells us that "Rome has become the capital of Christendom because it was there that St. Peter established his See"?

A. St. Leo the Great, Serm. I. in Nat. Apost.

Q. What clearly follows from the writings of those Fathers of the Church?

A. That the Popes or Bishops of Rome were always held to be the successors of St. Peter.

Q. Was the office of teacher, of priest, and of ruler in the persons of the other apostles also to continue throughout all time?

A. It was.

Q. How do we know this?

A. From the fact that Jesus Christ gave power to the Apostles to choose others, and ordain them as Bishops, and appoint them as rulers of His Church.

Q. In what words did he give this power?

A. In these: "As the Father hath sent me, I also send you."

Q. What is the meaning of those words?

A. The meaning is unmistakably this: As My Heavenly Father has empowered me to choose you to take My place on earth, so I empower you to choose others to take your place.

Q. From what other words of our Lord do we know that the threefold office of the Apostles was to continue to the end of the world?

A. From these words of our Lord: "Behold, I am with you all days, even to the end of the world" (Matt. xxviii. 20); that is, I am with you in your successors to the end of the world.

Q. When Jesus Christ chose the Apostles to preach His holy doctrine, and establish His Church all over the world, was it necessary for them to remember the whole doctrine of Christ, understand it perfectly, and preach it in that sense in which

Jesus Christ had preached it and wished it to be understood by the whole world?

A. Yes; this was absolutely necessary.

Q. Did Jesus Christ assure the Apostles that He would bestow upon them the grace to remember His whole doctrine, and understand it well?

A. He did.

Q. On what occasion did He give them this assurance?

A. When He said: "The Paraclete, the Holy Ghost, whom the Father will send in my name, he will teach you all things, and bring all things to your mind, whatsoever I shall have said to you." John xiv. 26.

Q. What effect, then, did the Holy Ghost work in the Apostles when He came down upon them on Whitsunday?

A. He reminded them of all that they had seen and heard from Jesus Christ, and He enlightened them so as to understand His doctrine, and preach it in that sense in which Jesus Christ wished it to be understood and practised.

Q. What is this grace, which the Holy Ghost bestowed upon the Apostles, called?

A. The grace or gift of infallibility in teaching.

LESSON IV.

INFALLIBILITY OF THE POPE.

Q. Did our Blessed Saviour foresee that certain men would corrupt or misinterpret His holy Doctrine?

A. He did.

Q. When certain men either corrupted or misinterpreted Christ's holy Doctrine, what was necessary to remove all doubts about its true meaning, and preserve it always pure and uncorrupted?

A. That there should be one particularly privileged by God to set forth and state plainly with *divine certainty* the true meaning of Christ's doctrine in all questions where His doctrine was concerned.

Q. What do we call such a privileged person?

A. The supreme judge in all points of divine law, from whose sentence there is no appeal.

Q. Why is such a judge necessary?

A. To put an end to all disputes about points of divine law.

Q. How so?

A. If every man in the country were to take the laws of the State, and to explain them as he pleased, there would be nothing but confusion and disorder in society. In like manner, if every man were to take the sacred, eternal law of God, the doctrine of Jesus Christ, and to interpret it as he pleased, there would be nothing but confusion in religion.

Q. What safeguard has human wisdom adopted to prevent confusion and disorder in society?

A. It has found it necessary to appoint a supreme judge to decide ultimately in all disputed points of civil law.

Q. What is the plain inference from this?

A. That if even human wisdom sees the necessity of appointing a supreme judge to decide ultimately in all points of civil law, it cannot be supposed that God, who is Infinite Wisdom, should neglect to appoint a supreme judge to decide ultimately in all points of divine law, in order thus to prevent all confusion in religion.

Q. Was there ever a time when men were left to themselves, to fashion their own religion, to invent their own creed, their own form of worship, and to decide in matters of religion?

A. No; there always existed on earth a

visible teaching authority, to which it was a bounden duty of every man to submit.

Q. Whom did God appoint to be this visible teaching authority before the coming of the Redeemer?

A. During the four thousand years that elapsed before the coming of the Redeemer, the doctrines that were to be believed, the feasts that were to be observed, the sacrifices, the ceremonies of worship, everything was regulated by the living, authoritative voice of the patriarchs, the priests, and the prophets.

Q. How do we know that God in the Old Law appointed a tribunal, presided over by the High-Priest, to judge in all controversies, both of doctrine and morals, and from whose decision there was no appeal?

A. The Jewish historian, Josephus, who was well acquainted with the laws and religion of his own nation, says: "The High-Priest offers sacrifice to God before the other priests; he guards the laws, judges controversies, punishes the guilty, and whoever disobeys him is punished as one that is impious towards God." Lib. 2, Contra Appium.

Q. Is there still a greater authority than Josephus bearing witness to the fact?

A. Yes; the Word of God itself bears witness to the fact. "If thou perceive," says holy Scripture, "that there be among you a hard and doubtful matter in judgment between blood and blood, cause and cause, and thou seest that the words of the judges within the gates do vary, arise and go up to the place which the Lord thy God shall choose. And thou shalt come to the priests, and to the judge that shall be at that time, and thou shalt ask them, and they shall show thee the truth of the judgment. And thou shalt do whatsoever they shall say, and thou shalt follow their sentence. Neither shalt thou decline to the right hand nor to the left hand. But he that will be proud and refuse to obey the commandments of the priest, who ministereth at the time to the Lord thy God, and to the decree of the judge, that man shall die, and thou shalt take away the evil from Israel." Deut. xvii. 8–12.

Q. What do we see from this?

A. Here we see clearly a tribunal appointed by Almighty God Himself to decide in the last resort; a tribunal from whose sentence there is no appeal. There is no exception, the rule is for all, the terrible sentence is pronounced against every transgressor. Whosoever shall refuse to abide by the decision of the High-Priest shall die the death.

Q. How long did this tribunal remain intact?

A. Until the coming of our Saviour.

Q. Who assures us of this?

A. Our blessed Redeemer Himself, in these words: "The Scribes and Pharisees have sat in the chair of Moses. All things therefore whatsoever they shall say to you, observe and do." Matt. xxiii. 2.

Q. Now, did our Lord Jesus Christ establish a supreme tribunal; did He give to the world an infallible judge and teacher, to decide ultimately in all controversies, both of faith and morals, whose decision is final, and without appeal?

A. Our Blessed Saviour came not to destroy the Law, but to make it perfect. He therefore established in the New Law that which in the Old Law was most necessary for the preservation of faith and morals. He gave to the whole world an infallible judge and teacher, to decide ultimately in all points of faith and morals.

Q. Whom did Jesus Christ appoint as the infallible judge and teacher in all points of faith and morals?

A. St. Peter, the Head of His Church.

Q. Were not all the successors of the Apostles to possess the gift of infallibility?

A. No; the successor of St. Peter, the Pope of Rome, only.

Q. How do we know that the successors of the other Apostles, the Catholic Bishops, were not endowed with the gift of infallibility?

A. Because Jesus Christ never promised it to them.

Q. How do we know that Jesus Christ never promised it to them?

A. Because no such promise is recorded either in Holy Scripture or tradition.

Q. Why did Christ not promise to the Bishops the gift of infallibility?

A. Because He does not multiply and dispense His gifts without necessity.

Q. Was not the gift of infallibility necessary to the Bishops?

A. By no means.

Q. Why not?

A. Because after the Apostles had preached the full doctrine of Christ, their successors had only to guard this doctrine, and deliver it uncorrupted to the faithful.

Q. What does the Apostle St. Paul write to the Bishop St. Timothy on this subject?

A. "Keep that which is committed to thy trust, avoiding the profane novelties of words, and oppositions of knowledge falsely so called." (1 Tim. vi. 20, and 2 Tim. i. 14.) "But evil men and seducers shall grow worse and worse, erring and driving into error. But continue thou in those things which thou hast learned, and which have been committed to thee." 2 Tim. iii. 13.

Q. But did not Christ promise the Apostles and their successors: "The Holy Ghost, the Spirit of Truth, shall be in you, and abide with you forever"? John xiv. 16.

A. He did so promise.

Q. If, then, according to this promise, the Spirit of Truth shall abide forever with the successors of the Apostles, are they not personally infallible?

A. By no means.

Q. Why not?

A. The Spirit of Truth may abide in a person, and yet that person may not be infallible. The Spirit of Truth may abide in a multitude, and yet not each individual of the multitude may possess it in its entirety.

Q. Give an example.

A. A million of men may not know the road to a certain city to which they wish to go. A single guide suffices to set this million on the right road. Once on it, they have only to follow their guide and they cannot go astray. Once the way is pointed out, all know it to be right, but one only could point out the right road to be followed.

Q. Do you mean that Christ wished that in this same manner the Spirit of Truth should abide with the Catholic Bishops?

A. Precisely so; for Christ gave them and all the faithful, in the person of the Head of His Church, an infallible teacher of all the truths which He and His Apostles taught. By invariably following this teacher the Spirit of Truth will always abide with them.

Q. How do we know that the Pope as successor to St. Peter possesses the gift of infallibility?

A. Christ Himself assured St. Peter and his successors of this.

Q. On what occasion?

A. When He told St. Peter that by His prayer to His heavenly Father He had obtained this gift of infallibility for him and all his successors. "I have prayed for thee (Peter) that thy faith fail not, and thou being once converted, confirm thy brethren." Luke xxii. 31, 32.

Q. Why did Christ pray to His Father that St. Peter and his successors should be endowed with the gift of infallibility ?

A. Because Christ wished that the never-failing faith of St. Peter and his successors should be forever the foundation-stone of His Church.

Q. On what occasion did Christ assure us of this ?

A. When He asked the Apostles: "Whom do you say that I am?" Matt. xvi. 15.

Q. Which of the Apostles made answer to this question ?

A. St. Peter.

Q. What was his answer ?

A. "Thou art Christ, the Son of the living God."

Q. What answer did Christ make to this reply of St. Peter ?

A. He said: "Blessed art thou, Simon Bar-Jona: because flesh and blood hath not revealed it to thee, but my Father who is in heaven. And I say to thee: that thou art Peter, and upon this rock I will build my Church."

Q. What is the meaning of these words of our Lord ?

A. Jesus Christ means to say that, as it is My Father who has made known to you, Peter, that I am His Son, I also make known to the whole world, that you and your successors will always know and understand who I am, and what I have taught.

Q. When did Christ build His Church upon Peter, that is, intrust him with the whole flock?

A. When He said to him: "Feed my lambs, feed my sheep." John xxi. 16.

Q. What is the meaning of this?

A. Christ says that His whole flock, teachers and hearers, priests and people, rulers and subjects, must believe and teach as Peter and his successors believe and teach.

Q. Why?

A. Because his faith, according to Christ's solemn words, shall not fail, since no power shall prevail against Peter or any of his successors so as to cause them to teach anything else than what Christ has taught. "The gates of hell shall not prevail against my Church," built upon Peter's faith. Matt. xvi. 18.

Q. What follows from this?

A. That where Peter, that is, the Pope, is,

there is the Church of Christ, or in other words, that all those who believe and teach as the Pope does, form the true Church of Christ. St. Ambrose.

Q. Who, by his own motion, often condemned heresies, both before and after the first general council?

A. The Pope.

Q. To whom did the Catholic Bishops always have recourse in all controversies both of faith and morals?

A. To the Pope.

Q. If the obstinacy of the party condemned by the Pope made it advisable to have recourse to general councils, were these councils, then, after the most mature deliberation, ever found to do anything else than to confirm the sentence already passed by the Pope?

A. They were not.*

Q. Did any Pope ever issue any decree concerning the truths of faith or sound morality, which was not afterwards received by the great body of the Bishops, as containing the most solid and wholesome doctrine?

A. Such a thing never happened.

Q. Could the greatest enemies of the Catholic faith ever prove that any Pope taught any doctrine contrary to the sacred truths taught by Jesus Christ and His Apostles?

* See Q. and A., p. 445.

A. Never.*

Q. What are we to understand from all this?

A. That it has always been the belief of the Catholic Church that the Pope, in his solemn decisions in matters of faith and morals, is infallible.

Q. If this be true, how then could it happen that some years ago a few Bishops and Priests were said not to have held this to be a doctrine of Catholic faith?

A. Because the divine tradition of this doctrine had not been as yet explicitly defined by the Holy Father.

Q. Did those Bishops, assembled in the Council of the Vatican, continue to oppose the dogma of the infallibility of the Pope, after it was defined?

A. No. All, without exception, freely and joyfully subscribed their names to the decrees of the council, and professed their faith in the infallibility of the Pope.

Q. If, then, in a general council, or assembly of all the Catholic Bishops, the meaning of a certain doctrine of Christ was to be set forth in precise language, and the majority of Bishops would explain it in one sense, and the minority in another, on which side would be the truth?

A. On that side, though it be the minority of Bishops, which agrees with the Pope.

* See Q. and A. p. 446.

Q. Why?

A. Simply because Christ bound Himself solemnly *only to Peter and his successors that their faith should never fail;* that is, that every one of them would always be so enlightened by the Holy Ghost as to understand the true meaning of His doctrine, and state and teach it plainly with divine certainty. " *Where Peter is, there is the Church.*"

Q. Must we, then, believe that such decisions of the Pope in matters of faith and morals are infallibly true?

A. Yes; because this is an article of faith, which we must believe, as firmly as we believe that there is a God.

Q. If any one should say, or even think otherwise, what would he be before God?

A. An apostate from the faith.

Q. Does the Pope then teach anything new, when in such misinterpretations of Christ's doctrine he declares what is to be believed?

A. No; he plainly states the truth in the sense in which Jesus Christ and the Apostles preached it.

Q. Can you now tell me whose office it is to guard the doctrine of Christ, as preached by the Apostles, and proclaim and apply it always and

everywhere, one and the same, and to defend the rights of God on earth against every enemy, at all times, and in all places ?

A. This is the Pope's office.

Q. Who is appointed by God Himself to declare and apply the invariable doctrine of Jesus Christ, and to govern all men and nations, kings and peoples, according to this invariable doctrine ?

A. The Pope.

Q. Must the Pope as guardian and judge of the law of God, resist with all his might every passion or tendency of every age, nation, community, or individual, whenever it leaves the law of God ?

A. He is bound in conscience to do so.

Q. When does the Pope speak "ex Cathedrâ," or infallibly ?

A. He speaks infallibly whenever in the discharge of his office of pastor and teacher of all Christians, he defines (that is, finally determines), according to his supreme apostolic authority, a doctrine concerning faith or morals, to be held by the Universal Church, or anything else that is conducive to the preservation of faith and morals.

Q. When the Pope, in accordance with the duty of his apostolic ministry and his supreme apostolic authority, proceeds, in briefs, encyclical letters, consistorial allocutions, and other apostolic letters,

to declare certain truths, to reprobate perverse doctrines, and condemn certain errors, must such declarations of truth, and condemnations of error, be considered as infallible, and as binding in conscience, and requiring our firm interior assent, although they do not express an anathema on those who disagree?

A. Such declarations of truth and condemnations of error are infallible, or *ex cathedrâ* acts of the Pope, and, therefore, are binding in conscience, and requiring our firm interior assent; to refuse which would be for us a mortal sin, since such a refusal would be a virtual denial of the dogma of infallibility, and we should be heretics were we conscious of such a denial. St. Alphonsus Liguori. Theol. Mor., Lib. I., 104.

Q. Are not such doctrinal utterances of the Pontiff of imperfect and incomplete authority until they are confirmed and accepted by the Bishops of the Church?

A. Nothing ever is farther from the thoughts of the Bishops than that the papal declarations of truth, and condemnations of error, should need the confirmation and acceptance of the pastors of the Church to be true utterances of the Holy Ghost, and binding in conscience, because their confirmation and acceptance does not add certainty to that which is already infallible.

Q. What does the Vatican Council teach on this subject?

A. It teaches that "the definitions of the Roman Pontiff, concerning faith and morals, are irreformable of themselves, and not by force of the consent of the Church thereto." Sess. iv., c. iv.

Q. What have the Fathers of the Church styled the Pope?

A. The mouth of the Church, ever living and open to teach the whole world;

The centre of Christian faith and unity, and the light of truth for the universe;

The Father of souls, the guide of consciences, and the sovereign judge of the religious interests of mankind;

The Prince of priests—a greater Patriarch than Abraham—greater than Melchisedech in priesthood—than Moses in authority—than Samuel in jurisdiction; a Peter in power, Christ by unction, pastor of pastors, guide of guides, the cardinal joint of all churches, the impregnable citadel of the communion of the children of God, the immovable corner-stone upon which the Church of God reposes.

Q. Why have the Fathers given these titles to the Pope ?

A. Because the Pope is the infallible teacher of the Church of Christ.

Q. What sentiments, then, should every Catholic express concerning the Pope ?

A. I acknowledge in the Pope an authority before which my soul bows, and yet suffers no humiliation.

LESSON V.

PROPAGATION OF CHRIST'S RELIGION.

Q. What did the Apostles do after they had received the Holy Ghost on Whitsunday ?

A. They went forth into the whole world to instruct all nations, according to the orders given them by Jesus Christ.

Q. What did they do with those who believed their doctrine ?

A. They gathered them into congregations.

Q. What came from these congregations of believers ?

A. There arose, in many places, communities of Christians, whose rulers were the Apostles.

Q. What did the Apostles do when those communities of Christians became very numerous?

A. They chose from amongst them men whom they ordained Bishops, appointing them everywhere as the spiritual rulers of the new Christian communities, with the commission likewise to ordain and appoint others to the like offices.

Q. Were all these communities united with one another?

A. Yes; because they all professed the same faith, partook of the same sacraments, and formed all together one great Christian community, under one common head, St. Peter.

Q. What did they call this great community of Christians under one common head?

A. The Catholic, that is, the universal Church, or, simply, the Church.

Q. What, then, is the Church at the present time?

A. The entire body of pastors and people, bound together by the same divine truths, laws, and means of grace, under one head, the Pope of Rome.

Q. Who are the true successors of the Apostles?

A. Only the Bishops of the Roman Catholic Church.

Q. Why?

A. Because they alone are rightly consecrated and in communion with the Pope, the Head of the Church.

Q. Did Christ appoint the Pope alone to govern His Church?

A. The Bishops, too, aid in governing the Church, but only with and under their head, the Pope. "Take heed to yourselves, and to the whole flock, wherein the Holy Ghost hath placed you Bishops, to rule the Church of God." Acts xx. 28.

Q. On what condition did Christ grant any power to His Apostles and their successors?

A. On condition that they would always believe and teach, as the visible Head of His Church believed and taught, and remain obedient to him.

Q. What does St. Irenæus say on this subject?

A. "The Apostles certainly delivered the truth and all the mysteries of our faith to their successors, the pastors. To these, therefore, we ought to have recourse to learn them, especially to the greatest church, the most ancient and known to all, founded at Rome by the two most glorious Apostles, Peter and Paul, *which retains the tradition which it received from them,* and which is derived through a succession of Bishops down to us. To this Church of Rome, on account of its chiefer principality, it is necessary that every church, that is, the faithful everywhere, address themselves, in which Church the tradition from the Apostles is everywhere preserved." Lib. iii. c. 3.

Q. What does St. Cyprian say?

A. "There is but one God and one Christ; there is but one Church and one See, founded upon Peter by our Lord Himself." Lib. i. ep. 8.

Q. What did St. Jerome write to Pope Damasus?

A. "I am attached to your Chair, which is the Chair of St. Peter. I know that the Church is built upon this rock. Whosoever does not eat the Lamb in this house is profane, and whoever does not enter into this Ark, will perish in the waters of the deluge. I do not know Vitalis, I am unacquainted with Meletius, and Paulinus is unknown to me—whoever is not with you is against Jesus Christ, and whoever gathereth not with you, scattereth."

Q. What conclusion are we forced to draw from this constant tradition of the Fathers?

A. That all Christian churches are bound to be in communion with the Church of Rome.

Q. Why is the Catholic Church called the Roman Church?

A. Because St. Peter established the See of his primacy in Rome, and because he handed down the same to be the See of all his successors.

Q. How do the Bishops rule the Church?

A. Each Bishop governs the diocese or bishopric assigned to him by the Pope, and according to the regulations of the Pope. They occasionally meet in council to give their opinion about the best way of advancing the welfare of the Church, and to make decrees and regulations, to be approved of by the Pope.

Q. Through whom do the Bishops exercise their office in the particular congregations (parishes) of their dioceses?

A. Through the priests or pastors whom they appoint.

Q. When may a priest discharge the duties of the priesthood?

A. When he has been expressly sent, or authorized, for that purpose, by his lawful Bishop.

Q. By what means are unity and good order maintained in the Church?

A. By the laity being always obedient to the priests, the priests to the Bishops, and the Bishops to the Pope. "Obey your prelates and be subject to them. For they watch as being to render an account of your souls." Heb. xiii. 17.

LESSON VI.

MARKS OF THE CHURCH.

Q. How many churches did Christ establish?

A. He established *only one* Church.

Q. How do we know this?

A. Because He said to St. Peter: "Upon thee I will build My Church."

Q. Was it a visible or an invisible Church that Christ established?

A. Christ established a visible Church.

Q. How do we know this?

A. Because Christ has commanded us "to

lay our complaints before the Church, that is, before her pastors, and abide by her decision" (Matt. xviii. 17); and because an invisible Church could neither *teach* the law of God nor administer the sacraments.

Q. How does it follow from this that Christ's Church is visible?

A. Because our Lord cannot command us to lay our complaints before *invisible* pastors.

Q. How, then, is the Church of Christ visible?

A. She is visible because all her pastors and members are visible, and have always suffered persecution because they were members of the Church of Christ.

Q. For how many years was this visible Church of Christ to last?

A. It was to last to the end of the world.

Q. How do we know this?

A. Because Jesus Christ said that His Church should last to the end of the world.

Q. What are His words?

A. "Behold I am with you all days, even to the end of the world" (Matt. xxviii. 20); and, "The gates of hell shall not prevail against my church." Matt. xvi. 18.

Q. What would happen, then, if the Church were not to last to the end of the world?

A. Jesus Christ would have told an untruth; to say which would be blasphemous.

Q. How old is the Church to-day?

A. Over eighteen hundred years.

Q. How is the Church so old?

A. Because it is now over eighteen hundred years since our Saviour ascended into heaven.

Q. In which of the religious societies do we find these marks of the Church of Christ?

A. Only in the Holy Roman Catholic Church.

Q. Can the Roman Catholic Church be traced as far back as eighteen hundred years?

A. It can; because we can trace an uninterrupted succession of Popes and Bishops from Pius IX. to St. Peter, and it is impossible to show that it was established at any later period.

Q. Did the Roman Catholic Church ever cease to exist?

A. Never; for she has always existed, and it would be impossible for one to name a period when she did not exist since the time of her establishment.

Q. Do all admit that the Catholic Church was the first Church, that it is the oldest Church, and, consequently the Church established by Jesus Christ?

A. All must aamit this; for it is a fact clearly proven by Scripture and by history.

Q. Who bear witness to this fact?

A. The Jews and the Gentiles bear witness to it, and even Protestants themselves acknowledge it.

Q. How do Protestants acknowledge it?

A. If asked why they call themselves Protestants, they answer: "Because we protest against the Catholic Church."

Q. What follows from this answer?

A. That the Catholic Church is older than Protestantism, otherwise they could not have protested against her.

Q. If we go still farther back, and ask the Greeks how they came to existence, what will be their answer?

A. They must answer: "We began by separating from the Catholic Church in the ninth century.

Q. What follows from this?

A. That the Catholic Church existed for eight hundred years before the Greek Church began, and, consequently, it is older than the Greek Church.

Q. If we thus go back to the very days of the Apostles, what do we find everywhere?

A. That every sect separated from the Catholic Church, and, consequently, that the Catholic Church existed before any of them.

Q. What follows from this ?

A. That the Catholic Church is the oldest Church, the first Church, and, consequently, the Church established by our Lord Jesus Christ.

Q. Can anything like this be said of any of the non-Catholic religious sects now existing ?

A. By no means; since the oldest of them was established only about three hundred years ago.

Q. Do you mean to say that the Protestant doctrine was not known before it was preached by Luther, Calvin, Henry VIII., and John Knox ?

A. I do, for it is impossible to show from history what society held this doctrine before Luther, Calvin, Henry VIII., and John Knox.

Q. If the Protestant religion was established fifteen hundred years later than the true Church of Christ, what follows from this ?

A. It clearly follows that the Protestant religion is *not* the true Church of Jesus Christ.

Q. But were, then, a Protestant to say to you that his doctrine is the same as that held by the Apostles and the Church during the first four centuries, what would you answer him ?

A. I would simply ask him whether or not he was foolish enough to believe that our Lord Jesus Christ and the Blessed Virgin and the Apostles were all Protestants.

Q. Are there still some other marks by which the true Church of Christ may be easily known?

A. Yes, by these four: She is one; she is holy; she is Catholic; she is apostolic.

Q. How many societies are there in this world, in which unity has always existed, and has never been broken?

A. There is only one such society, and this society is the Catholic Church.

Q. In what do her members differ from one another?

A. They differ in their character, their education, their modes of thought; they differ in their language, their habits of life, their sympathies, prejudices; in one word, they differ from one another in everything that distinguishes man from man.

Q. Is there one thing in which they do not differ from one another?

A. There is; they do not differ, and never have differed, from one another in their religion, in which alone they are all of one mind and one heart.

Q. How so ?

A. Because they believe all the same sacred truths contained in the Apostles' Creed, they are all bound by the same commandments of God and the Church, they have all recourse to the same means of grace, the seven sacraments and prayer, and they unite all in the same divine worship—in the holy sacrifice of the Mass.

Q. Can this union in religion ever be broken in the Catholic Church ?

A. Never; because the entirety of her faith will, according to Christ's promise, never fail in her Head—the Pope—from whom it will always flow in all its purity upon all her pastors, and through them upon the rest of the faithful; and the pastors, as well as their flocks, are, by the express command of Christ, all bound under pain of mortal sin to teach and to believe as the Pope teaches and believes, and to be perfectly submissive to him.

Q. How is the Roman Catholic Church holy ?

A. Because her founder, Jesus Christ, is holy, and she teaches His holy doctrine, offers to all the means of holiness, and is distinguished by the holiness of so many thousands of her children.

Q. What means the word Catholic ?

A. It means "universal."

Q. How is the Roman Church Catholic or universal ?

A. Because she exists in all ages, teaches all nations, and maintains all revealed truths, and, therefore, she always went by the name of Catholic, even among her bitterest enemies. "Your faith is spoken of in the whole world." Romans i. 8.

Q. How is the Roman Catholic Church apostolic ?

A. Because she has come down directly from the Apostles through the uninterrupted succession of her bishops; and because she received from the Apostles of Christ, who alone could give them, her doctrine, her orders, and her mission.

Q. Is any non-Catholic religious society one ?

A. No.

Q. Why can no non-Catholic religious society be one ?

A. Because to be one a religious society composed of various members must obey one infallible head only, submit absolutely to be governed by that common head, and obey the infallible teachings of that head. No non-Catholic religious society has or pretends to have such a head and such an infallible teacher.

Q. Give another reason why none of the Protestant sects can be one?

A. Every one of their members assumes to himself more power than Christ gave even to Peter and his successors.

Q. How so?

A. The founders of the Protestant sects and their successors after them, invariably taught their followers that every one has the right to interpret Holy Scripture as he pleases, and to believe as he pleases.

Q. What is the consequence of this freedom of interpretation and belief, as it is called?

A. That no two of them believe alike; that, according to them, Christ's doctrine contradicts itself, and that many of them have already become unbelievers.

Q. Is any non-Catholic religions society holy?

A. No.

Q. Why not?

A. Because their founders and their doctrine are unholy.

Q. Why are their founders not holy?

A. Because the founders of Protestantism

were bad Catholics, who fell away from the faith. "And of your ownselves shall arise men speaking perverse things to draw away disciples after them." Acts xx. 28.

Q. Why is their doctrine not holy ?

A. Because it makes our divine Lord Jesus Christ a liar; rejects and derides the means of holiness instituted by Him; and instead of leading men to holiness, leads them to unbelief and idolatry, by leaving every one free to believe whatever he chooses.

Q. Why cannot non-Catholic religious societies be called Catholic ?

A. Because they sprang up only in later years, and have not ceased to split again into countless sects, none of which is universally spread, or continually spreading in the manner ordained by Christ.

Q. What are the Calvinists, Arminians, Antinomians, Independents, Kilhamites, Glassites, Haldanites, Bereans, Swedenborgians, New-Jerusalemites, Orthodox Quakers, Hicksites, Shakers, Panters, Seekers, Jumpers, Reformed Methodists, German Methodists, Albright Methodists, Episcopal Methodists, Wesleyan Methodists, Methodists North, Methodists South, Protestant Methodists, Episcopalians, High Church Episcopalians, Low Church

Episcopalians, Ritualists, Puseyites, Dutch Reformed, Dutch non-Reformed, Christian Israelites, Baptists, Particular Baptists, Seventh-day Baptists, Hardshell Baptists, Softshell Baptists, Forty Gallon Baptists, Sixty Gallon Baptists, African Baptists, Free-will Baptists, Church of God Baptists, Regular Baptists, Anti-Mission Baptists, Six Principle Baptists, River Brethren, Winebremarians, Menonites, Second Adventists, Millerites, Christian Baptists, Universalists, Orthodox Congregationalists, Campbellites, Presbyterians, Old School and New School Presbyterians, Cumberland Presbyterians, United Presbyterians, The Only True Church of Christ, 573 Bowery, N. Y., up stairs, 5th story, Latter-day Saints, Restorationists, Schwentfelders, Spiritualists, Mormons, Christian Perfectionists, etc., etc., etc. ?

A. They are all so many sects that sprang up from Protestantism.

Q. Was any of the non-Catholic religious societies ever universally called Catholic ?

A. None of them ever was or can, by right, be called by that name.

Q. Why not ?

A. Because the name Catholic belongs to the true Church only ; for they who remained and remain always united with the ancient body of the faithful have retained their ancient name ; but they, on the contrary, who have separated from that body, received a new name, as a mark of their new departure.

Q. Why can none of the non-Catholic religious societies be called apostolic?

A. Because none of them sprang up until fifteen hundred years after the times of the Apostles. They cannot, therefore, trace their descent directly to the Apostles who were commissioned by Christ to teach, and of whom they have no lawful successors. Therefore their teachers, not being empowered by the Apostles or their lawful successors, are not sent by Christ, and are not to be believed and obeyed by Christians.

Q. If, then, none but the Roman Catholic Church has the marks of the one Church of Christ, what follows from this?

A. That the Roman Catholic Church *alone* is the true Church of Jesus Christ.

Q. Give a few proofs to show that the Roman Catholic Church alone is the true Church of Jesus Christ.

A. 1. The antiquity of the Roman Catholic Church.

2. Her establishment by poor fishermen all over the earth.

3. Her invariable duration from that time.

4. The miracles which are wrought in her.

5. The purity and holiness of her doctrines and precepts.

6. The holiness of all those who live according to her laws.

7. The deep science of her doctors.

8. The almost infinite number of her martyrs.

9. The peace of mind and happiness of soul experienced by those who have entered her bosom.

10. The fact that all Protestants admit that a faithful Catholic will be saved in his religion.

11. The frightful punishments inflicted by God upon all the persecutors of the Catholic Church.

12. The melancholy death of all the authors of heresies.

13. The constant fulfilment of the words of our Lord, that His Church would always be persecuted—all tend to convince every reasonable mind that the Roman Catholic Church alone is the true Church of Jesus Christ.

LESSON VII.

THE ROMAN CATHOLIC CHURCH CANNOT BE DESTROYED.

Q. What is the world in which we live?

A. It is the temple of God.

Q. What forms the carpeted floor of this temple?

A. The earth, with all its thousands of flowers.

Q. What forms the vaulted dome?

A. The blue sky above, with its millions of twinkling stars.

Q. For whom did God create this temple?

A. For man, that man might worship Him therein.

Q. What, then, is the world?

A. It is only the temple of religion, reared by God to His own honor and glory, and to the benefit of His servant, man.

Q. Does God watch over the world—the temple of His religion?

A. He watches over it with unceasing care, so that not even a grain of sand, not one atom of matter, has as yet been lost ever since the first morning of creation.

Q. Is it not of far greater importance for God to watch over the preservation of His religion?

A. It is.

Q. Why?

A. Because the preservation of the true religion, or of the true worship and service of God, is of greater importance than the preservation of the world—the material temple in which He is worshipped.

Q. How do we know this?

A. Because, to create the world God used no effort. He simply said: "Be it done," and it was done. But to create and establish His Church, the Son of God sacrificed wealth, honors, pleasure, and everything that man holds dear. He suffered poverty, contempt, persecution. He labored during His whole life, and at last died on a gibbet, and poured out every drop of His sacred blood.

Q. If God, then, preserves with such care the universe—the earthly, material temple, which cost Him nothing—will He not preserve with greater care His heavenly temple, His holy Church, which cost Him His blood and life?

A. He will, indeed, because the temple of this world without religion would be a sad mockery, a worthless encumbrance. It would have failed in the object for which God created it.

Q. What follows from this?

A. That before God allows His religion to be destroyed He must, of necessity, first destroy the world, which is the temple of religion; in other words, sooner shall the sun refuse its light, sooner shall the stars fall from the firmament; sooner shall the precious Blood of Jesus Christ lose its atoning power; sooner shall God cease to be God, than the Church of Jesus Christ cease to be the true Church.

Q. But let us suppose the Church of Jesus Christ had ceased to exist, who would be able to restore her to life?

A. God alone.

Q. Why?

A. Because to raise a dead person or the Church to life, is a far greater work than to preserve that person or Church in life; it is equal to the work of creation. Even the Apostles themselves could not give life to the Church; they could, with the assistance of God, only preserve that life which Jesus Christ had given her.

Q. How great, then, must be he who could restore that dead Church to life?

A. He must be greater than the Apostles; he must, at least, be equal to Jesus Christ Himself.

Q. But are there not men who tell us that they have raised the dead Church to life and restored her?

A. Yes; very many.

Q. Name some of these wonderful men.

A. Martin Luther, Henry VIII., Calvin.

Q. What did Martin Luther do?

A. He claimed to restore the Church to life; to reëstablish and reform her.

Q. How did our Lord Jesus Christ establish His Church?

A. By leading a life of poverty and pain. "He had not where to lay his head." By renouncing all that the world holds dear. By practising through His whole life the three great virtues of poverty, chastity, and entire obedience—obedience even to the death of the Cross.

Q. How did Luther establish his Church?

A. By doing the exact contrary of all this. By breaking his vows of poverty, chastity, and obedience.

Q. Can the church of Luther, then, be the Church of Christ?

A. No; unless the Son of God were to change His nature, which is impossible.

Q. Is not the Catholic Church the Kingdom of Jesus Christ on earth, which He has acquired with so much toil and labor and suffering?

A. Yes; it is that kingdom which He has purchased with His own blood, and which He has loved more than His own life.

Q. Will any power be able to tear this kingdom from Jesus Christ?

A. It would be blasphemous to think so.

Q. Is not the Catholic Church the sheepfold of which Jesus Christ is the Shepherd?

A. She is.

Q. Will the hellish wolf ever be able to take entire possession of the sheepfold in spite of her Divine Shepherd?

A. Sooner will the heavens and the earth pass away than that this will happen.

Q. Is not the Catholic Church the household of which Jesus Christ is the Master?

A. She is.

Q. Will Satan be able to take possession of this household in spite of its Divine Master?

A. No one can say so without blasphemy.

Q. Is not the Catholic Church the Body of Jesus Christ?

A. The Church, says St. Paul, is the Body of Christ.

Q. What follows from this?

A. That Christ is inseparably united with His Church.

Q. What, then, would it be for one to say that the Church could be destroyed?

A. It would be to say that Christ or God can be overcome, which would be the height of madness and blasphemy.

Q. How long will Christ protect and defend His own Body—the Catholic Church?

A. To the end of the world.

Q. In what words has He given us this assurance?

A. In these words: "Behold, I am with you all days, even to the end of the world" (Matt. xxviii. 20); and, therefore, "the gates of hell shall not prevail against my Church."

Q. Is there any other reason why the Catholic Church cannot be destroyed?

A. Yes; the true life of the Catholic Church is the Holy Ghost, the Spirit of Truth, who, according to the promise of Jesus Christ, will abide with His Church for ever.

Q. What is meant by this promise?

A. That the Holy Ghost will enlighten the

pastors of the Catholic Church to preserve and deliver her holy doctrine to the end of the world uncorrupted, and encourage them and the faithful to live up to it, and even to lay down their lives for it. St. John xiv. 16, and Gal. iv. 6.

Q. What follows from this ?

A. It follows that, although the hands of blind or wicked men may rob the Church, may pluck the crown from the Pontiff's brow, may drive her prelates into exile or death, may destroy and defile her sanctuaries, may persecute her children and massacre them by thousands, yet her faith, planted by the Son of God on earth, will gloriously shine and endure to the end of the world.

LESSON VIII.

WHAT CANNOT AND WHAT CAN BE REFORMED IN THE CHURCH.

Q. What follows from the fact that the holy Roman Catholic Church can never be destroyed by any created power ?

A. That it would be the sin of heresy for any

one to think or to say that a reform of the doctrine or the constitution of the Roman Catholic Church could ever become necessary.

Q. Can anyone change the doctrine of Jesus Christ, or the articles of faith, the commandments, or the sacraments?

A. To think so and to attempt to do so would be as foolish as it would be for one to attempt to reform the visible world and the laws which God has established to preserve and maintain it.

Q. Could some new doctrine, new commandment, or new sacrament be added; or could some of the articles of faith, some of the commandments, or some of the sacraments be left out?

A. By no means.

Q. Why not?

A. Because not even the Apostles themselves had power from Christ to add to, or leave out, any portion of Christ's doctrine.

Q. How do we know this?

A. Because Jesus Christ said to the Apostles: "Go and teach all nations, teach them to observe *all things whatsoever I have commanded you.*" Matt. xxviii. 19, 20.

Q. In what other words has our Blessed Saviour assured us that His holy doctrine will never suffer any change?

A. In these words: "Amen, I say unto you, till heaven and earth pass, one jot or one tittle shall not pass of the law, till all be fulfilled." Matt. v. 18. "Heaven and earth shall pass, but my words shall not pass." Matt. xxiv. 35.

Q. What does St. Paul say to assure us that nothing whatsoever can be added to, or left out of the doctrine of Jesus Christ?

A. He says: "But though we, or an angel from heaven, preach a gospel to you besides that which we have preached to you, let him be accursed. As we said before so now I say again: if any one preach to you a gospel besides that which you have *received*, let him be accursed." Gal. i. 8, 9.

Q. Is there nothing in the Catholic Church that may be reformed?

A. Nothing in the doctrine which was delivered to her from the beginning to teach, but the manners of such of her pastors and children as fail to live up to her teachings, may and ought to be reformed.

Q. May Priests and even Bishops, nay, even a Pope, fail to live up to Christ's holy doctrine?

A. They may, indeed; and certain periods

of the lives of some of them have been very disedifying.

Q. How can we easily account for this?

A. Because one can know and teach the true doctrine of Christ without practising it.

Q. What, then, is the answer to those who object to our religion because the lives of certain pastors of the Church have been disedifying?

A. The lives of the scribes and the Pharisees were very disedifying. Nevertheless our blessed Saviour told the multitudes and His disciples that "they have sitten on the chair of Moses. All things, therefore, whatsoever they shall say to you, observe and do: but according to their works do ye not: for they say and do not." Matt. xxiii. 2.

Q. Does the Lord make use of apostate Catholics, such as Martin Luther, Calvin, John Knox, Henry VIII., King of England, to reform the manners of the people?

A. The thought is absurd. The lives of those men were evil, and it is only the devil that makes use of them to pervert the people still more. The Lord makes use of His saints, such as a St. Francis of Assisium, a St. Dominick, a St. Ignatius, a St. Alphonsus, to convert the people and reform their evil manners by explaining to them the truths of faith, the commandments, and the necessity of receiving the sacraments with proper dispositions, and by setting them in their own lives the loftiest example of faith, purity, and all Christian virtues.

Q. Is it possible to reform men in any other way?

A. Since the coming of the Redeemer it has never been heard that men were reformed and made virtuous by any other means than those which Jesus Christ left to His Church.

LESSON IX.
THE FAITH OF THE ROMAN CATHOLIC.

Q. What do the words "I believe" mean?

A. They mean that I hold to be true that which another tells me.

Q. What must we know of a person to believe firmly all his words?

A. That he is truthful and knows well the things which he tells us.

Q. Is God truthful?

A. "He is Truth itself." Rom. iii. 4.

Q. Does God know all things well?

A. "He knows all things as they are." 1 John iii. 20.

Q. Why, then, must we firmly believe all that God has made known.

A. Because He can neither deceive nor be deceived. "God is not as a man, that he should lie." Numb. xxiii. 19.

Q. What is to believe God ?

A. It is to believe, without doubting, that whatever God has said is infallibly true.

Q. Can we of ourselves have this firm faith ?

A. No; it is a particular gift and light of God. "By grace you are saved through faith, and that not of yourselves, for it is the gift of God." Eph. ii. 8.

Q. What does this gift bring about in the soul ?

A. It enlightens the understanding, and moves the will of man to believe without doubting *all that God has made known.* "Faith is the evidence of things that appear not." Heb. xi. 1.

Q. To whom did God make known all that we must believe and do ?

A. Only to the Roman Catholic Church ?

Q. From whom, then, must all men learn all that they must believe and do ?

A. From the Roman Catholic Church, because she alone was appointed by God to teach the truths of salvation to all nations.

Q. Is to believe what the Roman Catholic Church teaches not the same as to believe God Himself?

A. It is, indeed.

Q. Why?

A. Because Jesus Christ has said to the pastors of the Church: "He who heareth you heareth me, and he who despiseth you despiseth me."

Q. What, then, is the faith of the Roman Catholic?

A. It is a grace and light of the Holy Ghost, which enables him to believe most firmly all that God teaches him by His Church.

Q. Is this faith of the Roman Catholic a divine or human faith?

A. It is divine faith.

Q. Why is it divine?

A. Because, by the light of grace, the Catholic knows for certain that the pastors of the Church are commissioned by God Himself to teach all men, in His name, authoritatively and infallibly, all the sacred and immutable truths of salvation, and, therefore, he feels himself bound in conscience to believe them without hesitation.

Q. Is this divine faith absolutely necessary for salvation ?

A. Yes; because it is only by divine faith that we can please God.

Q. Who assures us of this ?

A. Jesus Christ Himself.

Q. What are His words ?

A. "Go and teach all nations.—He that believeth not shall be condemned." Mark xvi.

Q. What does St. Paul say of those who do not believe God, when He speaks to them through those whom He appointed to teach men ?

A. That "it is impossible to please God without faith." Heb. xi.

Q. What, then, is the rule of faith which Jesus Christ gave to all men ?

A. To listen to His living voice, speaking through the pastors of His Church, and to believe them.

Q. Can men possibly have divine faith out of the Catholic Church ?

A. Out of the Catholic Church there can be none but human faith.

Q. What do you mean by human faith ?

A. To believe a man on his own authority.

Q. Do those who are out of the Church, and teach and preach to the people, teach and preach on their own authority ?

A. They do; because they are not sent by God, nor have they received any mission from His Church.

Q. What follows from this?

A. That those who believe them do not believe God, but man, and, therefore, their faith is only human, which availeth them nothing unto salvation.

LESSON X.

QUALITIES OF FAITH.

Q. When is our faith quite pleasing to God?

A. When it is *strong*, *lively*, *entire*, and *sound*.

Q. When is our faith strong?

A. When we believe without the least doubt, and choose to lose all, even our life, rather than fall away from it.

Q. When is our faith lively?

A. When we practise what our faith teaches.

Q. When is our faith entire?

A. When we believe all the truths which the Catholic Church teaches, as contained in the Holy Scripture or tradition.

Q. When is our faith sound?

A. When we avoid not only open heresy, but also diligently shun, and in our hearts dissent from, those errors which approach it more or less closely, and religiously observe those constitutions and decrees whereby such evil opinions, either directly or indirectly, have been proscribed and prohibited by the Holy See.

LESSON XI.

HOLY SCRIPTURE AND TRADITION.

Q. What do you mean by Holy Scripture?

A. A collection of books which were written by holy men, inspired by the Holy Ghost, and acknowledged by the Catholic Church to be the written Word of God.

Q. How is the Holy Scripture divided?

A. Into the books of the Old and the New Testament; or, of the Old and the New Law.

Q. What are we told in the books of the Old Testament?

A. In the books of the Old Testament we are told those truths which God made known before the coming of Christ.

Q. What are we told in the books of the New Testament?

A. Some of the truths which God made known through Jesus Christ and His Apostles.

Q. Is it easy for every one to understand the Holy Scripture?

A. There is nothing more difficult than to understand the true meaning of every passage of the Scripture.

Q. How do we know this?

A. From Holy Scripture itself, which says that "there are certain things hard to be understood, which the unlearned and unstable wrest to their own destruction." 2 Peter iii. 16.

Q. May not every one explain the Bible in his own private manner?

A. "No prophecy of the Scripture," says St. Peter, "is made by private interpretation." 2 Peter i. 20.

Q. To whom belongs the interpretation of the Holy Scriptures?

A. To the Catholic Church alone.

Q. Why?

A. "Because the Apostles carefully entrusted the Scriptures to their successors;

and to whom the Scriptures were entrusted, to them also was committed the interpretation of Scripture." St. Irenæus.

Q. How does the Church make known the meaning of any passage of Scripture?

A. She makes it known either directly by a solemn definition, or by the universal consent of the Church dispersed throughout the world; and she makes it known indirectly when she tells us that we are to interpret Scripture in such a way that our interpretation shall be in harmony with her teaching upon all other points of Christian doctrine.

Q. Have any great evils followed from the unrestricted private interpretation of the Bible?

A. Yes; numberless heresies and impieties.

Q. What have the chief pastors of the Church done to guard the faithful against corrupted Bibles, and against erroneous interpretations, sects, and schisms?

A. They have decreed—1. That, with regard to reading the Bible in the vernacular, we should have the learning and piety requisite for it. 2. That the translation should be approved by the Holy See, or accompanied with explanations by a Bishop.

Q. Why did you say that in the New Testament

we are told some of the truths, and not all the truths which God made known through Jesus Christ and the Apostles?

A. Because all the truths preached by Jesus Christ and the Apostles are not recorded in the Bible.

Q. How do we know this?

A. From the Bible itself, which says: "Many other signs also did Jesus in the sight of His disciples, which are not written in this book." John xx. 30.

Q. Why did the Apostles not write down all that Jesus had taught?

A. Because Jesus Christ had not commanded them to *write*, but to *preach* His doctrine. "Go ye into the whole world and *preach* the Gospel to every creature." Mark xvi. 15.

Q. What is the unwritten doctrine of Jesus Christ and the Apostles called?

A. Tradition.

Q. How did the unwritten doctrine of Jesus Christ come down to us?

A. The Apostles took great care to instruct their disciples thoroughly, and make them capable of so instructing others. Thus their pure doctrine was delivered to the first Bishops and priests of the Roman Catholic

Church. By these, it was in like manner handed down to their successors; and so on, unimpaired, to those who, at the present time, teach in the Catholic Church.

Q. How do we know this?

A. We know it from what St. Paul writes in his Second Epistle to the Bishop Timothy (chap. ii. 2), and from the early Fathers of the Church.

Q. What does St. Paul write?

A. "And the things which *thou hast heard of me* by many witnesses, the same commend to faithful men, who shall be fit to teach others also."

Q. Which of the early Fathers of the Church writes, when speaking of the ninety-first heresy: "All things are not found in the Holy Scripture, for the Apostles have taught us some by tradition, some by writing"?

A. St. Epiphanius.

Q. Who is it that writes: "Of the many truths of faith held by the Church, some have been received from the inspired writings, others from tradition; both sources are equally pure and certain"?

A. St. Basil, in his treatise on the Holy Ghost. Chap. xxvii.

Q. Is that which was taught by Jesus Christ and

His Apostles, but which is not written, less true than that which is written ?

A. The one is just as true as the other.

Q. Why ?

A. Because the Apostles taught the true doctrine of Jesus Christ not less by their preaching, than by their writings, and the Holy Ghost expressed His will, as well by their tongues as by their pens.

Q. What follows from this ?

A. That we must believe the unwritten Word of God as firmly as the written.

Q. Who assures us most emphatically of this ?

A. St. Paul, in these words: "Therefore, brethren, stand fast; and *hold the traditions* which you have learned, whether *by word,* or by our Epistle." 2 Thess. ii. 14.

Q. Was this also the belief of the Fathers of the Church ?

A. It was; for St. John Chrysostom writes, in his 4th homily on the Second Epistle of St. Paul to the Thessalonians: "Therefore it is evident that the Apostles taught many things *without writing,* which we must *believe as firmly* as those which are written."

Q. Name some of those truths of which the Bible does not speak, but which we believe from tradition?

A. We know only from tradition—1. That little children are to be baptized.

2. That we must keep holy the Sunday instead of the Saturday.

3. We know only from tradition those books which are divine, and contain the written word of God.

Q. But was it not possible that those truths which were taught by the Apostles, but which were not written, might easily be corrupted, or forgotten altogether, because not recorded in Holy Scripture ?

A. No; because God Himself took care that what He had taught should not be forgotten, but be handed down to us uncorrupted.

Q. Was there any written Word of God for two thousand years, from Adam down to Moses ?

A. There was not.

Q. How then did all that God spoke to Adam, Noah, etc., come down uncorrupted to Moses, who was the first to write down the Word of God ?

A. By tradition; that is, God took care that the Patriarchs, His faithful servants, should hand down by word of mouth His doctrine uncorrupted from generation to generation.

Q. Could not, and did not God do the same from the times of the Apostles down to us ?

A. He could, and did, by means of the faithful pastors of His Church.

Q. How did the pastors of His Church hand down to us the unwritten doctrine of the Apostles?

A. Partly by word of mouth and partly by their writings, in which they explain the doctrine of the Apostles, written and unwritten.

Q. What do we understand from this?

A. That, for example, the faith of the Catholic Church in the Real Presence of Jesus Christ in the Blessed Sacrament would have been at all times precisely what it is, had it pleased God that the passages in Holy Scripture, relating to it, had never been written; and so with all the rest of the teachings of the Catholic Church.

Q. Are the doctrines of the Catholic Church then entirely independent of Scripture?

A. They are; because she taught her doctrines, and they were believed by the early Christians before the New Testament was written—centuries, indeed, before the Bible was collected into its present form; and she would have done so, in precisely the same manner, had they never been written.

Q. When was the last part of the New Testament written?

A. It was written by St. John, *sixty-three* years after the Ascension of our Lord.

Q. When were the books of the Old and the New Testament, which we now call the Bible, or the Book, by pre-eminence, collected together, and declared to be the written Word of God?

A. They were so declared, for the first time, in the *great* Council of Nice, A. D. 325.

Q. If, then, to gain salvation, it were necessary to read the Bible, to interpret it by private judgment, and to form thereby a rule of faith and morals, how could all those thousands of Christians, who lived during those three hundred and twenty-five years, be saved? Or, how could those be saved who did not understand the true sense of the Bible, or who could not read the Bible, or get a Bible?

A. Thank God, it was not necessary to have a Bible; otherwise *all* would, inevitably, have been lost. The Bishops and priests taught them; they believed, and sealed their faith with their blood.

Q. What, then, is the principal motive why Catholics believe the truths of their religion: is it because these truths are found in Holy Scripture, or because the pastors of the Catholic Church teach them?

A. They believe these truths only because God teaches them through the pastors of the Church; so much so, that, as St. Augustine says, we would not believe even the Bible if the Catholic Church did not assure us that it was the written word of God.

Q. What are we to learn from all that has been said on the Scripture and tradition?

A. That the whole doctrine of Christ and His Apostles, written and unwritten, is to be found in the Roman Catholic Church alone.

Q. Why?

A. 1. Because it is she alone who received the Scripture and tradition from the Apostles, and has always, with the special assistance of the Holy Ghost, preserved them uncorrupted.

2. Because it is she alone who gives us undoubted security for their Divine origin.

3. Because in her alone Jesus Christ, in the person of St. Peter and his successors—the Popes—has left us an infallible interpreter of the whole doctrine of Christ, written and unwritten.

Q. What, then, do we mean when we say: "I believe the Holy Catholic Church"?

A. We mean that we firmly believe in the fact that Jesus Christ has established a visible church, endless in her duration, and infallible in her doctrine, which we must believe and obey without reserve, if we would obtain eternal salvation; and that this Church is no other than the Roman Catholic Church.

Q. How do people come to lose this faith?

A. 1. By want of instruction.

2. By neglect of prayer and other religious duties.

3. By worldliness and a wicked life.

4. By reading bad books.

5. By intercourse with scoffers at religion.

6. By mixed marriages.

7. By becoming members of secret societies.

8. By pride and subtle reasoning on the mysteries of our religion.

9. By want of submission to the Church.

10. By godless education.

LESSON XII.

NO SALVATION OUTSIDE OF THE ROMAN CATHOLIC CHURCH.

Q. Since the Roman Catholio Church alone is the true Church of Jesus Christ, can any one who dies outside of the Church be saved?

A. He cannot.

Q. Why not?

A. Because one who does not do the will of God cannot be saved.

Q. Is it, then, the will of God that all men should be Catholics?

A. Yes; because it is only in the Roman Catholic Church that they can learn the will of God; that is, the full doctrine of Jesus Christ, which alone can save them.

Q. Did Jesus Christ Himself assure us most solemnly, and in plain words, that no one can be saved out of the Roman Catholic Church?

A. He did, when He said to His Apostles: "Go and teach all nations, and teach them to observe all things whatsoever I have commanded you. He that believeth not all these things shall be condemned."

Q. Did Jesus Christ assure us in other words of the damnation of those who die out of His Church?

A. He did in these words: "He who will not hear the Church, let him be to thee as the heathen and publican." Matt. xviii. 17.

Q. Can you give some further proofs to show that no one can be saved out of the Roman Catholic Church?

A. From these words of Jesus Christ: "Other sheep I have who are not of this fold, them also I must bring, and they shall hear my voice, and they shall be one fold and one shepherd." John x. 16.

Q. How can you show from these words of our Lord that all who wish to be saved must be Roman Catholics?

A. Because in this passage He plainly declares that all those of His sheep who are not of His fold (that is, of His Church) must, as a *necessary* condition of their salvation, be brought to that fold.

Q. What do the Fathers of the Church say about the salvation of those who die out of the Roman Catholic Church?

A. They all, without exception, pronounce them infallibly lost for ever.

Q. What did St. Augustine and the other Bishops of Africa, at the Council of Zirta, A.D. 412, say about them?

A. "Whosoever," they said, "is separated from the Catholic Church, however commendable in his own opinion his life may be, he shall, for the very reason that he is separated from the Union of Christ, not see life, but the wrath of God abideth on him." John iii. 36.

Q. What does St. Cyprian tell us about the salvation of those who die out of the Roman Catholic Church?

A. He says that, "He who has not the Church for his mother cannot have God for his Father;" and with him the Fathers in general say, that "as all who were not in the ark of Noah perished in the waters of the deluge, so shall all perish who are out of the true Church."

Q. Who are out of the pale of the Roman Catholic Church?

A. All unbaptized persons, unbelievers, apostates, excommunicated persons, and all heretics.

Q. How do we know that unbaptized persons are not saved?

A. Because Jesus Christ has said: "Unless a man be born again of water and the Holy Ghost, he cannot enter into the kingdom of God." John iii. 5.

Q. How do we know that unbelievers are not saved?

A. Because it is said of them that they do not please God. "Without faith it is impossible to please God."

Q. How do we know that apostates are not saved?

A. Because to fall away from the faith is a great sin, which makes one lose the kingdom of heaven.

Q. How do we know that persons justly excommunicated, who are unwilling to do what is required of them before they are absolved, are not saved?

A. Because the sin of great scandal, for which they were as dead members expelled from the communion of the Church, excludes them from the kingdom of heaven.

Q. What is the meaning of the word heretic?

A. Heretic is a Greek word, and means simply a chooser.

Q. Who, then, is a heretic?

A. A baptized person who chooses among

the doctrines proposed to him by the Roman Catholic Church, to accept such doctrines as please him, and to reject the rest.

Q. How do we know that heretics are not saved?

A. Because St. Paul the Apostle assures us that such a chooser or heretic is condemned. "A man that is a heretic, after the first and second admonition, avoid; knowing that he who is such an one is subverted, and sinneth, being condemned by his own judgment." Tit. iii. 10, 11.

Q. Are there any other reasons to show that heretics, or Protestants who die out of the Roman Catholic Church, are not saved?

A. There are several. They cannot be saved, because

1. They have no divine faith.
2. They make a liar of Jesus Christ, of the Holy Ghost, and of the Apostles.
3. They have no faith in Christ.
4. They fell away from the true Church of Christ.
5. They are too proud to submit to the Pope, the Vicar of Christ.
6. They cannot perform any good works whereby they can obtain heaven.

7. They do not receive the Body and Blood of Christ.

8. They die in their sins.

9. They ridicule and blaspheme the Mother of God and His saints.

10. They slander the spouse of Jesus Christ —the Catholic Church.

Q. Why is it that Protestants have no divine faith?

A. Because they do not believe God in those whom He has appointed to teach.

Q. Who is the teacher among Protestants?

A. Every one is his own teacher, his own law-giver and judge in matters of religion.

Q. Was there ever a time when God left men to themselves, to fashion their own religion, to invent their own creed, and their own form of worship?

A. No; from the beginning of the world God established on earth a visible teaching authority, to which it was the bounden duty of every man to submit.

Q. What follows from this?

A. That Protestants, by refusing to submit to that divine teaching authority, cannot have divine faith.

Q. What is the act of faith of a Protestant?

A. O my God, I believe nothing except

what my own private judgment tells me to believe; therefore I believe that I can interpret Thy written word—the Holy Scriptures—as I choose. I believe that the Pope is anti-Christ; that any man can be saved, provided he is an honest man; I believe that faith alone is sufficient for salvation; that good works, and works of penance, and the confession of sins are not necessary, etc.

Q. Is this an act of divine faith?

A. It is rather a great blasphemy against God; it is the language of Luther, who, according to his own avowal, learned it from the devil.

Q. But if a Protestant should say—"I have nothing to do with Luther, or Calvin, or Henry VIII., or John Knox; I go by the Bible" what would you answer him?

A. In that case you adopt and go by the principles and spirit of these men, and you change the written Word of God into the word of man.

Q. How so?

A. Because every Protestant interprets Holy Scripture in his own private manner, giving it that meaning which he chooses to give it, and thus, instead of believing the Word of God, he believes rather his own private interpretation of it, which is but the word of man.

Q. Now, what is man without divine faith?

A. Such a man is profane, and devoid of all religion; and for refusing all obedience to his Sovereign Lord, he will never enjoy His presence, or see clearly what he is not willing to believe humbly.

Q. How do Protestants make a liar of Jesus Christ?

A. Jesus Christ says: "Hear the Church." "No;" says Luther and all Protestants, "do not hear the Church, protest against her with all your might."

Jesus Christ says: "If any one will not hear the Church, look upon him as a heathen and publican." "No," says Protestantism, "if any one does not hear the Church, look upon him as an apostle, as an ambassador of God."

Jesus Christ says: "The gates of hell shall not prevail against my Church." "No," says Protestantism, "'Tis false; the gates of hell have prevailed against the Church for a thousand years and more."

Jesus Christ has declared St. Peter, and every successor to St. Peter—the Pope—to be his Vicar on earth. "No," says Protestantism, "the Pope is anti-Christ."

Jesus Christ says: "My yoke is sweet, and my burden light." Matt. xi. 30. "No," said Luther and Calvin, "it is impossible to keep the commandments."

Jesus Christ says: "If thou wilt enter into life, keep the commandments." Matt. xix. 17. "No," said Luther and Calvin, "faith *alone*, without good works, is sufficient to enter into life everlasting."

Jesus Christ says: "Unless you do penance, you shall all likewise perish." Luke iii. 3. "No," said Luther and Calvin, "fasting, and other works of penance, are not necessary in satisfaction for sin."

Jesus Christ says: "This is My Body." "No," said Calvin, "this is only the figure of Christ's Body, it will become His Body as soon as you receive it."

Jesus Christ says: "I say to you, that whosoever shall put away his wife, and shall marry another, committeth adultery; and he that shall marry her that is put away, committeth adultery." Matt. xix. 9. "No," says Luther and all Protestants, to a married man, "you may put away your wife, get a divorce, and marry another."

Jesus Christ says to every man: "Thou shalt not steal." "No," says Luther to secular princes, "I give you the right to appropriate to yourselves the property of the Roman Catholic Church."

Q. How do Protestants make a liar of the Holy Ghost?

A. The Holy Ghost says in Holy Scripture: "Man knoweth not whether he be worthy of love or hatred" (Eccles. ix. 1); "Who can say: My heart is clean, I am pure from sin"? (Prov. xx. 9); and "Work your salvation with fear and trembling" (Philip. ii. 12). "No," said Luther and Calvin, "but whosoever believes in Jesus Christ, is in the state of grace."

Q. How do Protestants make liars of the Apostles?

A. St. Paul says: "If I should have faith, so that I could remove mountains, and have not charity, I am nothing." 1 Cor. xiii. 2.

"No," said Luther and Calvin, "faith *alone* is sufficient to save us."

St. Peter says that in the Epistles of St. Paul there are many things "hard to be understood, which the unlearned and unstable wrest, as also the other Scriptures, to their own perdition." 2 Eph. iii. 16. "No," said Luther and Calvin, "the Scriptures are very plain, and easy to be understood."

St. James says: "Is any sick among you? Let him bring in the priests of the church, and let them pray over him, anointing him with oil, in the name of the Lord." Ch. v. 14. "No," said Luther and Calvin, "that is a vain and useless ceremony."

Q. Now, do you think God the Father will admit into Heaven those who thus make liars of His Son Jesus Christ, of the Holy Ghost, and the Apostles?

A. No; He will let them have their portion with Lucifer in hell, who first rebelled against Christ, and who is the father of liars.

Q. Have Protestants any faith in Christ?

A. They never had.

Q. Why not?

A. Because there never lived such a Christ as they imagine and believe in.

Q. In what kind of a Christ do they believe?

A. In such a one of whom they can make a liar, with impunity, whose doctrine they can interpret as they please, and who does not care about what a man believes, provided he be an honest man before the public.

Q. Will such a faith in such a Christ save Protestants?

A. No sensible man will assert such an absurdity.

Q. What will Christ say to them on the day of judgment?

A. I know you not, because you never knew Me.

Q. Can a man be saved who has left the true Church of Christ—the Holy Catholic Church?

A. No; because the Church of Christ is the kingdom of God on earth, and he who leaves that kingdom shuts himself out from the kingdom of Christ in heaven.

Q. Have Protestants left the true Church of Christ?

A. They have, in their founders, who left the Catholic Church either through pride or through the passion of lust and covetousness.

Q. Who were the first Protestants?

A. 1. Martin Luther, a bad German priest,

who left his convent, broke the solemn vows of poverty, chastity, and obedience, which he had made to God, married a nun, and became the founder of the Lutherans.

2. Henry VIII., a bad Catholic king of England, who murdered his wives, and founded the Episcopalian or Anglican Church.

3. John Calvin, a wicked French Catholic, who was the founder of the Calvinists.

4. John Knox, a bad Scottish priest, who was the founder of the Presbyterians or Puritans.

Q. What great crime did these wicked men commit ?

A. They rebelled against the Church of Jesus Christ, and caused a great number of their Catholic countrymen to follow their bad example.

Q. What will be the punishment of those who wilfully rebel against the Holy Catholic Church ?

A. Like Lucifer, and the other rebellious angels, they will be cast into the everlasting flames of hell.

Q. Who has assured us of this ?

A. Jesus Christ Himself, the Son of God.

Q. What are His words ?

A. "He who will not hear the Church, let

him be to thee as the heathen and publican." Matt. xviii. 17.

Q. What does Jesus Christ tell us in these words?

A. He tells us plainly that he who is out of His Church, and does not obey her, is before Him as the heathen and publican.

Q. What follows from this?

A. It follows that, as the heathen is damned, so, also, all those will be damned who die out of the Church of Jesus Christ.

Q. Can a man be saved who is too proud to submit to the Head of the Church of Christ, and despises Jesus Christ in His representative—the Pope?

A. He cannot; because Jesus Christ says: "He who despiseth you (the Apostles and their successors) despiseth me."

Q. Do Protestants despise Jesus Christ in the person of St. Peter and his successors?

A. They do; for Luther taught them that whoever does not oppose the authority of the Pope cannot be saved. 1 Vol. Germ. Edit., f. 353.

Q. Do you think Christ can admit into Heaven him by whom He is despised?

A. This is impossible, and of such a one

is true what St. Paul says: "He that resisteth the power that is from God, resisteth the ordinance of God. And they that resist purchase to themselves damnation." Rom. xiii. 1, 2.

Q. Can any one enter into the Kingdom of Heaven without good works?

A. No.

Q. How do we know this?

A. Because on the last day of judgment Christ will say to the wicked: "Depart from me, ye cursed, into everlasting fire. For I was hungry and you gave me not to eat, I was thirsty and you gave me not to drink." Matt. xxv. 41, 42.

Q. Do not Protestants perform such good works?

A. Many of them do.

Q. Will they be saved on account of such good works?

A. By no means; because works, however good in themselves, performed outside of the church established by Jesus Christ, are not accompanied and vivified by divine faith, without which it is impossible to please God, and, therefore, they do not, they cannot merit the everlasting joys of Heaven. As faith without works is dead, so also works without faith are dead and cannot save the doer from damnation.

Q. What does Jesus Christ say of those who do not receive His Body and Blood?

A. Except you eat the Flesh of the Son of man and drink his Blood, you shall not have life in you. John vi. 54.

Q. Do Protestants receive the Body and Blood of our Lord?

A. No, because their ministers are not priests, and consequently have no power from Jesus Christ to say Mass, in which, by the words of consecration, bread and wine are changed into the Body and Blood of Christ.

Q. What follows from this?

A. That they will not enter into life everlasting, and deservedly so, because they abolished the holy sacrifice of the Mass.

Q. What was the consequence of the abolition of Mass?

A. By abolishing the Mass, they robbed God the Father of the infinite honor which Jesus Christ renders Him therein, and themselves of all the blessings which Jesus Christ bestows upon those who assist at this holy sacrifice with faith and devotion. "Wherefore the sin of the young men (the sons of

Heli) was exceeding great before the Lord, because they withdrew men from the sacrifice of the Lord." 1 Kings ii. 17.

Q. Do you believe that God the Father will admit into heaven these robbers of His infinite honor?

A. By no means; because if those are damned who steal the temporal goods of their neighbor, how much more will those be damned who deprive God of His infinite honor and their fellow-men of the infinite spiritual blessings of the Mass.

Q. Can a man be saved who dies in the state of mortal sin?

A. He cannot; because God cannot unite Himself to a soul in heaven who, by mortal sin, is His enemy.

Q. Do Protestants commit other mortal sins besides those above mentioned?

A. Very many besides.

Q. How do you prove this?

A. If it is a mortal sin for a Roman Catholic wilfully to doubt only one article of his faith, it is also, most assuredly, a mortal sin for Protestants wilfully to deny not only one truth, but almost all the truths revealed by Jesus Christ.

Q. Do they die in the sins of apostasy, blasphemy, slander, etc.?

A. They do, because all die in mortal sin who, having grievously offended Almighty God, are not willing to confess their sins.

Q. How do we know this?

A. Because Jesus Christ assures us that those sins which are not forgiven by His apostles and their successors, by means of confession, will not be forgiven. "Whose sins you retain they are retained." John xx. 22, 23.

Q. Are Protestants willing to confess their sins to a Catholic Bishop or priest, who alone has power from Christ to forgive sins? "Whose sins you shall forgive, they are forgiven them."

A. No, for they generally have an utter aversion to confession, and therefore their sins will not be forgiven throughout all eternity.

Q. What follows from this?

A. That they die in their sins and are damned.

Q. If any one loves God, will he also love the Mother of God and all His Saints?

A. He will, undoubtedly.

Q. Do Protestants love the Mother of God and the Saints?

A. They do not, or they would not ridicule

and blaspheme the Mother of God and the Saints.

Q. What follows from this?

A. That Protestants will never be admitted into the company of the Saints in heaven, whom they have ridiculed and blasphemed on earth.

Q. Would a great king of this world punish most severely one who slanders the queen?

A. He would.

Q. Is the Catholic Church the Spouse of Jesus Christ, the King of heaven and earth?

A. She is, and St. Paul assures us that "Jesus Christ loves His church, that He died for her in order that He might have a glorious church, having neither spot nor wrinkle, but holy and without blemish." Eph. v. 25–27.

Q. Have Protestants ever ceased to slander her?

A. Never.

Q. How do they slander the Spouse of Jesus Christ?

A. The Protestant Episcopalian book of homilies, for instance, says: "Laity and clergy, learned and unlearned, all ages and degrees of men, women, and children of entire Christendom had been drowned in abominable idolatry."

Q. Is idolatry a grievous sin?

A. It is one of the most grievous sins that can be committed.

Q. Could Protestants ever prove that the Catholic Church, the Spouse of Christ, became guilty of this sin?

A. Never; on the contrary, all know that the Catholic Church has abolished idolatry and has always held it in abomination.

Q. What follows from this?

A. That Protestants commit the great sin of slander against the Spouse of Christ.

Q. Can they commit this great sin without accusing Jesus Christ at the same time of having abandoned that glorious Spouse, whom He loves so ardently?

A. They cannot.

Q. What follows from this?

A. That the vengeance of Jesus Christ shall sooner or later overtake Protestants for committing the sins of a horrid blasphemy and slander.

Q. But is it not a very uncharitable doctrine to say that none can be saved out of the Church?

A. On the contrary, it is a very great act of charity to assert this doctrine most emphatically.

Q. Why?

A. Because Jesus Christ Himself and His apostles have taught it in very plain language.

Q. Is it not great charity to warn one's neighbor when he is in danger of falling into a deep abyss?

A. It is, indeed.

Q. Are not all those who are out of the Church in very great danger of falling into the abyss of hell?

A. They are.

Q. Is it not, then, great charity to warn them of this danger?

A. It would be as great a cruelty not to warn them.

Q. Are all those who are out of the Church equally guilty and damnable before God?

A. No; some are more guilty than others.

Q. Who are least guilty and damnable?

A. Those who, without any fault of theirs, do not know Jesus Christ or His doctrine at all.

Q. Who are most guilty and damnable?

A. Those who know the Catholic Church to be the only true Church, but do not embrace her faith, as also those who could know her if they would candidly search, but who, through indifference and other culpable motives, neglect to do so.

Q. What are we to think of the salvation of those who are out of the pale of the Church without any fault of theirs, and who never had any opportunity of knowing better?

A. Their inculpable ignorance will not save them; but if they fear God and live up to their conscience, God, in His infinite mercy, will furnish them with the necessary means of salvation, even so as to send, if needed, an angel to instruct them in the Catholic faith, rather than let them perish through inculpable ignorance.

Q. Is it then right for us to say that one who was not received into the Church before his death, is damned?

A. No.

Q. Why not?

A. Because we cannot know for certain what takes place between God and the soul at the awful moment of death.

Q. What do you mean by this?

A. I mean that God, in His infinite mercy, may enlighten, at the hour of death, one who is not yet a Catholic, so that he may see the truth of the Catholic faith, be truly sorry for his sins, and sincerely desire to die a good Catholic.

Q. What do we say of those who receive such an extraordinary grace, and die in this manner?

A. We say of them that they die united, at least, to the soul of the Catholic Church, and are saved.

Q. What, then, awaits all those who are out of the Catholic Church, and die without having received such an extraordinary grace at the hour of death?

A. Eternal damnation, as sure as there is a God.

Q. But are there not many who would lose the affections of their friends, their comfortable homes, their temporal goods, and prospects in business, were they to become Catholics? Would not Jesus Christ excuse them under such circumstances from becoming Catholics?

A. As to the affections of friends, Jesus Christ has solemnly declared that: "He who loveth father or mother more than me, is not worthy of me; and he that loveth son or daughter more than me, is not worthy of me," Matt. x. 37; and as to the loss of temporal gain He has answered: "What shall it profit a man if he gain the whole world and suffer the loss of his soul?" Mark viii. 36.

Q. But would it not be enough for such a one to

be a Catholic in heart only, without professing his religion publicly ?

A. No; for Jesus Christ has solemnly declared that, "He who shall be ashamed of me and of my words, of him the Son of Man shall be ashamed when he shall come in his majesty, and that of his Father, and of the holy angels." Luke ix. 26.

Q. But might not such a one safely put off being received into the Church till the hour of death ?

A. This would be to abuse the mercy of God.

Q. What might be the punishment for this sin ?

A. To lose the light and grace of faith, and die a reprobate.

Q. What else keeps many from becoming Catholics ?

A. It is this: they know very well that, if they become Catholics, they must lead honest and sober lives, be pure, and check their sinful passions, and this they are unwilling to do. "Men love darkness rather than light," says Jesus Christ, "because their deeds are evil." There are none so deaf as those that will not hear.

Q. What follows from what has been said on salvation in the Roman Catholic Church alone ?

A. That it is very impious for one to think and to say that it matters little what a man believes provided he be an honest man.

Q. What answer can you give to a man who speaks thus?

A. I would ask him whether or not he believed that his honesty and justice was so great as that of the Scribes and Pharisees in the Gospel?

Q. In what did the honesty and justice of the Scribes and Pharisees consist?

A. They were constant in prayer, they paid tithes according to the law, gave great alms, fasted twice a week, and compassed sea and land to make a convert and bring him to the knowledge of the true God.

Q. What did Jesus Christ say of this justice of the Pharisees?

A. He says: "Unless your justice shall exceed that of the Scribes and Pharisees you shall not enter into the kingdom of heaven." Matt. v. 20.

Q. Was, then, the righteousness of the Pharisees very defective in the sight of God?

A. Most undoubtedly. Their righteousness was all outward show and ostentation. They did good only to be praised and admired by men; but within, their souls were full of impurity and malice. They were lewd hypocrites, who concealed great vices under the beautiful appearance of love for God, charity to the poor, and severity to themselves. Their devotion consisted in exterior acts, and they despised all who did not live as they did; they were strict in the religious observances of human traditions, but scrupled not to violate the commandments of God.

Q. What are you then to think of those men who say: "It matters little what a man believes, provided he be honest"?

A. That their exterior honesty, like that of the Pharisees, may be sufficient to keep them out of prison, but not out of hell.

Q. Should a non-Catholic say: "I would like very much to believe the doctrine of the Catholic Church, but I cannot," how would you answer?

A. That, without doubt, it is the will of God, that "all men be saved, and come to the knowledge of the truth." 1 Tim. ii. 4; but it is, at the same time, the will of God that you should earnestly employ all the proper means to acquire this necessary knowledge; otherwise, you plainly show that you do not sincerely desire to believe.

Q. What are the means you speak of?

A. Sincerity of heart which must prove itself,

1. By a most earnest desire to know the true religion,

2. By a diligent and persistent search for it,

3. By fervent and frequent prayer to God for the gift of faith,

4. And lastly, by a firm resolution to trample under foot every obstacle that might hinder or retard one from embracing the known truth.

Q. But will one not lose his dear liberty if he believes and does what the Roman Catholic Church teaches?

A. No; on the contrary, he will then only enjoy true liberty, for he only is free whom the truth makes free.

Q. Cannot God do all things that He pleases?

A. He can.

Q. Why?

A. Because He is supreme Liberty itself.

Q. But can God sin?

A. He cannot.

Q. Are not the angels and saints in heaven free?

A. They are perfectly free, because they partake of the liberty of God.

Q. But can the saints sin?

A. They cannot.

Q. Is it, then, a mark of liberty to be under the power of sin, in following your passions, and so going to perdition?

A. This is no power or mark of liberty at all.

Q. What is it, then?

A. It is rather a mark of weakness and misery.

Q. What does the power of sin imply?

A. The possibility of becoming a slave of sin and the devil.

Q. Are those then truly free who are greatly under the power of sin, and thus go to hell?

A. They are rather the miserable slaves of sin and of their passions.

Q. What must necessarily become of them if they remain under this power of sin and of their passions?

A. They will become the slaves of the devil in hell for all eternity.

Q. Who, then, can call himself truly free?

A. He who wills and does what God wishes him to do for his everlasting happiness.

Q. If God, then, as we have seen, wishes that men should be saved only in the holy Roman Catholic Church, does a man lose, or does he enjoy liberty, when he believes and does what the Church teaches ?

A. Then, indeed, he enjoys true liberty, and makes a proper use of it.

Q. What do you say of a man whose power of will is very great, and who hardly experiences any difficulty in following the teaching of the Church ?

A. Such a man is truly *free.*

Q. Do Catholics, then, who faithfully live up to the teaching of the Church, enjoy greater liberty than Protestants and unbelievers, who believe and do as they please ?

A. They do, indeed, because they are the children of the light of truth, that leads them to heaven, whilst those who live out of the Church are the children of the darkness of error, that leads them finally into the abyss of hell.

Q. If no one can be saved except in the Roman Catholic Church, what are all who are out of it bound to do ?

A. They are obliged to become members of the Church.

Q. Does not common sense tell this to every non-Catholic ?

A. It does.

Q. How so ?

A. Because every non-Catholic believes that every practical member of the Catholic Church will be saved.

Q. What follows from this ?

A. It clearly follows that when there is question about eternal salvation and eternal damnation, a sensible man will take the surest way to heaven.

Q. Will every one who is a member of the Catholic Church be saved ?

A. No; only practical members will be saved; but those who are dead members, that is, bad Catholics, will be condemned to hell.

Q. Who is a practical member of the Catholic Church ?

A. He who firmly believes all the truths contained in the Apostles' Creed, keeps the commandments of God and of the Church, and uses the means of grace, that is, the sacraments and prayer.

Q. Where do you learn all this ?

A. In the Christian doctrine.

Q. Whose duty is it to teach the Christian doctrine ?

A. This is the duty of the pastors of the Catholic Church.

Q. Is it very pleasing to God to instruct men in the Christian doctrine ?

A. Yes ; it is one of the holiest works, and most pleasing to God.

Q. Whose duty is it to attend to the explanation of the Christian doctrine ?

A. This is the duty of all, but especially of those who are more or less ignorant of the Christian religion.

Q. Is God much pleased with those who eagerly listen to the explanation of the Christian doctrine ?

A. God is so pleased with them that He often showed His pleasure by miracles.

Q. Is God also much displeased with those who do not care for the Christian doctrine ?

A. God is so displeased with them that He often showed His displeasure by frightful punishments.

Q. What should we do when we hear the Christian doctrine explained ?

A. We should listen to it with the intention of profiting by it.

Q. What do you call the book which briefly contains the Christian doctrine in the form of questions and answers ?

A. The Catechism.

Q. Of what, then, does the Catechism treat?

A. The Catechism treats of what we must believe, of what we must do, and of the means of grace which we must use; that is, of the sacraments and prayer.

FAMILIAR EXPLANATION

OF

CHRISTIAN DOCTRINE.

PART II.

WHAT WE MUST BELIEVE.

LESSON I.

ON GOD.

Q. What did the Apostles do before they went into the whole world to instruct all nations ?

A. They made the Symbol or Creed.

Q. What is this Symbol or Creed of the Apostles ?

A. It is a summary of the whole Christian Doctrine, in these terms:

1. I believe in God, the Father Almighty, Creator of heaven and earth ;

2. And in Jesus Christ, His only Son, our Lord;

3. Who was conceived by the Holy Ghost, born of the Virgin Mary;

4. Suffered under Pontius Pilate, was crucified, dead and buried;

5. He descended into hell; the third day He arose again from the dead;

6. He ascended into heaven, sitteth at the right hand of God, the Father Almighty;

7. From thence He shall come to judge the living and the dead.

8. I believe in the Holy Ghost;

9. The Holy Catholic Church; the Communion of Saints;

10. The forgiveness of sins;

11. The resurrection of the body;

12. And life everlasting. Amen.

Q. How is the Apostles' Creed divided?

A. Into twelve parts or articles.

Q. Which is the first article of the Creed?

A. I believe in God the Father Almighty, Creator of heaven and earth.

Q. What is God?

A. God is the *Independent Spirit,* Who is of Himself, and is infinite in all His Perfections.

Q. Why do we call God a Spirit?

A. Because God has understanding and free will, but no body.

Q. Why do we call God the "Independent" Spirit?

A. Because all things depend on God, but He depends on no one.

Q. Why is God called Almighty?

A. Because He can do all things whatsoever by *merely willing* them to be.

Q. Is God eternal?

A. Yes, because He has no beginning; He always was and always will be.

Q. Is God immense?

A. Yes, because He is in heaven, on earth, and in all places.

Q. Does God know and see all things?

A. God knows and sees all things, even our most secret thoughts and desires.

Q. Does God know how to dispose all things so as to bring about whatever He wills?

A. He does, because He is infinitely wise.

Q. Does God love and will only what is good, and hate all that is evil?

A. He does, because He is infinitely holy.

Q. Does God leave a sinful act without due punishment, and a good work without due reward?

A. He does not, because He is infinitely just.

Q. Is God infinitely good?

A. He is, because He is all love to those who love Him, and He cannot be more bountiful than He is.

Q. Does God most willingly and readily forgive all truly sorrowful sinners who are ready to comply with the condition on which He has promised pardon?

A. He does, because He is infinitely merciful.

Q. Is God infinitely true?

A. Yes, because He makes known nothing but truth, and can neither deceive nor be deceived.

Q. Does God surely keep His promises and carry out his threats?

A. He does, because He is infinitely faithful.

Q. Are there more gods than one?

A. No, there is but one God.

Q. Can we see God?

A. No; we cannot see God with the eyes of our body, because He is a Spirit.

Q. Since we cannot see God, how have we come to know God and His Perfections?

A. Because God has made Himself known to man in a natural, and especially in a supernatural manner.

Q. How has God made Himself known to man in a natural manner?

A. By the visible world, which He has created, and continually governs.

Q. How do we see from the creation and government of the world that there is a God?

A. Because no sensible man will think that the world made itself, or that its regular and perfect order came and continues by itself.

Q. Does God make Himself known to man in any other natural manner?

A. Yes, by the voice of man's conscience, which tells him that there is a Supreme Being, who rewards the good and punishes the wicked.

Q. What else does the voice of conscience create in us?

A. It fills us with remorse after secret crimes, and with fears of the judgments of God, whilst it makes us feel delight after performing good works.

Q. What follows from this?

A. That conscience comes from that holy and just Being, who created us, and formed our heart.

Q. How has God made Himself known to man in a supernatural manner?

A. By all that He has made known to us by the Patriarchs, prophets, and at last by His Son.

LESSON II.

THE THREE DIVINE PERSONS.

Q. Why do we call God Father?

A. Because God is our invisible Father in heaven, and because in God there are more persons than one, the first of whom is called the Father.

Q. How many persons are there in God?

A. There are three persons in God.

Q. How are they named?

A. God the Father, God the Son, and God the Holy Ghost.

Q. Is each one of the three persons God?

A. Yes; the Father is true God, the Son is true God, and the Holy Ghost is true God.

Q. Are these three persons, then, three Gods?

A. No; the three persons are but one and the same God.

Q. Why are the three persons but one God?

A. Because there is but one and the same divine nature, or essence, in the three persons.

Q. Is any of these persons older, or greater than the others ?

A. No, all three persons are from all eternity; and each person is as great as the other, because all three are but one and the same God.

Q. What are the three persons in one God called?

A. The Holy Trinity.

Q. What works are chiefly attributed to each of the Divine Persons ?

A. Of God the Father we say that He created the world; of God the Son, that He redeemed it; and of God the Holy Ghost, that He sanctified it, although the works of creation, redemption, and sanctification are common to all three Persons.

LESSON III.

CREATION AND GOVERNMENT OF THE WORLD.

Q. Why is God called Creator of heaven and earth ?

A. Because He made heaven and earth, and all things out of nothing, by His mere word.

Q. In how many days did God create the world ?

A. In six days.

Q. Why did God make the world?

A. For His own glory, and for man's use and benefit.

Q. What does God still do in order that the world may not fall back into nothingness?

A. He preserves and governs it.

Q. How does God preserve the world?

A. By the same power of His will with which He made the world He also causes it to last in the manner He pleases and as long as He pleases.

Q. How does God govern the world?

A. He takes care of all things, orders and directs all things without labor and inconvenience to that end for which He made them.

Q. If God orders and directs all things in the world, why then is there so much evil done? Does God will evil?

A. God wills no evil, but He permits it because He created man free, and knows also how to draw good from evil.

Q. What do we call this care of God in preserving and governing the world?

A. Divine Providence.

LESSON IV.

THE ANGELS.

Q. Did God create anything else besides this visible world?

A. God has also created countless spirits, called angels.

Q. In what state were the angels when God created them?

A. They were all good and happy, and endowed with excellent gifts and graces.

Q. What did God command the angels to do?

A. He commanded them to adore the Son of God, who was to be made man.

Q. Did all the angels obey this command?

A. No; Lucifer, through pride, refused to obey, and seduced a very great number of the angels to join with him in his rebellion against God.

Q. How did God punish these rebellious angels?

A. They were at once banished from heaven, and condemned forever to hell.

Q. Was there any hell before the angels sinned?

A. No; hell was made only to punish sin.

Q. What are these rebel angels called?

A. They are called demons or devils.

Q. How do they occupy themselves?

A. In tempting men to sin.

Q. For what purpose ?

A. To make them partners of their torments and rebellion against God.

Q. How can we overcome the temptations of the devil ?

A. We must instantly turn to God, and ask His assistance.

Q. What was the reward of the faithful angels ?

A. They were immediately confirmed in the enjoyment of the heavenly glory.

Q. In what are they employed in heaven ?

A. In enjoying God as He is, and in loving Him, and praising Him for ever.

Q. How are they employed on earth ?

A. They carry out the orders of God, they protect us in dangers, pray for us, and help us to become good.

Q. What are those angels who protect us called ?

A. Guardian angels.

Q. What is our duty towards our guardian angel ?

A. We should have great reverence for our guardian angel, have confidence in his protection, thank him every day, and ask him always to assist us and never to abandon us.

LESSON V.

ADAM AND EVE, OUR FIRST PARENTS, AND THEIR FALL.

Q. How did God make the first man ?

A. He made a body of the slime of the earth, and breathed into it an immortal soul, created to His own image and likeness, and called him Adam.

Q. Of what did God make Eve ?

A. He made Eve from a rib of Adam.

Q. Were Adam and Eve holy and happy when God created them ?

A. They were very holy, and very happy, and were never to die.

Q. Where did our first parents live ?

A. God placed them in the garden of Paradise, giving them to understand that thence they should be taken up to heaven if they were always obedient to Him.

Q. How did God try their obedience ?

A. He forbade them to eat the fruit of only one tree, which He pointed out to them.

Q. Did Adam and Eve obey God's command ?

A. No; they were disobedient, and ate of the forbidden fruit.

Q. Who tempted them to eat of it?

A. The devil, in the shape of a serpent, persuaded Eve to eat of it.

Q. What did Eve then do?

A. She gave to her husband to eat of it.

Q. Did God punish this disobedience?

A. Yes; He punished Adam and Eve in body and soul.

Q. What was the punishment of the body?

A. Immediate banishment from Paradise, all manner of pains, diseases, and death.

Q. What was the punishment of the soul?

A. The loss of God's grace, and of all right to heaven; darkness in the understanding; weakness in the will; and strong inclination to evil.

Q. Did the sin of our first parents pass to all mankind?

A. Yes; as children of a rebellious father we were all made partakers of his sin and punishment.

Q. What is the sin of our first parents called?

A. Original sin.

Q. What is original sin?

A. It is a privation of God's grace, in punishment of the disobedience of Adam, so that we are all born children of wrath and enemies of God.

Q. Are all men conceived in sin?

A. Yes, except the Blessed Virgin Mary, who, by a special privilege of God, through the merits of her Son, was conceived without the stain of original sin.

Q. What would have become of man had not God shown him mercy?

A. All men would have been lost for ever.

Q. How did God show mercy to mankind?

A. He promised them a Saviour, who should take away their sin, and regain for them the grace and friendship of God and the right to the kingdom of heaven.

Q. To whom did God first make this promise?

A. To Adam and Eve immediately after their fall, and afterwards to the Patriarchs.

Q. Through whom did God, in the course of time, renew this promise?

A. Through the prophets who foretold the time of the coming of the Saviour, and the exceedingly great blessings He would bestow upon mankind.

Q. When did the Saviour come?

A. About four thousand years after the fall of our first parents.

LESSON VI.

Q. Which is the second article of the Creed?

A. "And in Jesus Christ His only Son our Lord."

Q. Who was the Redeemer promised by God?

A. Jesus Christ, our Lord.

Q. Who is Jesus Christ?

A. He is God the Son, made man for us.

Q. Is Jesus Christ truly God?

A. Yes; He is truly God.

Q. Why is Jesus Christ truly God?

A. Because He has one and the same nature with God the Father.

Q. Was Jesus Christ always God?

A. Yes; He was always God: born of the Father from all eternity.

Q. Which Person of the Blessed Trinity is Jesus Christ?

A. He is the Second Person of the Blessed Trinity.

Q. Is Jesus Christ truly man?

A. Yes; He is truly man.

Q. Why is He truly man?

A. Because He has the nature of man, having a body and soul like ours.

Q. Was the Son of God always man?

A. No; He was man only from the time of His Incarnation.

Q. What do you mean by His Incarnation?

A. I mean His taking to Himself our human nature.

Q. How many natures, then, are there in Jesus Christ?

A. There are two; the nature of God, and the nature of man.

Q. Are there also two persons in Jesus Christ?

A. No; in Jesus Christ there is only one Person, which is the Person of God the Son.

Q. Did Jesus Christ fast, pray, and suffer for us as God or as man?

A. He did all this for us as man.

Q. Can we not with strict propriety say, that it was God who fasted and prayed, suffered and died?

A. Most certainly we can.

Q. Why so?

A. Because works are always attributed to the person, and the person of Jesus Christ is God.

Q. What are we to understand from this?

A. That all the works of Jesus Christ were of infinite value and infinite merit.

Q. Why was God the Son made man?

A. To redeem us from sin and hell.

Q. What means the Holy name Jesus?

A. It means the Saviour, or Redeemer.

Q. What means the name CHRIST?

A. The anointed.

Q. Why is Jesus Christ called our Lord?

A. Because He is our God and Saviour.

LESSON VII.

Q. Which is the third article of the Creed?

A. "Who was conceived by the Holy Ghost, born of the Virgin Mary."

Q. What is the meaning of this article?

A. It means that God the Son had no man for His father; but took flesh and was made man by the power of the Holy Ghost, in the womb of the Blessed Virgin Mary, who is, therefore, the mother of God.

Q. How was she informed that she should be the mother of Christ?

A. By the angel Gabriel, whom God sent to her on that message.

Q. How did she consent to it?

A. After the angel had assured her that she should remain a virgin.

Q. What happened then to her?

A. The WORD was made flesh.

Q. What is the WORD?

A. The Son of God.

Q. What means "He was made flesh"?

A. It means that He became man like us.

Q. Where was our Saviour born?

A. In a stable at Bethlehem.

Q. Upon what day was He born?

A. Upon Christmas day.

Q. Who came first to adore the Infant Jesus?

A. Pious shepherds from the neighborhood; then came the Magi, or the three kings from the East.

Q. How did the Shepherds and the Magi learn the birth of Christ?

A. The shepherds heard it from an angel, and the Magi were informed of it through the agency of a miraculous star.

Q. How did Herod, King of Jerusalem, learn the news of the birth of Christ?

A. He learned it from the Magi.

Q. What did the Magi tell the king?

A. That they had come to adore the divine Infant, who was born King of the Jews.

Q. How did Herod receive the news of the birth of Christ?

A. Fearing that the Infant might soon become King of the Jews, he sought to destroy it by causing all the male infants in and around Bethlehem to be murdered.

Q. How was Jesus saved?

A. St. Joseph, admonished by an angel, retired with Him and His mother into Egypt, and did not return till after the death of Herod.

Q. Who was St. Joseph?

A. St. Joseph was the foster-father of Jesus, and the spouse of the Blessed Virgin Mary.

Q. Where did Jesus spend His childhood after His return from Egypt?

A. At Nazareth.

Q. How did He live there?

A. He lived obedient to His Virgin Mother and St. Joseph. St. Luke ii. 51.

Q. What did He do when He was twelve years old?

A. He went with His parents to Jerusalem and spent there three days in the Temple.

Q. What did Jesus do when He was thirty years old?

A. He went to the river Jordan to be baptized by John the Baptist.

Q. What did Jesus do after His baptism?

A. He went into the desert.

Q. What did He do there?

A. He fasted and prayed there forty days and forty nights.

Q. What happened to Him there?

A. He was tempted by the devil.

Q. Why did He permit the devil to tempt Him?

A. To teach us by His example how to overcome the temptations of the devil.

Q. What did He do after He had left the desert?

A. He began to teach in public, and from those who followed Him He chose twelve men whom He called His Apostles, or messengers.

Q. What did Jesus Christ teach?

A. He taught all the truths we must believe, the commandments we must keep, and the means of grace we must make use of in order to be saved.

Q. What did Jesus say of Himself?

A. He said that He was the Promised Redeemer, the Son of God Himself, and He proved His assertion from the writings of the prophets, who had foretold all the circumstances of His life.

Q. Who else bore witness to the fact that Jesus Christ was the Son of God?

A. His heavenly Father Himself.

Q. On what occasion?

A. When He was baptized in the river Jordan, and transfigured on Mount Tabor, a voice from heaven was heard, saying: "This is my beloved Son, in whom I am well pleased; hear ye him." Matt. iii. 17, and xvii. 5.

Q. How did Jesus Christ prove the truth of His doctrine?

A. He proved it by the sanctity of His life, by His prophecies and miracles.

Q. Name some of His miracles?

A. He changed water into wine; with five loaves He fed several thousands; with one word He calmed the winds and the waves; cured diseases of all sorts; cast out devils, and raised the dead to life.

Q. Why are such works called miracles?

A. Because they are of such an extraordinary character that they cannot be done by material powers, and can be performed only by the direct power of God.

Q. Mention some of the prophecies of Jesus Christ?

A. Jesus Christ foretold His betrayal by Judas; His denial by Peter; the manner of His death; His resurrection; His ascension into heaven; the destruction of Jerusalem; the spreading of the Gospel; the persecution and the duration of His Church.

Q. Did many follow Jesus Christ when preaching in the towns and villages?

A. The people came from all parts in crowds to see and hear Him.

Q. Had he any enemies?

A. Yes; the carnal Jews.

Q. Who were the carnal Jews?

A. Those who served God merely for interest.

Q. What notion had they of the coming and of the reign of Christ?

A. They believed that He would come and reign as a powerful King upon earth, that He would reduce all other nations under subjection to the Jews, and that He and they with Him, would live in the enjoyment of riches, honors, and pleasures.

Q. Why did they hate Jesus Christ?

A. Because He reprimanded them for their sins and vices, and preached to them humility and poverty.

Q. Who were the greatest enemies of Christ?

A. The Scribes, or the doctors of the law; the Pharisees, or those who pretended to keep the law better than others, and the Sadducees, who denied the resurrection of the body and the existence of spirits.

Q. Did the Pharisees lead a good life?

A. No; they were, for the greatest part, rank hypocrites.

Q. How far did these enemies go in their hatred against Jesus?

A. They went so far as to resolve upon taking away His life.

Q. Who promised to betray Jesus Christ?

A. His Apostle Judas Iscariot.

Q. For what reward?

A. For thirty pieces of silver.

Q. What did Jesus do when He saw that the end of His life was drawing near?

A. He gave, at the Last Supper, His body and blood to the Apostles as food and drink for their souls.

Q. How did He give His body to them?

A. He took bread, blessed and gave to them, saying: THIS IS MY BODY.

Q. How did He give His blood to them?

A. He took the cup with some wine, blessed and gave to them, saying: Drink ye all of this, for this is my blood, the blood of the new covenant. Matt. xxvi. 28.

LESSON VIII.

Q. Which is the fourth article of the Creed?

A. "Suffered under Pontius Pilate, was crucified, dead, and buried."

Q. What does the fourth article of the Creed teach us?

A. It teaches us that Jesus Christ suffered for us, died on the cross, and was laid in the grave.

Q. What did Jesus do after the Last Supper?

A. He went into the Garden of Olives to pray.

Q. What happened to Him while He was praying?

A. Large drops of blood covered His body like sweat.

Q. What did Judas do in the meanwhile?

A. He brought armed men to take Jesus.

Q. Whither did they lead Him?

A. To Caiphas the High Priest, and from him to Pilate.

Q. How was He treated by Pilate?

A. Pilate had Him scourged, and suffered Him to be crowned with thorns, and, at last, condemned Him to die upon the Cross.

Q. When and where was Jesus crucified?

A. On Good Friday, on Mount Calvary.

Q. What happened at His death?

A. The sun was darkened, the earth shook, and many of the dead rose to life.

Q. Was Jesus Christ forced to suffer death?

A. No; Christ suffered death of His own free will.

Q. What are our duties to Jesus Christ?

A. Our duties to Jesus Christ are sovereign worship, entire confidence, and ardent love.

Q. What kind of worship do we owe to Jesus Christ?

A. We owe to Him divine worship and supreme adoration.

Q. Why should we have entire confidence in Jesus Christ?

A. Because He is the only MEDIATOR of justice, properly speaking, between God and us.

Q. How do you show that He is our only Mediator?

A. Because He alone, by His life and death, has atoned for original sin as well as for all the other sins of mankind, and He alone has merited for us all the graces of which we stand in need.

Q. Could none of the saints, of themselves alone, have atoned either for original sin, or for the other sins of men ?

A. No; not all the saints and angels united could render satisfaction for one single sin.

Q. How so ?

A. Because the more dignified the person offended is, the more grievous is the offence; and the less dignified the person is who makes the satisfaction, the less the satisfaction is.

Q. What follows from this ?

A. That the satisfaction of all the saints together could never satisfy for an offence offered to God.

Q. Was Jesus Christ able to satisfy for all sins ?

A. He was; because being a divine Person He could render to God honor and glory infinitely greater than the offence and insult offered by the sins of all mankind.

Q. What has Christ gained for us through His sufferings and death ?

A. 1. He has reconciled us with God.

2. Re-opened heaven to us.

3. Merited abundant graces for us, to enable us to lead a holy life and gain eternal happiness.

Q. How do you show that Jesus Christ has merited for us all these graces?

A. St. Paul tells us that God showers down upon us His blessings and graces through Jesus Christ. Ephes. i.

Q. Why do we owe to Jesus Christ an ardent love?

A. Because he has delivered us from sin, from the power of the devil, and from the eternal damnation which we had deserved by sin.

Q. How do Catholics show that they truly honor and love Jesus Christ?

A. By the honor and love they pay Him in His person, in His saints, and in His images.

Q. How do we truly honor the Person of Jesus Christ?

A. By adoring and worshipping Him upon our altars in the Blessed Sacrament.

Q. How do we honor Jesus Christ in His saints?

A. By venerating the saints as His friends and servants.

Q. How do we honor Jesus Christ in His images?

A. By entertaining the greatest respect for the crucifix, as well as for every other image of our Divine Saviour.

Q. How do we show that we place all our confidence in the merits of Jesus Christ?

A. By the many feasts which we observe in commemoration of the Passion and sufferings of our Divine Saviour, as also by the fact that we assist at the holy Sacrifice of the Mass and receive the sacraments, whereby the merits of Jesus Christ are applied to our souls.'

Q. Why do we so often make the sign of the Cross?

A. To show that we look for grace and assistance only through the merits of the Cross and the sufferings of Jesus Christ.

Q. Why do we always end our prayers, "Through Jesus Christ our Lord"?

A. To show that we hope to obtain every grace only through the merits of our Saviour.

Q. Has Christ merited grace and eternal salvation for those only who are really saved?

A. No; He has merited grace and salvation for all men, without exception, because He died for all without exception.

Q. If Christ has merited eternal salvation for all men, why are not all men saved?

A. Because men have their share also in the work of salvation, and Jesus Christ has taught them how to gain it; but all do not believe His doctrine, keep His commandments, and make use of the means of grace.

Q. What became of the body of Christ after His death?

A. It was taken from the Cross and laid in the grave.

Q. By what sign do we profess our faith in Jesus crucified?

A. By the sign of the Cross.

Q. What puts us in mind that Christ suffered for us on the Cross?

A. The very form of the Cross which we make on ourselves.

Q. For what other reason do we make the sign of the Cross?

A. To put us in mind of the Blessed Trinity.

Q. What puts us in mind of the Blessed Trinity when we make the sign of the Cross?

A. We invoke the Blessed Trinity when we say: In the name of the Father, and of the Son, and of the Holy Ghost.

Q. Should we often make the sign of the Cross?

A. It is good and wholesome to make it often with devotion, especially when going to and rising from bed, before and after prayer, before every important action, and in all temptations and dangers.

Q. Why is it wholesome often to make the sign of the Cross ?

A. Because by devoutly making the sign of the Cross we draw upon ourselves the blessing of Jesus Christ, and receive strength to conquer the temptations of the devil.

LESSON IX.

Q. Which is the fifth article of the Creed ?

A. "He descended into hell, the third day He rose again from the dead."

Q. What means "He descended into hell"?

A. It means that the soul of Jesus Christ, after His death, went into Limbo.

Q. What do you mean by Limbo ?

A. A place of rest.

Q. Who were in Limbo ?

A. The souls of the saints who died before Christ.

Q. Why did Christ go to the saints in Limbo ?

A. To convey to them in person the joyful tidings of their redemption.

Q. Why could not the souls of the saints who died before Christ go to heaven immediately after their death ?

A. Because heaven was shut against them on account of the sin of our first parents, and could not be opened to any one save by the death of Christ.

Q. When did the souls of the saints who died before Christ go to heaven ?

A. When Christ ascended into heaven.

Q. Where was Christ's body while His soul was in Limbo ?

A. In the grave.

Q. When the body and soul of Christ were separated from each other, were they also separated from Christ's Divinity ?

A. No ; the Divine Person always remained inseparably united with His body and with His soul.

Q. What means "The third day He rose from the dead" ?

A. It means that on the third day after His death, Christ reunited, by His own power, His soul to His body, and rose again from the grave.

Q. How did Christ rise again ?

A. He came forth glorious and immortal from the grave.

Q. Did Christ retain in His glorified body the marks of His sufferings ?

A. He still retained in His hands, feet, and side the marks of His wounds.

Q. Why has He retained those marks?

A. 1. In testimony of His victory over hell.

2. As a proof that He rose again in the very same body in which He had suffered.

3. To show them on the day of judgment, for the consolation of the just, and for the confusion of the wicked.

Q. How do we know that Christ rose from the dead?

A. From the testimony of the Apostles and His disciples, who, during forty days, often saw Him, touched Him, ate, spoke, and conversed with Him; and St. Paul tells us that our Saviour "was seen by more than five hundred at once." 1 Cor. xv. 6.

Q. What should we learn from the Resurrection of Christ?

A. 1. That Christ is true God..

2. That we, too, shall one day rise from the dead.

3. That we should rise from the death of sin to a new and holy life.

LESSON X.

Q. Which is the sixth article of the Creed?

A. "He ascended into heaven, sitteth at the right hand of God the Father Almighty."

Q. What means "He ascended into heaven"?

A. It means that Christ, by His own power, with soul and body, went up into heaven.

Q. On what day did Christ go up to heaven?

A. On Ascension Day, forty days after His resurrection.

Q. From what place did Christ go up to heaven?

A. From Mount Olivet, in the presence of His disciples.

Q. Why did Christ ascend into heaven?

A. 1. To take possession of His glory as conqueror of death and hell.

2. To be our Mediator and Advocate.

3. To send the Holy Ghost to His disciples.

4. To open heaven and to prepare a place for His followers.

Q. What means "sitteth at the right hand of God"?

A. It means that Christ, even as man, is

exalted above all created things, and shares in the power and glory of the Divine Majesty.

Q. Is Christ, then, not present in all places?

A. As God He is everywhere, but as God-Man, He is only in Heaven and in the Holy Eucharist.

LESSON XI.

Q. Which is the seventh article of the Creed?

A. "From thence He shall come to judge the living and the dead."

Q. What does this article teach us?

A. That Jesus Christ, at the end of the world, will come down again from heaven to judge all men.

Q. What do you call this judgment?

A. The general or last judgment.

Q. When will the day of the last judgment come?

A. Of that day and hour no one knoweth, not even the angels of heaven.

Q. What are the things which Christ will judge?

A. All our thoughts, words, works, and omissions.

Q. What will Christ say to the just?

A. Come, ye blessed of My Father, possess the kingdom which is prepared for you.

Q. What will He say to the wicked?

A. Depart from Me, ye cursed, into everlasting fire.

Q. Why will there be a general judgment?

A. 1. That God's wisdom and justice may be acknowledged by all men.

2. That Jesus Christ may be glorified before the whole world.

3. That the good may be honored worthily, and the wicked confounded, as they have deserved.

Q. Will not every man be judged at his death as well as at the last day?

A. Yes: "it is appointed unto men once to die, and after this is the judgment." Heb. ix. 27.

Q. Whither does the soul go after this particular judgment?

A. Either to Purgatory, or to Heaven, or to Hell.

Q. What do you mean by Purgatory?

A. A place where souls suffer for a time on account of their sins.

Q. Which souls go to Purgatory?

A. Those souls who leave this world without having fully paid the debt of temporal punishment due to their sins, the guilt of which has been forgiven by the sacrament of penance.

Q. What do you mean by temporal punishment?

A. That which will have an end, either in this world, or in the world to come.

Q. How do we know that there is a Purgatory?

A. Holy Scripture tells us that "It is a holy and wholesome thought to pray for the dead, that they may be loosed from their sins." 2 Machab. ii.

Q. What do we learn from this passage?

A. That besides heaven and hell, there also is a third place.

Q. Why so?

A. Because the souls in heaven have no need of our prayers, and those in hell cannot be benefited by them. Therefore it is clear that there is another place where departed souls can be benefited by prayer.

Q. What other proofs have we that there is a Purgatory?

A. Jesus Christ declares that: "He who shall speak against the Holy Ghost, it shall not be forgiven him, neither in this world, nor in the world to come." Matt. xii. 32.

Q. What are we to understand from this passage?

A. That there are some sins which are forgiven in the next world.

Q. Can sin be forgiven in heaven?

A. No; for no sin whatever is allowed to enter into heaven.

Q. Can sin be forgiven in hell?

A. It cannot; for, out of hell there is no redemption.

Q. What follows from this?

A. That there is a third place, which we call Purgatory, where sin is forgiven.

Q. What says St. Paul in his Epistle to the Philippians?

A. That at the name of Jesus every knee should bend, of those that are in heaven, on earth, and in hell.

Q. What do we learn from these words of St. Paul?

A. Those who are in hell do not bend the knee at the name of Jesus—it is therefore to be understood of those who are in Purgatory, and who love and revere that holy name.

Q. What do we read in the twenty-first chapter of the Apocalypse?

A. "There shall not enter into heaven anything defiled."

Q. What do we learn from this passage?

A. That there is a place in which the soul is cleansed from its stains.

Q. Why so?

A. Because it cannot be supposed that those who die suddenly have either the time or the dispositions necessary to atone for all their faults. Therefore the divine goodness has made a place in the world to come, in which the soul is cleansed from her little faults and imperfections.

Q. What other proof of Purgatory can you give?

A. The universal custom of the Catholic Church, from her very beginning, to offer up prayers, and especially the holy Sacrifice of the Mass for her deceased members, and the tradition of the Fathers of the Church.

Q. What does St. Augustine say, in his book on heresies?

A. Arius was the first who dared teach that neither prayers nor sacrifices ought to be offered for the dead—and this, says he, "was the fifty-third heresy."

Q. What answer, then, can we give those who pretend that the doctrine of Purgatory was invented by priests?

A. We reply to them in the words of St. Augustine, that "the fifty-third heresy consisted in denying the necessity of prayers for the dead."

Q. Will Purgatory continue to exist after the general judgment?

A. No. After the general judgment there will be only Heaven and Hell.

Q. Which souls go to heaven immediately after death?

A. Those souls who, on departing this life, are quite pure and undefiled in the sight of God.

Q. Which souls go to hell immediately after death?

A. Those souls who depart this life in the state of mortal sin.

LESSON XII.

Q. Which is the eighth article of the Creed?

A. "I believe in the Holy Ghost."

Q. Who is the Holy Ghost?

A. The Holy Ghost is the third person of the Blessed Trinity.

Q. From whom does the Holy Ghost proceed?

A. The Holy Ghost proceeds from the Father and the Son from all eternity.

Q. Is He equal to them?

A. Yes. He is the same Lord and God as they are.

Q. Which is the chief gift of the Holy Ghost?

A. The love of God, which we receive by His grace.

Q. What effect does this love produce in us?

A. It makes us take pleasure in doing the will of God.

Q. Is this pleasure natural to us?

A. No; we naturally take pleasure in doing our own will, and gratifying our senses.

Q. How then can we do good works and lead a holy life?

A. Only by the grace of God, which is the gift of the Holy Ghost.

Q. What are the particular gifts of the Holy Ghost?

A. They are seven. 1. Wisdom. 2. Understanding. 3. Counsel. 4. Fortitude. 5. Knowledge. 6. Godliness or Piety. 7. The Fear of the Lord.

Q. On what day and in what manner, did Christ send down the Holy Ghost upon His Apostles?

A. On Whitsunday or Pentecost, the Holy Ghost descended upon the Apostles in the form of tongues of fire.

Q. Why did the Holy Ghost come down upon the Apostles?

A. To enable them to preach the Gospel and plant the Church of Jesus Christ.

Q. Is the Holy Ghost still sent at the present time?

A. Yes, whenever He enters with His sanctifying grace into our souls in order to dwell there.

Q. How long does the Holy Ghost dwell in the soul?

A. As long as the soul is free from mortal sin.

Q. Where, then, is the Holy Ghost?

A. The Holy Ghost is everywhere because He is God; but, as He is the dispenser of grace, He is especially with the Catholic Church, and in the souls of the just.

LESSON XIII.

Q. Which is the ninth article of the Creed?

A. "The Holy Catholic Church; the communion of Saints."

Q. What does this article teach us?

A. It teaches us that the holy religion of the Catholic Church was revealed by Jesus Christ, and entrusted to the chief pastors of His Church, who are divinely commissioned to teach all men authoritatively and infallibly, all its sacred and immutable truths—truths which we are consequently bound in conscience to receive without hesitation.

Q. Are only the faithful on earth united together as one Society or Church?

A. With the faithful on earth are also spiritually united the Saints in heaven and the souls in Purgatory.

Q. In what does this spiritual union consist?

A. It consists in this, that all are members of one body, whose Head is Jesus Christ, and that, therefore, the different members share in one another's spiritual good.

Q. What is this spiritual union called?

A. The communion of the Saints.

Q. Why are all the members of this communion styled Saints?

A. Because all are called to be Saints, and have been sanctified by baptism, and many of them have already arrived at perfect sanctity.

Q. What benefit do we reap from communion with the Saints in heaven?

A. We partake of the merits which they acquired while on earth, and are assisted by their prayers to God in our behalf.

Q. What benefit do the souls in Purgatory receive from our communion with them?

A. We come to the assistance of these our suffering brethren, in order that their pains may be mitigated and shortened.

Q. By what means can we assist the poor souls in Purgatory?

A. By prayers, alms-deeds, and other good works, especially by the Holy Sacrifice of the Mass, and the application of indulgences.

Q. What profit do we draw from the communion of the faithful on earth?

A. We share in all the Masses, prayers, and good works of the Catholic Church, and, in general, in all her spiritual goods.

Q. Do sinners also, as long as they are not cut off from the Church, share in this communion?

A. Sinners as dead members forfeit, indeed, most of the spiritual goods; nevertheless, in virtue of their union with the Church, they still receive various blessings and graces, which help to their conversion.

LESSON XIV.

Q. Which is the tenth article of the Creed?

A. "The forgiveness of sins."

Q. What is meant by this article?

A. That in the Catholic Church there is forgiveness of sins and of the punishments due to them.

Q. What sins can be forgiven in the Catholic Church?

A. All sins, without exception.

Q. To whom has Christ given power to forgive sins?

A. To the Apostles and their lawful successors—the Bishops and priests of His Church.

Q. By what sacraments are sins forgiven?

A. Principally by baptism and penance.

LESSON XV.

Q. Which is the eleventh article of the Creed?

A. "The resurrection of the body."

Q. What means the resurrection of the body?

A. That we shall rise again with the same bodies at the day of judgment.

Q. Why will our bodies rise again united to our souls?

A. That they may share in the soul's everlasting reward or punishment.

Q. How are the bodies of the saints to rise?

A. They will be glorious and immortal.

Q. Are the bodies of the damned also to be glorious?

A. No; but they will be immortal, to suffer for ever the torments of hell.

LESSON XVI.

Q. Which is the twelfth article of the Creed?

A. "And life everlasting."

Q. What means this article?

A. That the good shall live for ever happy in heaven.

Q. What is the happiness of heaven?

A. To see, love, and enjoy God for evermore.

Q. And shall not the wicked also live for ever?

A. They shall live and be punished for ever in the flames of hell.

Q. What are the pains of the damned?

A. They suffer, 1. An inward torture and despair at the thought of all the evil they have done, and of the many graces they have abused. Wisd. v. 1–15; Matt. viii. 12.

2. They suffer sadness and misery, because they have, by their own fault, forfeited the eternal enjoyment of God. Luke xiii. 25–28.

3. They suffer everlasting horror at the dismal company of the devils, and of all the damned. Matt. xxv. 41; and

4. They suffer the most intolerable torments of the senses without any hope of relief or end; for their fire shall not be extinguished, and their worm shall not die. Mark ix. 47; Apoc. xx. 9, 10.

Q. How do we know that the pains of the damned are eternal?

A. From the words of Jesus Christ and the Apostles.

Q. What are the words of Jesus Christ?

A. "Depart from me, ye cursed, into everlasting fire—and they shall go into everlasting punishment." Matt. xxv. 41, 46.

Q. What does St. John write on the eternity of hell?

A. "And the smoke of their torments shall go up for ever and ever." Apoc. xiv. 11.

Q. What does the Church teach concerning the eternity of hell?

A. She has solemnly condemned the wilful errors of those heretics who taught that the pains of the devils and of the damned would in time have an end.

Q. Why are the pains of the damned everlasting?

A. 1. Because only the everlasting pains of hell are a sufficient means to inspire man with a proper fear, to avoid sin even in secret.

2. Because all who die in sin remain for ever fixed in sin.

3. Because the offence against the *Infinite* Majesty of God demands of His justice a punishment without end; and

4. Because God hates evil no less than He loves what is good, and, therefore, punishes vice eternally, as He eternally rewards virtue.

Q. Will the pains of all the damned be the same?

A. No; each one will suffer in proportion to his sins, and to the ill use he has made of the graces bestowed upon him.

Q. Will all those who are damned be damned through their own fault?

A. Yes; because all men may be happy for ever if they avail themselves of the abundant graces which God gives them.

Q. What means "Amen"?

A. So it is, or, so be it.

Q. What do we mean by the word "Amen," at the end of the Creed?

A. That we firmly believe all that is contained in the Creed, and that we are resolved to live up to this belief and to die in it.

FAMILIAR EXPLANATION
OF
CHRISTIAN DOCTRINE.

PART III.

WHAT WE MUST DO.

LESSON I.

Q. Will faith alone save us?

A. No; we must also keep the commandments of God.

Q. How do we know this?

A. Jesus Christ says: "If thou wilt enter into life, keep the commandments." Matt. xix. 17.

Q. How are we enabled to keep the commandments?

A. By the grace of God, which He gives to all who ask for it.

Q. Which is the greatest commandment?

A. To love God with our whole heart above all things, and our neighbor as ourselves.

Q. What is, to love God above all things?

A. It is to be willing to lose all things, even life itself, rather than to offend God by sin.

Q. Why are we bound to love God?

A. Because He is our Creator, our Redeemer, and our Supreme Happiness for time and eternity, and not to love Him is to be unhappy for ever.

Q. How many kinds of love of God are there?

A. Two kinds—perfect and imperfect love.

Q. When is our love of God perfect?

A. When we love God chiefly for His own sake.

Q. When is our love of God imperfect?

A. When we love God chiefly for the sake of His gifts and blessings.

Q. May we love God and ourselves at the same time?

A. We may.

Q. In what manner?

A. If we always do the will of God, take more care of our souls than of our bodies, and do not seek our own good to the prejudice of our neighbor.

Q. What is, to love our neighbor as ourselves?

A. If we do as Jesus Christ has said: "All things, therefore, whatsoever you would that men should do to you, do you also to them." Matt. vii. 12.

Q. Who is our neighbor?

A. All men are our neighbors.

Q. Are we also bound to love our enemies?

A. Yes, we must forgive them, pray for them, and show charity towards them as well as we are able.

Q. Is it a sin not to forgive him who has injured us, or to wish him some harm, or to manifest hatred or to take revenge?

A. It would be very wrong for us to do anything of the kind.

Q. How should we behave towards such a one?

A. If we were accustomed to speak to him, we should not pass him by without speaking, or in some way showing him that we forgive him, provided such conduct does not make matters worse, or is not an occasion of sin.

Q. Is it a sin for us to feel a dislike for a person?

A. If we try to put away the dislike, and are kind to him, it is no sin to feel a dislike of which we cannot rid ourselves.

Q. Who has commanded us to love our enemies?

A. Jesus Christ, in these words: "I say to you, love your enemies, do good to them that hate you, and pray for them that persecute and calumniate you: That you may be the children of your Father, who is in heaven, who maketh his sun to rise upon the good, and raineth upon the just and the unjust." Matt. v. 44, 45.

Q. For which class of persons should we always show a particular love?

A. For the poor, orphans, widows, and in general, for all those who are in temporal or spiritual need.

Q. What sin is it, to give nothing to the poor, to save up all one's money in order to become rich?

A. It is a mortal sin.

Q. How should we help the needy?

A. By corporal as well as by spiritual works of mercy.

Q. Which are the corporal works of mercy?

A. 1. To feed the hungry. 2. To give drink to the thirsty. 3. To clothe the naked. 4. To harbor the harborless. 5. To visit the sick. 6. To visit the imprisoned. 7. To bury the dead.

Q. Which are the spiritual works of mercy?

A. 1. To convert the sinner. 2. To instruct the ignorant. 3. To counsel the doubtful. 4. To comfort the sorrowful. 5. To bear wrongs patiently. 6. To forgive injuries. 7. To pray for the living and the dead.

Q. Who is it that truly loves God and his neighbor?

A. He who keeps the commandments of God and of the Church.

LESSON II.

Q. Say the ten commandments.

A. 1. I am the Lord thy God; thou shalt have no God but Me.

2. Thou shalt not take the name of the Lord thy God in vain.

3. Remember that thou keep holy the Sabbath day.

4. Honor thy father and thy mother.

5. Thou shalt not kill.

6. Thou shalt not commit adultery.

7. Thou shalt not steal.

8. Thou shalt not bear false witness against thy neighbor.

9. Thou shalt not covet thy neighbor's wife.

10. Thou shalt not covet thy neighbor's goods.

Q. Who gave the ten commandments?

A. God gave them to the Jews, through Moses, on Mount Sinai.

Q. Are Christians also bound to keep them?

A. They are; for Jesus Christ says: "If thou wilt enter into life keep the commandments." Matt. xix. 17.

Q. What do these commandments teach us?

A. They teach us to avoid evil and to do good.

Q. Which is the first commandment?

A. I am the Lord thy God; thou shalt have no God but Me.

Q. What are we commanded by the first commandment?

A. By the first commandment we are commanded to know and profess the four great truths of religion, because no one can go to heaven without so doing.

Q. What are these four great truths?

A. 1. That there is but one God.

2. That there are three persons in God: The Father, the Son, and the Holy Ghost.

3. That the Second Person, the Son of God, was made man and died to save us from hell.

4. That God will reward the good and punish the wicked.

Q. What else should every Christian know?

A. The Apostles' Creed. The commandments of God and of the Church. The seven sacraments, but especially Baptism, the Holy Eucharist, Penance, and any other sacrament which he is about to receive; the prayers known as the Our Father and Hail Mary, and the duties of his state.

Q. What are we commanded to do by the first commandment?

A. By this commandment we are commanded to adore but one true and living God, and serve Him all our days.

Q. How are we to worship God?

A. By faith, hope, and charity.

Q. How do we worship God by faith?

A. By believing firmly all that He teaches us through the Catholic Church, and by worshipping and adoring Him as the only true, eternal Lord, and Creator of heaven and earth.

Q. What are the sins against faith?

A. Infidelity, heresy, apostasy, indifference to faith, and wilful doubt of any article of faith, all of which are mortal sins.

Q. What is infidelity ?

A. Infidelity is the want of the true faith in an unbaptized person.

Q. What is heresy ?

A. Heresy is the obstinate clinging to error of a baptized person, in opposition to a truth taught by the Catholic Church.

Q. What is apostasy ?

A. Apostasy is a formal renunciation of the Catholic faith.

Q. What is indifference to faith ?

A. Indifference to faith is, not to care for any religion at all, or to consider all equally good; or to neglect to attend religious instruction when one stands in need of being instructed.

Q. How may we commit sin against the worship and adoration of God ?

A. By worshipping false gods or idols, or by giving to any creature whatsoever the honor which is due to God alone, to do which is always a mortal sin.

Q. May one commit sin against the adoration of God in any other way ?

A. Yes; by attending the false worship of any non-Catholic religious society, by sacrilege and irreverence, by simony, superstition, witchcraft, and spiritualism.

Q. What is sacrilege?

A. Sacrilege is the profanation of holy things, holy persons, or holy places; for instance, to receive a sacrament unworthily, to ill-treat a priest or religious, to desecrate a church or sacred vessel, or to use sacred things for the purpose of committing sin.

Q. Are his sins forgiven, who, through fear or shame, conceals a mortal sin in confession?

A. No; his sins are not forgiven, but he has added to them the sin of sacrilege, which he is bound to confess, and make his confession over again.

Q. What is irreverence?

A. By irreverence is understood ill-behavior in the church, or towards priests and religious, or sacred things; for instance, to crucifixes and religious ceremonies, the Holy Scripture, the relics of the saints, sacred pictures, beads, etc.

Q. What is simony?

A. Simony is the buying or selling of

anything sacred, for example, a relic of a saint, to do which is a mortal sin.

Q. What is superstition?

A. Superstition is to believe that some things or persons have a certain power which they cannot have either by nature, or by the prayers of the Church, or from God.

Q. Can you give some instances of this?

A. When we go to fortune-tellers and ask them to tell us our fortune by cutting cards, or by looking at our hands; or when we ask those who use charms, or signs, or toss cups; or when we pay attention to dreams, lucky days, vain and foolish signs and practices, in order to know hidden things, or to obtain luck or health. The sin is still greater when, for such a purpose, we use even holy names and blessed things.

Q. Is such superstition a grievous sin?

A. It is generally a mortal sin for him who practises such things, because he usually expects the assistance of the evil spirit, if not openly, at least secretly; at all events, he places in idle or delusive practices that confidence which he ought to place in God alone.

Q. Is it also a mortal sin to ask fortune-tellers to

tell your fortune, or to find out hidden things, or things to come?

A. For the reason just given, it would be a mortal sin firmly to believe in such superstitious practices.

Q. How do people become guilty of witchcraft?

A. When they try, with the help of the evil spirits, to find hidden treasures, to injure others, or to work wonderful things.

Q. What should one do if he is in doubt whether the use of suspicious means for curing diseases, or discovering certain things, is allowed or not?

A. He should ask the priest or his confessor.

Q. What is spiritualism or spiritism?

A. Spiritism is to believe that the spirits or souls of the dead communicate with men by rapping and moving furniture, or by writing, seeing, and speaking mediums.

Q. Are those spirits thus communicating with men really the souls of the dead?

A. No; they are all evil spirits.

Q. How do we know this?

A. These spirits often tell palpable lies, and communicate impious principles, which lead the devotees of spiritualism and its mediums to immorality. When in presence of some supernatural power they cannot manifest themselves through their mediums, and the manifestations through rapping, tipping, writing, or entranced mediums, have a baneful influence upon the followers of spiritualism.

Q. What clearly follows from this ?

A. That those spirits are no holy spirits or angels, because holy spirits tell no lies, and do not communicate impious principles to men, nor do they cause any harm to them in body and mind.

Q. What, then, are we to think of spiritualism ?

A. That it is nothing else than satanism or dealing with the devil; it is real necromancy, that is, the evocation of the dead.

Q. What, then, are our modern spiritualists ?

A. They are real necromancers, real diviners, attempting, by means of evoking the dead, to divine secrets whether of the past or the future, unknown to the living.

Q. Is spiritualism or necromancy a great sin ?

A. Holy Scripture tells us that necromancy or spiritualism is an abomination in the sight of God.

Q. In what words has the Lord pronounced temporal and eternal woe upon this sort of dealing with the devil ?

A. In these words: "Let there not be found among you," says the Lord, "any one that consulteth soothsayers, or observeth dreams and omens; neither let there be any wizard, nor charmer, nor any one that consulteth pythonic spirits, or fortune-tellers, or that seeketh the truth from the dead, for the Lord abhorreth all these things." "The soul that shall do these things, I shall set my face against that soul, and destroy it out of the midst of its people." "A man or woman that hath a familiar spirit, or is a wizard, dying, let him die, they shall stone them, and their blood shall be upon them." Deut. xviii. 10-12; Leviticus xix. 20; and xx. 27.

Q. Is it wrong to be present, through curiosity, at the circles or meetings of spiritualists?

A. It is; for it is a sin to give countenance to spiritism even in the most casual manner, and therefore no one is allowed, through curiosity, ever to be present at its circles, for they who enter the house of the devil, have every reason to fear that they will be deluded by his devices, and enslaved to his command.

LESSON III.

ON HOPE.

Q. What is hope?

A. Hope is a virtue which God infuses into our souls, and by which we firmly expect, from God's mercy, everlasting life through the merits of Jesus Christ, and the good works which we perform with God's assistance.

Q. What, then, is the primary object of Christian hope?

A. Life everlasting, that is, God Himself, whom we hope to enjoy for ever.

Q. What are the secondary objects of Christian hope?

A. The secondary objects of Christian hope are the means to obtain everlasting happiness, which are the divine grace, and our good works, performed with the assistance of grace.

Q. What are the motives of Christian hope?

A. 1. The Omnipotence of God, by which He is able to save us. 2. His mercy, by which He wishes to save us; and 3. The faithfulness of God to His promise to bring us to glory, through the merits of Jesus Christ, provided we pray to Him for salvation through the merits of Jesus Christ.

Q. How, then, do we worship God by hope?

A. By expecting with firm and immovable confidence that God will give us salvation, and all things necessary to obtain it, if we do what He requires of us.

Q. When is our hope of salvation firm and immovable?

A. When we have no doubt at all that God, on His part, will not fail to fulfil His promise of saving us through Jesus Christ, our Redeemer, provided we employ the great and necessary means of salvation.

Q. What is this great and necessary means of salvation?

A. Prayer.

Q. Why is prayer the great and necessary means of salvation?

A. Prayer is the great means of salvation because God has promised to grant us all the graces necessary for salvation if we pray for them; it is the necessary means because God has made prayer the ordinary and necessary means of salvation.

Q. For whom, then, is the infallible promise of

God the strongest motive of his hope of salvation?

A. Only for him who prays sincerely.

Q. What follows from this?

A. That as God has made us the infallible promise to give us all the graces we need, if we only pray for them, and as He has given the grace of prayer to every one, no one can reasonably fear to be lost, if he really perseveres in prayer.

Q. What are the sins against hope?

A. Despair and presumption.

Q. What is despair?

A. Despair is the loss of all hope in God's goodness and mercy.

Q. What is presumption?

A. Presumption is a rash and foolish confidence of salvation, without endeavoring to live up tc the faith and the commandments of God.

Q. May we confidently hope to obtain from God life everlasting and yet have some fear of being lost?

A. We have every reason to hope confidently that God will give us all the graces necessary for salvation, provided we duly ask for them; but, at the same time, we may, and ought to have a wholesome fear that, through our own culpable failure in not faithfully corresponding to these graces, we may eventually be lost. St. Paul himself trembled lest he would become a cast-away.

Q. How do we worship God by charity ?

A. By loving God above all things for His own sake, and our neighbor as ourselves for the love of God.

Q. What are the sins against charity ?

A. All mortal sins in general; but in particular, 1. Indifference and aversion to God and divine things; and 2. Hatred and repugnance to Him and His paternal dispensations.

LESSON IV.

THE VENERATION AND INVOCATION OF THE SAINTS.

Q. Do Catholics adore the saints ?

A. God forbid! They are far from rendering them any such homage.

Q. What kind of worship do they render to the saints ?

A. They merely honor them as the servants of God.

Q. Do not Catholics, however, build and consecrate churches to them?

A. No; they build and consecrate churches to God alone, although under the invocation of the saints.

Q. Do they not offer the Sacrifice of the Mass to the saints?

A. No; the priest offers this sacrifice to God alone, although he makes a commemoration of the saints.

Q. Do Catholics believe that the saints of themselves can obtain graces for them?

A. No; but they believe that the saints can obtain graces for them by their prayers-- Jesus having already merited those graces for them by His passion and death.

Q. Is the honor which Catholics render to the saints altogether proper?

A. Undoubtedly it is.

Q. But does it not seem that, by invoking the saints, we abandon God?

A. By praying to the saints we no more abandon God than when we beg the prayers of the living.

Q. But at least is it not, in some measure, lessening the merits of Jesus Christ, to beg the intercession of the saints?

A. It is no more lessening the merits of

Jesus Christ to beg the prayers of the saints, than it is to beg the prayers of men.

Q. But when we pray to the saints do we not place our confidence in creatures?

A. Not more than we do when we recommend ourselves to the prayers of men.

Q. Is it, then, wrong for any one to say that Catholics, by praying to the saints, substitute them for Jesus Christ?

A. The idea that Catholics, by praying to the saints, put them in the place of Jesus Christ is utterly false, because Catholics do not ask the saints to grant them any graces, but to obtain them from God.

Q. How do you prove this?

A. Because Catholics when praying to God never say to Him as they say to the saints, "Pray for us," but, "Grant us," "Hear us," "Have mercy on us."

Q. Is there any saint in heaven, in whose prayers Catholics have more confidence than in those of all the other saints?

A. They have greater confidence in the prayers of the Blessed Virgin Mary, and love and honor her more than all the other saints.

Q. Why?

A. Because, as Mother of God, she is placed

in dignity above all the saints and angels, and has greater power with her Son Jesus Christ, than all the Saints united.

Q. Why do you say that Catholics do not substitute the saints for Jesus Christ?

A. Because they know very well that it is not the saints, but Jesus Christ alone, who has merited the graces for which they ask.

Q. Are, then, the merits of the saints of no avail to us?

A. They certainly are of great service to us, for their prayers for us are so much the more powerful as their merits are more pleasing in the sight of God.

Q. What place, then, do we wish the saints to take when we pray to them?

A. Our own place.

Q. How so?

A. By entreating them to pray for us, in order that we may the more readily obtain what we ask for.

Q. Is there any benefit to be derived from invoking the saints?

A. If the prayers of the living are of benefit to us, it is evident that the prayers of the saints must also be extremely beneficial.

Q. How do we know that the prayers of the living are beneficial to us?

A. This is clear from what God said to the friends of Job: "Go to my servant Job—and he shall pray for you, that folly be not imputed to you." Job xlii. 8. It is also clear from what St. Paul writes: "Brethren, pray for us." 1 Thess. v. 25. "Pray for me that speech may be given me, that I may open my mouth with confidence, to make known the mystery of the Gospel." Ephes. vi. 19.

Q. What do we learn from this?

A. That it is pleasing to God to see us have recourse to the intercession of the saints, and that He is ever ready to hear their prayers.

Q. From what else do we know that it is pleasing to God to seek His graces through His saints?

A. From the many wonderful favors spiritual and corporal, which He has granted, and still does grant to those who ask them through the intercession of His saints, and especially through that of His holy Mother.

Q. Was the invocation of the saints an ancient practice in the Church?

A. It was, as we know from the writings of the Fathers of the Church.

Q. What says St. Basil in his sermon on the forty martyrs.

A. "If any one is afflicted, let him pray to

these holy martyrs, in order that he may be relieved."

Q. What says St. John Chrysostom?

A. "Even he that is clad in purple, comes to the tombs of the saints to implore their intercession before the Lord." (Vol. 66, ad pop. Ant.)

Q. What says St. Gregory of Nyssa in his panegyric on the Martyr Theodorus?

A. "We stand in need of many graces: be our intercessor, and pray to the Lord for our country."

Q. What says St. Augustine?

A. "We do not offer our prayers *for* the martyrs, but we recommend ourselves to their prayers." (Tract 84, in Joan).

Q. What follows from all that has just been said?

A. That the invocation of the saints is a good and salutary practice, since all who have been most eminent in learning and in sanctity have both taught and practised it.

Q. Do the saints know when we pray to them?

A. If the angels are aware of the good works of men, without doubt the saints enjoy the same knowledge.

Q. How do we know that the good works of men are known to the angels?

A. From these words of Christ: "There shall be joy in heaven upon one sinner that doth penance, more than upon ninety-nine just." Luke xv. 7.

Q. In what way may the saints learn when we are praying to them?

A. Either God Himself or our guardian angel makes it known to them, or they see it in God as we see in a mirror what is passing around us.

Q. Of what use are pictures and images?

A. They serve to decorate the churches, to instruct the ignorant, and to excite devotion.

Q. Does not the Scripture say: "You shall not make to yourselves any graven thing"?

A. It does, but immediately adds: "To adore it."

Q. Do Catholics adore images?

A. No; they are far from doing so.

Q. Do they invoke them?

A. They do not invoke them.

Q. Do they not seek grace and assistance from them?

A. No; they ask nothing of them, and they expect nothing from them.

Q. Do Catholics believe that there is any virtue or power in images?

A. They do not.

Q. If images have no virtue in themselves, what is meant by miraculous images?

A. It is not to be supposed that images, which are senseless and lifeless things, can work miracles; but God sometimes grants special graces to those who pray with fervor before certain images.

Q. What honor is paid to images?

A. We bow our heads, or kneel before them, to adore Jesus Christ, and show our reverence for the saints who are represented by these images.

Q. Is it improper to have images on the altar?

A. No; for Solomon placed two Cherubim upon the Ark of the Covenant, by the order of God Himself.

Q. Is it not improper to kneel before images?

A. Josue knelt down before the Ark of the Covenant—there is no impropriety in doing the same before images.

Q. Is there any benefit to be derived from pilgrimages?

A. Yes, when they are made in a spirit of true devotion.

Q. But what use is there in pilgrimages? Is not God everywhere?

A. God, of course, is everywhere; but we know that He has been pleased to bestow many graces and benefits in certain places, and therefore we feel ourselves animated to pray there with greater fervor and confidence.

Q. To perform a pilgrimage is to do something that God does not command. Now, how can this give glory to God?

A. God may be more glorified by actions which he does not command, and which are performed of our own accord, without any compulsion.

Q. Give an instance of this?

A. David is related to have thrown away some cold water when he was burning with thirst, and this action, though not obligatory, glorified God.

Q. Can you give another example?

A. The Blessed Virgin took the vow of chastity—and this act, which was voluntary, did certainly glorify God.

Q. Is there any instance recorded in Scripture, of one leaving home to go to some distant place in order to pray?

A. Yes, Elcana and Anne went every year to Silo, there to offer their prayers; and

Jesus and Mary went every year to Jerusalem to pray in the Temple.

Q. What abuses are to be avoided in making pilgrimages?

A. We should not make them through a spirit of curiosity; we should not make them in the company of dangerous or suspicious companions; we should not for their sake neglect other more important duties, which may require us at home.

Q. In what manner do Catholics honor the relics of saints?

A. They honor them as precious remains, which recall to their minds their great sanctity; or they honor them as precious tokens which increase the confidence they have in the intercession of the saints.

Q. Did the first Christians honor relics?

A. They did, and from them we have learned the practice of venerating the relics of the saints.

Q. What says St. Augustine, writing to Quintian?

A. "I send you," he says, "the relics of St. Stephen, martyr, which you will honor as it is proper." (Epist. 103.)

Q. Do relics possess any hidden virtue?

A. No; but God often grants through them great favors.

Q. Can you quote an instance of this from Scripture?

A. It is related in the Fourth Book of Kings, that a dead man being cast into the tomb of the prophet Eliseus, was restored to life as soon as he touched the bones of the prophet.

Q. Mention another instance taken from the New Testament?

A. A woman was cured by touching the garment of our Saviour. Matt. ix. 20.

Q. Are there not other instances recorded in the Acts of the Apostles?

A. Yes, many persons are there recorded to have been cured by the shadow of St. Peter, and by touching the handkerchiefs of St. Paul. Chap. i. xv. and xix. 12.

Q. Is it not superstitious to wear images, medals of the saints, blessed articles of devotion, or relics?

A. On the contrary, it is praiseworthy, if it is done with a pious intention, that is to say, with confidence in God, in the intercession of the saints, or in the prayers and blessing of the Church.

LESSON V.

Q. Which is the second commandment?

A. "Thou shalt not take the name of the Lord thy God in vain."

Q. What are we commanded by the second commandment?

A. We are commanded to speak with reverence of God, of His saints and priests, of religion, its practices and ceremonies, and of all holy things, and to keep our lawful oaths and vows.

Q. Is it a sin to say: Good God! or, O Lord!?

A. To say so habitually and without respect, is a venial sin.

Q. What is blasphemy?

A. Blasphemy is to speak ill of God or the saints, or holy things; for example, to say that God is cruel or unjust, or takes no care of us—to express the wish that there was no God—to say the sacraments are of no use, the Holy Scriptures contain lies, or to damn anything sacred.

Q. Is blasphemy a great sin?

A. It is a mortal sin to utter these and like blasphemies, if one knows the evil of what he is saying, and that it is an injury to God.

Q. What is meant by cursing?

A. Cursing means, to wish any evil either to ourselves, or to our neighbor, or to any of God's creatures, whereby the name of God is frequently dishonored.

Q. Is every curse a great sin?

A. Curses—that people may die, never stir, or about the devil, or hell, or bad luck to you, if not said from the heart, are venial sins; but if they are said from the heart, and really some grievous harm to a person is meant, then they are mortal sins.

Q. If one repents of the habit of saying a bad word, and it slips out of his mouth against his will, is such a word also a sin?

A. No; but when this happens he must do his best to correct himself.

Q. What is an oath?

A. An oath is to call God or a sacred thing to witness that what we say is true, or that we will do something, or fulfil the promise which we make; for example, to swear on the Bible, or—By the name of God, or the Holy Name—By Heaven—On my soul—So help me God.

Q. Is it wrong for one to say in conversation: Faith—On my life—On my conscience—True as I

stand here—True as Gospel; or to say in talking: I swear—God's truth—God knows—I declare to God?

A. To say such words is commonly a venial sin, but not an oath, unless God is called to witness the truth.

Q. Is it a mortal or venial sin to take an oath, not false or bad, but without any necessity?

A. Such an oath is a venial sin.

Q. Is it a mortal or venial sin to take a false oath, especially in a Court of Justice?

A. Such an oath is always a mortal sin.

Q. Is it a mortal or venial sin to take an oath to do something which is a sin, and must such an oath be kept?

A. Such an oath is also a mortal sin and must never be kept.

Q. Is it also a great sin not to keep, when you can, an oath in an important matter?

A. It is.

Q. Is it a sin to take an oath on a proper occasion; for example, in a Court of Justice?

A. Such an oath is no sin, but a good and meritorious act.

Q. Is it a very bad thing to have the custom of taking oaths in conversation?

A. It is, and a most decided mark of vulgarity.

Q. What is a vow?

A. A vow is a deliberate promise made to God to do something pleasing to Him, which one is not obliged to do.

Q. Are we bound to keep our vows?

A. Yes, we are bound to keep them; and it would be a mortal sin to break a vow in a grave matter. But it is a venial sin to break a vow in a small matter; for instance, a vow to say the Hail Mary; or to break a vow even in an important matter is but a venial sin, if we bound ourselves only under pain of a venial sin.

Q. What should one do before making a vow?

A. It would always be well to ask the advice of one's confessor or some other prudent priest.

LESSON VI.

Q. Which is the third commandment?

A. "Remember that thou keep holy the Sabbath day."

Q. What are we commanded by the third commandment?

A. We are commanded to keep the Lord's day holy.

Q. Which is the Lord's day?

A. In the Old Law, it was the seventh day of the week, or the Sabbath day; but in the New Law, it is the first day of the week, or the Sunday.

Q. Who made this change?

A. The Apostles made this change to distinguish the Christians from the Jews, and also because Jesus Christ rose from the dead and sent the Holy Ghost on a Sunday.

Q. How are we to keep the Sunday holy?

A. By resting from servile works and hearing Mass.

Q. Why are we commanded to rest from servile works?

A. That we may have time and opportunity for prayer, receiving the sacraments, hearing instructions, and reading good books.

Q. Which works are servile and forbidden?

A. All bodily works which are commonly performed by servants, day-laborers, and tradesmen.

Q. Is it servile work to write, or teach, or draw, or sing, or travel?

A. No; because works by which the mind is principally exerted, are not numbered amongst the servile works.

Q. Is it a sin to be paid for this kind of work?

A. If a person does on Sunday what is not servile work, it is not a sin to be paid for it.

Q. Is it never lawful to do servile work on Sunday?

A. It is lawful—1. When the pastors of the Church, for weighty reasons, give a dispensation; 2. As often as the honor of God, the good of our neighbor, or grave necessity requires it.

Q. Mention some cases in which there is a necessity to do servile work?

A. 1. In case of certain works which cannot be interrupted without great inconvenience, such as the work of certain manufactories.

2. If a person has not food enough for the day.

3. In case of a funeral and the like.

4. Poor people who have no other time are allowed to wash and mend their clothes.

5. Servants may do household work, cooking, etc.

6. If it becomes necessary to avoid a great loss—for example, if a farmer's hay or corn, or fruit is in danger of being destroyed or much injured by the weather.

7. In buying, or selling, if there is any custom permitted by the Bishop.

8. It is allowed to sell things on Sunday which are necessary, as medicines, food, etc.

Q. Is it a venial or mortal sin to work on Sunday without necessity?

A. It is a mortal sin to work without necessity, for a considerable time, but it is only a venial sin to work for a short time.

Q. Are those only guilty who themselves do forbidden work?

A. No; those also are guilty, and even more so, who without necessity make their inferiors, as servants, day-laborers, or tradesmen, do such work, or allow them to do it; for God says: "That thy man-servant and thy maid-servant may rest, even as thyself."—Deut. v. 14.

Q. Who is bound under pain of mortal sin to hear Mass on Sundays?

A. Every Catholic from the age of seven is bound to hear Mass on Sundays, unless lawfully excused.

Q. Who are excused from hearing Mass?

A. 1. Those who are sick, or so weak that it is dangerous for them to go to church.

2. Those who have the care of the sick, if they cannot conveniently leave them.

3. Servants who cannot leave the house without very great inconvenience.

4. Those who must stay at home in order to cook, or mind children, take care of cattle, etc.

5. Children are excused if hindered by their parents, or wives by their husbands.

6. Soldiers, people in prison and work-houses, if they cannot go to Mass.

7. Those who are on a journey, and cannot interrupt it without great inconvenience.

8. Those who cannot go to Mass without exposing themselves to the danger of some great temporal or spiritual evil.

9. Those who live far from a church, especially if they are weak, or the weather is bad.

Q. What should servants and other people do when engaged in the service of masters who seldom or never let them go to Mass and the Sacraments?

A. They are not bound to leave them immediately if they cannot easily find another situation, but they should try their best to get another place where they can comply with their Christian duties.

Q. Is it a sin wilfully to lose any part of a Mass of obligation?

A. If a person through his own fault loses much of the Mass on Sundays or on days of obligation, he commits a mortal sin, unless he knows that he can hear another Mass, and really hears it.

Q. Is it just as great a sin to lose Mass, or to do unnecessary servile work on a Holy Day of obligation as on a Sunday?

A. Yes; it is just as great a sin.

Q. Is it also a mortal sin to play or talk during a great part of a Mass of obligation, so that you cannot attend to it?

A. It is a mortal sin.

Q. Does he who sleeps during the principal parts of Mass fulfil the precept?

A. He does not; but he who is troubled with sleepiness hears Mass if he can give some attention to it.

Q. Is helping at Mass, by serving, singing, playing the organ, a hindrance to hearing Mass?

A. It is not.

Q. Is the Sunday profaned only by servile work and staying away from Mass?

A. The Sunday is also profaned by debauchery, intemperance, and extravagant games, sports, and amusements, which make of the Lord's day a day of revelry and public scandal.

Q. What should make every one afraid of profaning the Sunday ?

A. 1. The temporal and eternal punishments with which God threatens those who break the Sabbath.

2. That it is unpardonable heedlessness not to give even so much as one day to the care of our immortal soul, after the body has been taken care of for six days.

3. That the observance of the Sunday is a public profession of Christian faith, and that, therefore, by profaning the Lord's day we bring disgrace on our holy religion, and give great scandal to our fellow-Christians.

LESSON VII.

Q. Which is the fourth commandment ?

A. Honor thy father and thy mother.

Q. What are we commanded by the fourth commandment ?

A. We are commanded to love, honor, and obey our parents and superiors in all that is not sinful.

Q. Why must children love, honor, and obey their parents ?

A. Because, next to God, their parents are their greatest benefactors, and they hold for them the place of God, from whom parents have power to direct, instruct, and correct their children.

Q. How should children love their parents?

A. 1. They should be grateful to them, and wish them well from their heart.

2. They should endeavor to make them happy by their good conduct.

3. They should help them in their necessities, and take care of them in their old age as well as they are able.

4. They should bear with their faults and weaknesses.

Q. How should children honor their parents?

A. They should look upon them as those who hold the place of God in their regard, and should, therefore, always show them respect in word and deed.

Q. How should children obey their parents?

A. 1. They should do what their parents tell them to do, and not do what they forbid, provided they order nothing that is bad.

2. They should readily follow their advice and willingly receive their corrections.

Q. What is promised by God to children who faithfully keep the fourth commandment?

A. God's protection and blessing in this life, and eternal happiness in the next.

Q. When do children sin against the love they owe to their parents?

A. 1. When they wish, or do them evil.

2. When, by their bad behavior they give them trouble, and bring disgrace upon them, or otherwise give them great sorrow, or put them into a passion.

3. When they do not help them in their sickness, or poverty, or old age.

4. When they do not bear with their failings.

5. When they do not pray for their parents, whether living or dead.

Q. When do children sin against the honor and respect they owe to their parents?

A. 1. When in their heart they despise them, or disregard them, as they do when they look sullen and give disrespectful answers, or threaten or scold them, and cast up their faults to them, or do not speak to them, through pride.

2. When they speak ill of them.

3. When they treat them harshly, as they

do when they marry secretly, strike them, or mock them, or the like, through spite and contempt, or in their hearing curse them or call them very bad names, such as fools, beasts, drunkards, to do which is a mortal sin.

Q. When do children sin against the obedience they owe to their parents?

A. When they obey badly, or not at all, or do not willingly listen to their admonitions, and offer resistance to their corrections.

Q. When is it very bad for children to disobey their parents?

A. When they disobey them in an important matter, such as going out at night, or into bad company, or to dancing-houses and the like, or playing about in the streets with any one they meet, or leaving their parents.

Q. What should a child do if he knows that his brothers or sisters go into bad company, or do other bad things?

A. He should tell his parents about it.

Q. What should children do if their parents set them a bad example?

A. They must not follow their bad example, but pray for their conversion.

Q. What will fall upon those children who do not fulfil their duties towards their parents?

A. In this life, the curse of God, disgrace, and shame will fall upon them, and eternal damnation in the life to come.

Q. What other superiors besides our parents must we love, honor, and obey?

A. Our guardians, tutors, teachers, employers, masters, and mistresses, and all our spiritual and temporal superiors.

Q. What are our duties towards these superiors?

A. We should consider them as the representatives and assistants of our parents, and therefore our duties towards them are like those which children owe to their parents.

Q. What are the duties of servants to their masters and mistresses?

A. They should, for God's sake, show them love, respect, obedience, and faithfulness.

Q. How do servants sin against their masters and mistresses?

A. 1. By disobedience.

2. By laziness, by pilfering dainties, and by wasting and embezzling their goods.

3. By slander, detraction, and tale-bearing, and most of all, by teaching evil to the children, by seducing them, by assisting them to do evil, or by conniving at it.

Q. What are our duties towards our spiritual superiors?

A. 1. We should love and respect them as the representatives of God, and as our spiritual fathers.

2. We should submit to their ordinances.

3. We should pray for them, and provide for their support in the manner established by law and custom.

Q. When do we sin against our spiritual superiors?

A. 1. When by word or deed we fail in reverence due to them, or when, by speaking ill of them, we lower their character.

2. When we oppose them, and thereby may be the cause of schism and scandal.

3. When, contrary to our duty, we refuse to contribute towards their support, and to provide for the Divine service and the good of religion.

Q. What are our duties towards our civil magistrates?

A. We are bound—1. To show to our civil magistrates respect, fidelity, and conscientious obedience.

2. To assist our country in its necessities and dangers, and even to sacrifice our prop-

erty and life for its defence against all its enemies.

Q. How do we sin against our temporal rulers?

A. 1. By hatred and contempt. 2. By reviling and cursing them. 3. By refusing to pay the taxes justly imposed. 4. By resistance and rebellion, or conspiracy, against our sovereign and country.

Q. When are parents, superiors, and sovereigns not to be obeyed?

A. When they command anything unlawful before God.

Q. How should young people behave towards the aged?

A. They should treat the aged respectfully, listen to their good advice, and, as far as possible, lighten the burden of their old age.

Duties of Parents, Masters, and Superiors.

Q. Did God give the fourth commandment only for children and inferiors?

A. No. He gave it also for fathers and mothers.

Q. What are the duties of fathers and mothers towards their children?

A. The first and most sacred duty of parents

is, to bring up their children for God and for heaven. Therefore they must not delay having them baptized in the Catholic Church. They must teach them when very little, and make them say their prayers. When their children are seven years old, parents must make them go to Confession, to Mass, to Catechism, or Sunday-school. They must not let their children say bad words or go into bad company, or keep dangerous company with persons of the other sex, or play about in the streets. They must correct them for their faults, and not keep in the house bad or irreligious books or pamphlets or story-papers and the like.

Q. What other duty have parents towards their children ?

A. They must see to the temporal welfare of their children.

Q. How do parents sin against the love they owe their children for their spiritual welfare ?

A. 1. By showing hatred and cruelty toward them, beating them too much, or without cause, or in a passion.

2. By cursing them and setting them a bad example.

3. By showing too much love and fondness for any particular one of them, or by letting them have their own way.

4. By neglecting to instruct them or to have them instructed in their religion.

5. By putting brothers and sisters in the same bed.

6. By sending them to schools forbidden by Bishops and parish priests.

7. By hindering their children from following the call which God gives them to become priests or nuns, or by hindering, without just reason, their marriage, or forcing them to marry, to do which is a mortal sin.

Q. How do parents sin by neglecting the temporal welfare of their children?

A. 1. By not taking proper care of them before and after their birth.

2. By unjustly depriving a child of his inheritance.

3. By sending them out to beg instead of bringing them up to some trade, or employment.

4. By inconsiderately squandering their property and not taking proper care of the food, clothing, or health of their children.

5. By abandoning their children, which is a great sin for parents.

Q. What are the duties of masters and mistresses towards their servants ?

A. They should—1. Not ill-treat them by harsh, unkind words, or by overworking them, or not giving them food enough.

2. They should not keep wicked servants, to have the care of children, nor should they allow servants to use bad words, or go into bad company and stay out at night, nor should they ask them to do anything forbidden by the law of God.

3. Masters and mistresses must make their servants attend to their religious duties, and give them time to do so, and when it is necessary that some one should stay at home, it would be wrong not to allow each in turn to have an opportunity of going to Mass.

4. They must not make their servants do servile work on Sundays without necessity.

Q. What are the obligations of civil magistrates or temporal rulers ?

A. Temporal rulers are ordained by God for the good of their fellow-citizens, therefore they should—

1. Promote the welfare of the people to the best of their power.

2. They should perform the duties of their office with wisdom and justice.

3. They should punish evil, and be to all a pattern of a Christian life.

LESSON VIII.

Q. Which is the fifth commandment?

A. "Thou shalt not kill."

Q. What does the fifth commandment forbid?

A. God forbids us by this commandment to do any injury to ourselves, or to our neighbor, in body or soul.

Q. How do we injure ourselves in our bodies?

A. 1. By exposing ourselves to danger of death without necessity.

2. By suicide, or by trying to take away our life.

3. By wilfully injuring our health and shortening our lives by intemperance in eating and drinking, debaucheries, etc.

Q. What sin is committed by him who deliberately takes away his own life?

A. He commits three horrible crimes. 1.

A crime against God, who alone has power over life and death.

2. A crime against human society, and especially against his relations, on whom he brings inexpressible grief and disgrace.

3. A crime against his own soul, which he unmercifully casts into everlasting hell-fire.

Q. What is the punishment of the Church for the suicide or self-murderer ?

A. She refuses him Christian burial.

Q. Are we never allowed to expose our life or health to danger ?

A. Never, without some just reason.

Q. May we wish for our death ?

A. If such a wish proceeds merely from impatience, or want of resignation to the will of God, or from despair, it is a sinful wish; but it is not sinful, if it proceeds from a true desire to go to heaven or be free from the occasion of sin, or from some temporal evil which may lead to despair or some other great sin.

Q. What sin is committed by him who wilfully gets quite drunk ?

A. It is a mortal sin for one wilfully to get quite drunk so as to lose his senses, and he is answerable for all the sins he could foresee he was likely to commit while in that state of drunkenness.

Q. What sin is it to get half drunk?

A. To get half drunk is in itself but a venial sin; but it may sometimes be a mortal sin; for instance, for a father of a family who frequently gets half drunk, and thus injures his health and shortens his life by slow degrees, or commits other sins, or induces others to follow his example, or greatly grieves and scandalizes his family, whose goods he unreasonably squanders.

Q. How do we injure our neighbor in his body?

A. By fighting, unjust shedding of blood, and wilful murder.

By all that leads to such sins, as quarrelling, hatred, anger, revenge, etc.

Q. What sin is committed by him who unjustly takes away his neighbor's life?

A. He commits a most heinous sin, that cries to heaven for vengeance; for, 1. He takes to himself the right of God; 2. He undermines the safety of human society; and, 3. He casts his neighbor into the greatest temporal, and, possibly, into eternal ruin.

Q. Is it ever lawful to take away the life of another?

A. Yes, it is lawful—1. For the supreme civil authority to do so in the execution of criminals. (Rom. xiii. 4.) 2. For others, in a just war in defence of their country, or when necessary to defend a person's own life, or another's life, chastity, or property of great value, when unjustly attacked.

Q. Is it also lawful to send a man a challenge, or to accept his, to a duel in defence of our honor?

A. No; for such a duel is always a great crime, which is directly opposed to all order established by God and man.

Q. How does the Church punish those who fight duels, and those who are accessory to, and voluntary witnesses of them?

A. They all incur excommunication.

Q. Is it wrong to desire that some temporal misfortune may befal another?

A. It is not a sin to do so, if he desires that his neighbor may be converted, or may cease to give scandal, and to persecute the good.

Q. When do we injure our neighbor in his soul?

A. When we scandalize him; that is to say,

when we cause him in any way to commit sin.

Q. Who make themselves guilty of the sin of scandal?

A. 1. Those who use impious or filthy language, or dress very immodestly, or introduce such a mode of dress.

2. The authors of bad books, songs, pamphlets, novels, story-papers, newspapers, etc.

3. Those who spread abroad, or give such bad writings to others to read.

4. Those who introduce an unchristian or godless system of education.

5. Those who approve of, and support by word and deed, such a system of education.

6. Those who open their houses to thieves, drunkards, gamblers, or other wicked men, for their unlawful meetings.

7. Those superiors who give bad example, or do not hinder evil, as they are in duty bound to do.

Q. What should keep every one from giving scandal?

A. 1. The thought that he who gives scandal is an agent of Satan, who destroys those souls which Jesus Christ has ransomed with His Blood.

2. The dreadful consequences of scandal, since those who are led into sin generally lead others into it also, and thus sin is continually spreading.

3. The dreadful words of Jesus Christ against those who give scandal: "It were better for them that a mill-stone should be hanged about their neck and that they should be drowned in the depth of the sea." Matt. xviii. 6.

Q. What must we do when we have injured our neighbor in his body or in his soul?

A. We must not only be sorry and confess the sin, but we must also, to the best of our power, repair the evil we have done.

Q. What is commanded by the fifth commandment?

A. It commands us to live in peace and union with our neighbor; to promote, according to our ability, his spiritual and temporal welfare; and also to take reasonable care of our life and health.

LESSON IX.

Q. Which is the sixth commandment?

A. "Thou shalt not commit adultery."

Q. What is forbidden by the sixth commandment?

A. The sixth commandment forbids—1. Adultery and all sins of uncleanness; as all wilful, unchaste looks, words, jests, immodest touches and liberties with any person or thing, or with one's self alone, and whatsoever is against the virtue of chastity. 2. Everything that leads to impurity.

Q. What is it that generally leads to impurity or the sin of uncleanness?

A. 1. Not putting away bad thoughts and desires immediately.

2. Curiosity to know, and see, and hear bad things.

3. Immodesty of dress, drunkenness and revelry, idleness and effeminacy.

4. Nightly interviews, and indecent plays.

Q. What else leads to the sin of uncleanness?

A. Obscene songs, books, pictures, and the like.

Q. May one keep those things?

A. No, such things must be destroyed.

Q. What else leads to the sin of uncleanness ?

A. Scandalous things.

Q. Can you name some things that are scandalous ?

A. 1. It is a great sin for women or girls to go wilfully and unnecessarily into company where they know that liberties will be taken with them, although these liberties are against their will.

2. It is a great sin to do anything to raise bad thoughts in the minds of others.

3. It is a sin for men to make women think they are going to marry them when they have no such intention.

4. Girls should take care when men or boys come to them when alone, especially if they say anything which may have a bad meaning, or ask them to walk alone with them. So, let girls when they fear anything evil, try to escape all danger.

Q. Is there anything else that leads to the sin of uncleanness ?

A. Yes; dangerous places and things, such as dancing-houses, bad wakes, gambling-houses, theatres, houses of assignation, grog-shops, public houses, sometimes boarding-houses, and the streets at night, or shows, if there is anything bad in them.

Q. What else often leads to the sin of impurity?

A. 1. The reading of novels and romances is often very dangerous.

2. It is better for girls not to go to schools taught by men unless the priest approves of these schools.

3. The playing of boys with girls.

4. It is very dangerous for men and women to keep company, especially if alone.

5. In some cases it is very dangerous for girls or women to receive presents or letters from men.

6. On many occasions when women or girls have to make visits, it is very proper for some one else to be with them; the same may be said of many occasions when they have to receive visits.

7. The time before marriage is very dangerous. Those engaged to be married should avoid taking improper liberties, and it is advisable that they should not be in company alone, but with their parents, or some well-behaved persons. They will learn each other's character much better by inquiring, than by

being alone, for, before marriage, people seldom show themselves to be what they really are.

Q. Why must we guard most carefully against the sin of uncleanness ?

A. Because no sin is more shameful; and because no sin is attended with such dreadful consequences.

Q. Why is this sin so shameful ?

A. Because, by this sin man degrades himself to the level of an unclean animal, disfiguring his soul, the image of God, in a most shameful manner.

Q. What are the evil effects of the sin of uncleanness ?

A. 1. It robs man of his innocence, and ruins body and soul.

2. It leads him to many other sins, and often to despair and murder.

3. It casts him into all kinds of misery and shame, and at last into hell.

Q. Is every sin of uncleanness a great sin ?

A. Yes, every sin of uncleanness which one commits knowingly and wilfully, either with himself, or with others, is a mortal sin.

Q. Are all sins of uncleanness equally grievous ?

A. No; some are more grievous than others, according to the persons with whom the sin is committed; or, according as the sin is more heinous and unnatural, and its effects are more hurtful.

Q. What are we to do when we doubt whether or not anything is a sin against purity or chastity?

A. We must ask our confessor, and, in the meanwhile, carefully avoid that of which we are in doubt.

Q. What are we commanded by the sixth commandment?

A. It commands us to be pure and modest in all our thoughts, desires, looks, words, and actions, and most carefully to preserve the innocence of our soul as the greatest treasure and the most beautiful ornament of man.

Q. What means should we make use of in order to preserve our innocence?

A. 1. We should shun all bad company and all occasions of sin.

2. Carefully guard our senses, especially our eyes.

3. Never be idle, but practise humility and the mortification of the senses.

4. Receive the sacraments frequently.

5. In temptation against purity, call immediately on Jesus and Mary to help us to overcome the temptation.

Q. What means should be adopted by those who have become addicted to the sin of impurity ?

A. They should use the means just mentioned, and moreover return, if possible, to the same confessor.

LESSON X.

Q. Which is the seventh commandment ?

A. "Thou shalt not steal."

Q. What does the seventh commandment forbid ?

A. All unjust taking away, or keeping what belongs to another, as also all manner of cheating in buying and selling, or any other way of wronging our neighbor in his temporal goods.

Q. Who are guilty of stealing ?

A. 1. Those who steal much at once.

2. Those who take and keep things by little and little.

3. Those who help others to steal.

4. Those who let others steal what they themselves have in charge.

5. Those who receive stolen goods or things from servants, or from persons who have no right to give them away.

6. Those who keep a thing found without trying to find the owner.

7. Those who destroy or injure wilfully what belongs to another.

8. Those who cause a person to lose anything by lies, detraction, or other unjust means: for example, to cause a servant to lose her place, or a shop-keeper his customers.

9. Those who steal by force, or from a church, or anything sacred, commit a great sin different in kind.

Q. Who are guilty of cheating their neighbor?

A. 1. Those who are not sufficiently experienced in their employment or profession, and thus injure others, as an ignorant doctor or druggist.

2. Those who make a bargain or contract to do what is sinful, or to do something which they are unable to do.

3. Those who cheat in fulfilling a contract, for example, by using unsound materials, or doing the work ill, or doing only part, and taking the whole price.

4. Those who break an agreement without just reason.

5. Those who cheat in buying and selling; that is, who sell for more, or buy for less than a reasonable price; who lend or sell what is hurtful to the buyer, for example, bad books, medicines, liquors; who sell what is in itself bad or useless to the buyer; who sell what is imperfect for the same price as if it were perfect, except in some cases where there is a common understanding that a thing is to be sold for what it will bring.

6. Those who do not pay wages to servants or others.

7. Those who charge too much interest in lending money, or sell provisions to the poor on credit, and overcharge them.

8. Those who imitate any writing for some bad purpose.

9. Those who knowingly pass false money.

10. Those who beg under the false pretext of being poor.

11. Those who carry on unjust law-suits.

12. Those who break a promise of marriage.

13. Those who get into debt, not meaning to pay, or to pay at proper time when they

are able, or do not lessen their expenses in order to pay.

Q. What sin is it to steal or cheat?

A. 1. It is a venial sin if the amount stolen be very small.

2. It is a mortal sin to steal or cheat, when the matter is grave; for example, to steal from a workman a day's wages, or to steal less from a poor man, or more from a rich man, or from parents.

3. If any one often steals a little, it is a sin each time, and when the little sums altogether make up a large sum, then it becomes a mortal sin.

4. It is also a mortal sin to steal a little if at the same time one has the will and intention to steal much if he could.

5. Those who break a promise of marriage without just reason, commonly commit a mortal sin.

6. To break a simple promise to give something to another is commonly not more than a venial sin, and many promises are no more than the expressions of one's intention.

7. A promise to give does not bind at all, if it is about anything hurtful, unlawful, or

useless, or when things change so much afterwards, that if we had foreseen the change, we would not have made the promise. At the same time one should be very careful how he makes such promises.

Q. May servants give alms of what belongs to their masters?

A. No, unless they know that their masters would have no reasonable objection to it.

Q. What must we do when we have stolen anything, or are in possession of ill-gotten goods, or have injured our neighbor?

A. If we have injured any one in his person, character, honor, or goods, we must make just amends.

Q. When are we not obliged to restore?

A. We are not obliged to restore if the injury we did was by accident, and we did not mean to do it.

Q. May restitution sometimes be delayed for some time?

A. We may delay restitution if we cannot make it immediately without very great difficulty; for example, if a workman would have to sell his tools, or if a person would lose his character thereby; but we must have the will and intention to do it as soon as possible, at least by little and little, otherwise we could not be forgiven.

Q. How much must we restore?

A. 1. If we have knowingly and unjustly taken or kept back our neighbor's goods, we must make full amends; that is to say, restitution must be made, not only of the things stolen, or, if consumed, of their value, but also of the profits they have in the meantime produced, the expense, however, being deducted, which was made for the preservation and valuable improvements of the goods. And, in general, the owner must be compensated for all the profits which he has been deprived of, and for all the losses he has suffered.

2. If we did it unknowingly or unwillingly we must, as soon as we come to know that it is another man's property, restore all that is still left, and as much more as our wealth has been increased by it, after having, however, deducted our own expenses for the preservation of such property and its valuable improvements.

Q. To whom must ill-gotten goods be restored?

A. Ill-gotten goods must be restored to the person injured, or his heirs, or if this cannot be done, they must be spent in works of charity.

Q. What should we bear in mind in order not to become guilty of stealing, or of neglect in making restitution?

A. 1. That death will wrest all ill-gotten goods from us, and perhaps, sooner than we expect.

2. That goods ill-gotten always bring upon us misfortune, uneasiness, and troubles of mind.

3. That there is no greater folly than to lose heaven for the sake of perishable goods, and cast ourselves into everlasting hell fire.

Q. What is commanded by the seventh commandment?

A. To pay our lawful debts, and give every one his due.

LESSON XI.

Q. Which is the eighth commandment?

A. "Thou shalt not bear false witness against thy neighbor."

Q. What does the eighth commandment forbid?

A. All false testimony, that is to say, giving

evidence in a court of justice that we know to be untrue.

Q. How are we to give evidence in a court of justice?

A. We must tell the truth just as we know it, and neither more nor less.

Q. What else is forbidden by the eighth commandment?

A. Lies and hypocrisy, all calumny and slander, detraction, tale-bearing, rash judgment, unjust suspicions, and contumely.

Q. What is a lie?

A. A lie is to say knowingly and deliberately what is not true.

Q. Is it ever lawful to tell a lie?

A. It is never lawful to tell a lie, either for our own benefit or for that of another, either in jest or earnest; because every lie is essentially opposed to God, who is Truth Itself.

Q. When is a lie a mortal sin?

A. A lie is a mortal sin when by it a grievous injury is done to another, and it is of such lies that the Holy Scripture speaks when it says: "The mouth that lieth killeth the soul." Wisd. i. 11.

Q. How do we sin by hypocrisy?

A. By pretending to be better or more pious

than we really are, in order thereby to deceive others.

Q. How do we sin by calumny or slander?

A. By injuring much or taking away any one's character by a lie, telling faults of our neighbor, of which he is not guilty, or exaggerating those of which he is guilty.

Q. What sin is it to do this?

A. It is a mortal sin.

Q. How do we sin by detraction?

A. We sin by detraction if we injure much, or take away any one's character by making known to others something very bad about him, which is true, but which was not known before we made it known.

Q. What sin is such detraction?

A. It is a mortal sin, except in case when we ask advice, or wish to prevent a great evil, or tell a superior that he may correct his subject. In all cases such detraction is only lawful when it is binding on our conscience to disclose our neighbor's grave fault, and when it is certain that such disclosure is necessary, or may benefit him; if made only out of a spirit of malicious or idle gossip, it is a grave and mischievous sin.

Q. Is every calumny or detraction equally sinful?

A. No, the sin is greater—1. The greater the fault is, and the higher the person of whom the fault is told.

2. The greater the loss and injury which he suffers by it.

3. The more people there are who hear it.

4. The worse our intention is in making it known.

Q. Is it also a sin, even to listen to detraction or calumny?

A. Yes, it is a sin—1. To be pleased with hearing the detraction or calumny through curiosity, and it is even worse if we are pleased with the injury done to a person's character.

2. To encourage others who detract; for example, by asking them questions, or by approving of their detraction.

3. Not to prevent it when it is in our power to do so.

Q. Who are bound to prevent calumny and detraction?

A. 1. Superiors must not let their inferiors detract. 2. Parents must hinder their children from detracting; and, 3. Masters their servants.

Q. What must we do when we have taken away another's character by slander?

A. We must recall the lie; we might say we were mistaken, or the like.

Q. What must we do when we have injured another's character by detraction?

A. We must repair it as well as we can; for example, by praising the good qualities of such a person.

Q. When do we sin by tale-bearing?

A. When we relate to a person what another has said of him, or of somebody else, and thus do some great harm by it, such as changing friends into enemies, to do which is a very detestable sin. It is often done in jest, but such jesting is always dangerous.

Q. When do we sin by rash judgment?

A. When, for little or no reason, we firmly believe something bad about a person.

Q. When do we sin by unjust suspicions?

A. When, without sufficient reason, we think to ourselves that our neighbor is guilty of something bad.

Q. Are such unjust suspicions great sins?

A. They are seldom great sins, unless they

are quite wilful, and about something very bad, such as murder; if there is some foundation for a suspicion, it is not a sin.

Q. When do we sin by contumely ?

A. When we dishonor or insult any one by striking him or calling him bad names, or the like, or if we scoff and laugh at people.

Q. What else is forbidden by the eighth commandment ?

A. Telling a secret and reading the letters or private papers of others.

Q. Is it a sin to do this ?

A. Yes; and it is a great sin to tell a great secret, and its telling does great harm or gives great sorrow. To read the letters or private papers of others is also a sin, and it is a great sin if we know that these letters or papers are of importance, and that their owners would feel exceedingly displeased at our knowing their contents.

Q. Is it never lawful to tell a secret ?

A. It is not wrong to tell a secret to some one for a good reason, such as to ask necessary advice.

Q. What is commanded by the eighth commandment ?

A. It commands us to speak the truth in all

things, to be deeply interested in the good character of our neighbor, and to bridle our tongue.

Q. How should we be interested in our good character?

A. As far as the honor of God, the good of our neighbor, and the duties of our state of life demand.

Q. In what manner should we take care of our reputation?

A. We should take care of it only by making use of the lawful means to preserve it, especially by leading a virtuous life, and by avoiding, to the best of our ability, even the very appearance of evil.

Q. In what manner may we best avoid the sins of the tongue?

A. 1. By never talking thoughtlessly, bearing in mind that we have to give an account of every idle word; and, 2. By keeping our heart free from ambition, envy, hatred, vengeance, and all inordinate affections.

LESSON XII.

Q. Which is the ninth commandment?

A. "Thou shalt not covet thy neighbor's wife."

Q. What does the ninth commandment forbid?

A. The ninth commandment forbids all lustful thoughts and desires, and all wilful pleasure in the irregular motions of the flesh.

Q. Is every bad thought a sin?

A. A bad thought, which is not wilful, is no sin at all, and a bad or impure thought in the mind, for some moments before we can be sufficiently on our guard against it, is not a mortal sin; but not to try to put away the bad thought when we think of our duty of doing so, and to take pleasure in it and consent to it, is a sin.

Q. When do we sin by lustful desires?

A. We sin by lustful desires when we voluntarily wish to see, hear, or do, something that is contrary to chastity.

Q. What should we do when we are tempted by lustful thoughts and desires?

A. We should immediately pray to Jesus and Mary to obtain grace to banish them, and, if we cannot get rid of them, we must not feel discouraged, but pay attention to our will, that it may not take any delight in them.

Q. Next to invoking Jesus and Mary, what is the best cure for thoughts and desires of this nature?

A. Healthy and active occupation of body and mind.

Q. What is commanded by the ninth commandment?

A. It commands us to think of such things only as are modest and holy.

LESSON XIII.

Q. Which is the tenth commandment?

A. "Thou shalt not covet thy neighbor's goods."

Q. What does the tenth commandment forbid?

A. All covetous thoughts and unjust desires of our neighbor's goods and profits.

Q. What is commanded by the tenth commandment?

A. It commands us to be contented with what is our own, and not to envy others what belongs to them.

Q. How can the poor easily content themselves with what is their own?

A. By remembering—1. That a pure conscience is the greatest treasure in this world. 2. That our true home is in the other world. 3. That if they were well off they might incur the curse of the Gospel: "Woe to the rich." 4. That Christ has become poor for our sake, and that one day He will not fail to bestow the richest reward in heaven upon all those who patiently suffer poverty for His sake.

Q. Why does God forbid, not only all evil actions, but also all evil thoughts and desires?

A. Because evil thoughts and desires defile the soul and lead but too often to bad actions.

LESSON XIV.

THE SIX COMMANDMENTS OF THE CHURCH?

Q. Who is bound to obey the Church?

A. All baptized persons, for we are commanded by Jesus Christ Himself to obey His Church.

Q. What are His words?

A. "He who will not hear the Church, let him be to thee as the heathen and the publican." Matt. xviii. 17. And addressing the pastors of His Church, He says: "He that heareth you, heareth me, and he that despiseth you, despiseth me." Luke x. 16.

Q. What says St. Paul in his Epistle to the Hebrews?

A. "Obey your prelates. For they watch as being to render an account of your souls." Chap. xiii. 17.

Q. What do we understand from these passages?

A. That we are bound in conscience to keep the commandments of the Church.

Q. But are not the commandments of the Church, merely the commandments of men?

A. We are also bound to keep the commandments of men when God orders it.

Q. Show this by a comparison.

A. The command of a father or of a civil magistrate is but the command of a man, yet God requires us to obey it.

Q. Does not our Saviour say: "In vain do they worship me, teaching doctrines and commandments of men?" Matt. xv. 9.

A. Our Saviour speaks here only of such

commands as are either contrary to the law of God, or else vain and useless.

Q. Has the Church also the power to punish those who break her commandments?

A. The Church has a right to punish them. She can refuse them the sacraments, expel them from her society, deprive them of Christian burial, etc.

Q. Which are the chief commandments of the Church?

A. 1. To hear Mass, and to rest from servile works on Sundays and holy days of obligation.

2. To keep the fast in Lent, on the Ember days, the Fridays in Advent in most of our dioceses, and eves of certain festivals, and to abstain from flesh meat on Fridays, and other appointed days of abstinence.

3. To go to confession at least once a year.

4. To receive the Blessed Sacrament during the Easter time.

5. To support our pastors.

6. Not to marry within certain degrees of kindred, nor privately, without witnesses; nor to solemnize marriage at the forbidden times.

Q. Why did the Church give these commandments?

A. They are intended to make us keep the commandments of God; for whilst God requires us to fast, to confess our sins, to receive holy communion, etc., the Church points out to us the time and manner of complying with these sacred duties.

Q. Has the Church the power of instituting festivals?

A. She certainly has as much right as the Jewish Church had; and that the Jewish Church exercised such power, may be seen from the 9th Chapter of the Book of Esther, and from the last chapter of the Book of Judith.

Q. Is there anything else to say in favor of this power of the Church?

A. If the Church did not possess such power by what authority did she command that Sunday should be kept holy instead of Saturday?

LESSON XV.

THE FIRST COMMANDMENT OF THE CHURCH.

Q. How are we to keep the holy days of obligation which the Church has instituted in honor of our Lord and of His saints ?

A. In the same manner as the Sundays.

Q. Why did the Church institute the feasts of our Lord ?

A. To bring before our mind the mysteries of the life of our Lord, to thank Him for His graces, and make us renew our zeal in serving Him, and thus render ourselves more worthy of the fruits of His life and death.

Q. Why did the Church institute the feasts of the saints ?

A. That we may—1. Praise the Lord for the graces He has bestowed upon the saints, and through them also upon us: 2. Represent to our mind their virtuous life on earth and their happiness in heaven, and resolve to follow their example; and, 3. To ask their prayers with God.

Q. Can the Church also abolish holy days ?

A. As she has full power to institute holy days, so she has also the power to abolish them, to transfer them, or to limit them to certain places, as time and circumstances may require.

LESSON XVI.

THE SECOND COMMANDMENT OF THE CHURCH.

Q. Has the Church also the power of instituting fasting days?

A. She has: and St. Augustine charges Arius with heresy for calling in question this right of the Church.

Q. Has the Church the power of forbidding certain kinds of food?

A. She has: and she exercised it even in the time of the Apostles, as we read in Acts xxv., where the use of "blood and things strangled" is forbidden.

Q. Would Christians have sinned in eating such food?

A. They would, without doubt, since they would have broken the commandment of the Church.

Q. Might they not have said, "that which goeth into the mouth defileth not a man"?

A. It is not the food, but the disobedience, that defiles a man.

Q. What should Catholics answer to Protestants and infidels when they make the same reproach to them?

A. That it is not the food, but the disobedience, that defileth a man.

Q. Of what food does our Saviour speak when He says: "Not that which goeth into the mouth defileth a man"? Matt. xv. 11.

A. He speaks of food that is taken with unwashed hands, and not at all of that which is taken contrary to the precepts of the Church.

Q. Why does the Church forbid the use of flesh-meat on certain days?

A. In order that we may mortify our bodies.

Q. Is flesh-meat an unclean food?

A. No, it is the flesh of God's creatures, which is to be used with thanksgiving.

Q. Who were they that believed it to be unclean, and a creature of the devil?

A. The Marcionites and Manicheans.

Q. What does the Apostle call this doctrine?

A. He calls it a diabolical doctrine.

Q. How long is it since Catholics began to abstain from flesh?

A. This practice began with Christianity itself, as we learn from St. Epiphanius, who says: "It is ordained, by the law of the Apostles, to fast two days of the week."

Q. Has abstinence always been kept by the whole church on Fridays and Saturdays?

A. No; in some places it was observed on Wednesdays and Fridays.

Q. What says St. Jerome?

A. That we are to follow, in this particular, the usage of the country in which we live.

Q. Why do we practise abstinence on Fridays?

A. To honor the death and burial of our Lord Jesus Christ.

Q. Did not St. Paul reprove the Colossians for saying—"Touch not, taste not"? Chap. ii. 21.

A. He reproved them only for making use of these words in the sense of the Old Law.

Q. Does not the same Apostle say, in the same chapter—"Let no man judge you in meat, or in drink, or in regard of a festival day"?

A. He speaks here only of the Jewish law, which was no longer binding upon Christians.

Q. Again the same Apostle says—"Where the spirit of the Lord is, there is liberty." Why, then, are we subjected to the laws of the Church?

A. "Be ye free," says St. Peter, "and not

as making liberty a cloak of malice, but as the servants of God." 1 Eph. ii. 16.

Q. By whom was Lent established?

A. By the Apostles, as may be shown from the rule of St. Augustine, and from the testimony of the Fathers of the Church.

Q. What rule has St. Augustine left us?

A. Every usage, says he, that is received by the whole Church, and the introduction of which cannot be traced to any Bishop, or Pope, or Council, must be considered as coming from the Apostles.

Q. What do you prove from this rule?

A. That Lent, which is received by the whole Church, and the introduction of which cannot be traced to any Bishop, or Pope, or Council, is an apostolical institution.

Q. What would you say to those who pretend that the Council of Nice introduced Lent?

A. I would answer, that such could not be the case, since Tertullian and Origen, who lived long before this Council, make mention of Lent.

Q. Do you know of any Fathers of the Church, who expressly declare that Lent was instituted by the Apostles?

A. Yes; St. Jerome and St. Leo expressly

declare it: "We keep," says St. Jerome, "a fast of forty days, according to the apostolical institution." And St. Leo says: "It was the Apostles, who, by the inspiration of the Holy Ghost, established Lent."

Q. Was fasting binding even then?

A. Yes; it was binding in conscience.

Q. What are the words of St. Jerome?

A. "The Montanists keep three Lents, whilst we keep but one. Not that it is unlawful for one to fast the whole year if he likes; but it is one thing to fast of one's own free choice, and another, to fast because one is obliged to it."

Q. What says St. Augustine?

A. We are at other times free to fast, or not to fast, but it is sinful not to fast in Lent.

Q. Why was Lent instituted?

A. 1. To honor the fast of our Saviour. 2. To honor his Passion. 3. To prepare us for the celebration of the feast of Easter.

Q. Why are we bound to fast on Ember days?

A. Because on those days the Church administers Holy Orders, and therefore has dedicated those days to public prayers and fasting.

Q. Why are we to fast on certain vigils, or the eves of great festivals?

A. To prepare ourselves for the devout keeping of the feast following.

Q. In what manner must we fast?

A. 1. We must abstain from flesh meat. 2. We must take but one meal, and that meal is to be taken about noon.

Q. How much are we allowed to eat at supper?

A. We can take only a small collation, generally not exceeding eight ounces.

Q. What kind of food may be taken at this collation?

A. In general, only light food, such as is permitted by the Bishop of the Diocese in which we live.

Q. Are we permitted to take breakfast, or luncheon, on fasting days?

A. No; we are forbidden to do so.

Q. Is it allowed to take a warm drink, for instance, some hot coffee, or thin chocolate, with a little food not exceeding two ounces?

A. Yes; if such is the custom of the country, or if without it we could not easily keep the fast.

Q. Who is obliged to fast?

A. Every Christian from the age of twenty-one to the age of sixty, except those who are sick, convalescent, or have hard labor, or cannot get a full meal in the day, or would, by fasting, not be able to discharge the duties of their calling.

Q. Who are bound to abstain from flesh meat on Fridays and on all fasting days ?

A. All Christians from the age of seven, unless they are ill, or can get nothing else.

Q. What sin is it to break fast or abstinence ?

A. It is a mortal sin, unless one does it by mistake or forgetfulness, or for some lawful reason.

Q. What ought they to do who cannot fast or abstain from flesh meat ?

A. They should apply for a dispensation, and perform some other good work instead.

Q. Why does the Church command us to fast ?

A. Because fasting is pleasing to God and very wholesome to us.

Q. How do we know that fasting is pleasing to God ?

A. 1. Because God has often recommended fasting, and has shown His favor and mercy to those who practised it.

2. Because Jesus Christ, the Apostles, and the saints of all times, have fasted.

Q. How is fasting wholesome to us ?

A. Because, 1. By fasting we satisfy the

justice of God for our sins, and thus avert the punishment due to the same. 2. Because fasting humbles our pride and weakens our sensual desires and passions; and, 3. Because, by fasting, we obtain the more certainly the grace of God and eternal salvation.

Q. In what spirit should we spend the fasting days?

A. We should spend them in the spirit of penance, and sanctify them by prayer and good works.

Q. How should we answer those who rail at us about fasting and abstinence?

A. We should answer them with this passage: "He who does not hear the Church, let him be to thee as the heathen and the publican."

Q. What may we say to Protestants to make them feel the absurdity of their railing at us?

A. We may ask them on what ground they keep the Sunday holy, and still refuse to abstain from flesh meat on Fridays.

Q. Might they not answer that we are commanded in the Scriptures to keep Sunday holy, but that we are nowhere commanded to keep abstinence on Fridays?

A. The Scriptures speak of the Sabbath as

a day of obligation, but nowhere is Sunday styled a day of obligation.

Q. What else may we say to them ?

A. We may say to them, you keep holy the Sunday because it is an ancient usage of the Church ; why, then, do you not abstain on Fridays for the same reason ?

LESSON XVII.

THIRD AND FOURTH COMMANDMENT OF THE CHURCH.

Q. What are we obliged to do by the third and fourth commandment of the Church ?

A. To make a good confession of our sins, at least once a year, and to receive Holy Communion worthily during Easter time.

Q. To what priest must we make our confession ?

A. To any priest authorized by his Bishop to hear confessions.

Q. How soon are children bound to go to confession ?

A. As soon as they come to the use of reason, and have committed a mortal sin.

Q. When are children generally supposed to come to the use of reason ?

A. About the age of seven years.

Q. How soon are Christians bound to receive the Blessed Sacrament?

A. As soon as they are capable of being instructed in that sacred mystery.

Q. Why does the Church command us to receive holy Communion during the Easter time?

A. 1. Because Jesus Christ instituted the Holy Eucharist within this time; and, 2. Because within this time, He died, rose again from the dead, and, therefore, we too, should die to sin, and lead a new life.

Q. When does the Easter time begin and end in this country?

A. It begins on the first Sunday in Lent, and ends on Trinity Sunday.

Q. Is it a great sin to neglect one's Easter Communion?

A. Yes; it is a great sin.

Q. What must those do who are sick or disabled so that they cannot go to church during Easter time?

A. They must send for the priest and make their Easter Communion at home.

Q. Should those who have missed their Easter Communion wait until next year?

A. No; they must go as soon as possible.

Q. Is it not enough to go to Communion at Christmas?

A. No; all are bound under pain of mortal sin to go to Communion during the Easter time.

Q. What must those do who have wilfully made a bad confession and Communion during the Easter time?

A. They must go again and make a good communion.

Q. What is the punishment of those who neglect their Easter Communion?

A. They are threatened with excommunication, and when they die, their body cannot be blessed and buried in consecrated ground.

Q. Is it enough for one to receive Holy Communion once a year?

A. One Communion is enough to comply with the command of the Church, but it is certainly not enough to comply with the intention of the Church, and the desire Jesus Christ has to come into our soul, nor is it enough for the spiritual wants of our soul.

Q. Why is it, then, that the Church does not command us to go oftener than once a year?

A. 1. Because the love for Jesus Christ in the Blessed Sacrament, and the care for our souls, should alone be sufficient to urge us to go often. 2. Because the Church wishes to prescribe, under pain of excommunication, only what she deems absolutely necessary.

Q. How often should we go to Holy Communion?

A. As often as possible, with due preparation.

LESSON XVIII.

THE FIFTH COMMANDMENT OF THE CHURCH.

Q. Why is it just and reasonable that the faithful should contribute to the temporal support of their pastors?

A. Because the pastors are bound in conscience to labor for the salvation of those who are entrusted to their care, and therefore it is just and reasonable that they should be supported by those for whom they labor.

Q. How do pastors labor for the faithful?

A. 1. They offer daily their prayers for them, and frequently the holy sacrifice of the Mass.

2. They administer to them the sacraments and instruct them in their holy religion.

3. They console the afflicted, attend the sick, and do so often at the risk of their lives, and in order to comply with these duties, they are forbidden to marry and to engage in worldly business.

Q. What does Christ say on this subject?

A. The laborer is worthy of his hire.

Q. What does St. Paul say on the same subject?

A. He says: "The Lord ordained that they that preach the Gospel, should live by the Gospel."—1 Cor. ix. 14.

Q. What are we to understand from these words of our Lord and the Apostle?

A. That the faithful are bound in conscience to keep this commandment of the Church, just as conscientiously as any other.

(About the sixth commandment of the Church, see the Sacrament of Matrimony.)

LESSON XIX.

VIOLATION OF THE COMMANDMENTS.

Sin.

Q. What is sin?

A. A wilful offence in thought, word, deed, or omission against any law of God, or of the Church.

Q. How many kinds of sin are there?

A. Two; original and actual sin.

Q. What is original sin?

A. It is the sin in which we were conceived and born.

Q. What is actual sin?

A. Every sin which we ourselves commit.

Q. How is actual sin divided?

A. Into mortal sin and venial sin.

Q. What is mortal sin?

A. It is a sin by which we forfeit the grace and friendship of God.

Q. Why is it called mortal?

A. Because it destroys the spiritual life of the soul by robbing it of the grace of God, and making it liable to eternal punishment.

Q. What is venial sin?

A. That sin which does not entirely deprive the soul of God's grace, but makes it displeasing to Him.

Q. Why is it called venial?

A. Because it is more easily pardoned than mortal sin.

Q. Why should we avoid mortal sin?

A. Because of its great malice and evil consequences.

Q. Are we able to understand the great malice of mortal sin?

A. We shall never be able properly to understand the malice of mortal sin, because we are not able to comprehend the infinite greatness of God, who is offended by sin.

Q. From what does the malice of mortal sin clearly appear?

A. 1. From the punishments which God has inflicted on the rebellious angels, on our first parents, and the other terrible chastisements recorded in the Scriptures; 2. From the everlasting punishment of hell, which every mortal sin deserves; and 3. From the bitter Passion and Death which Jesus Christ our Lord suffered for our sins.

Q. What are the evil effects of mortal sin?

A. Mortal sin—1. Separates us from God,

and robs us of His love and friendship; 2. It disfigures in us the image of God, and disturbs the peace of our conscience; 3. It robs us of all merits, and renders us unfit to perform any work meritorious of heaven, and makes us lose our right to heaven; 4. It draws down upon us the judgments of God, and lastly, eternal damnation.

Q. Why should we also carefully avoid venial sin?

A. 1. Because, next to mortal sin, venial sin is the greatest of all evils, for it is also an offence against God.

2. Because it weakens the will of man to do good and resist evil.

3. On account of venial sin God withholds from us many graces which He intended to give us—graces that we may need to overcome strong temptations, the loss of which may lead us to mortal sin and eternal ruin.

LESSON XX.

DIFFERENT KINDS OF MORTAL SIN.

Q. How many kinds of mortal sin are there?

A. Four.

Q. What are they?

A. 1. The seven capital or deadly sins.

2. The six sins against the Holy Ghost.

3. The four sins crying to heaven for vengeance.

4. The nine ways of being accessory to another person's sins.

Q. Which are the seven capital sins?

A. 1. Pride; 2. Covetousness; 3. Lust; 4. Anger; 5. Gluttony; 6. Envy; 7. Sloth.

Q. Why are they called capital sins?

A. Because they are so many main sources from which all other sins flow.

Q. When do we sin by pride?

A. When we think too much of ourselves, do not give God the honor He deserves, and when we despise our neighbor.

Q. When do we sin by covetousness?

A. When we inordinately seek and love money or other worldly goods, and are hard-hearted towards the poor.

Q. How do we sin by lust?

A. By indulging in immodest or impure thoughts, desires, words, or actions.

Q. When do we sin by anger?

A. When we are exasperated at what displeases us, when we fly into a passion, and suffer ourselves to be carried away by a violent desire of revenge.

Q. When do we sin by gluttony?

A. When we eat or drink too much.

Q. When do we sin by envy?

A. When we repine at our neighbor's good, and are sad when he enjoys temporal and spiritual blessings, but are glad when he is deprived of them.

Q. When do we sin by sloth?

A. When we give way to our natural repugnance to labor and exertion, so as to neglect our duties.

Q. What kind of sloth is particularly hateful to God?

A. Lukewarmness, or laziness in all that concerns the service of God, or the salvation of our soul.

Q. Which are the six sins against the Holy Ghost?

A. 1. Presumption of God's mercy. 2. Despair. 3. Resisting the known Christian truth. 4. Envy at another's spiritual good. 5. Obstinacy in sin. 6. Final impenitence.

Q. Why are they called sins against the Holy Ghost?

A. Because by these sins we resist in an

especial manner, the Holy Ghost, since we knowingly and willingly despise, reject, or abuse His grace.

Q. Why should we particularly avoid those sins?

A. Because, being the greatest hindrance to God's grace, they harden the heart, and therefore render its conversion extremely difficult.

Q. Which are the four sins crying to heaven for vengeance?

A. 1. Wilful murder. 2. Sodomy. 3. Oppression of the poor, of widows and orphans. 4. Defrauding laborers of their wages.

Q. Why are they called sins crying to heaven for vengeance?

A. Because the malice of each is so great, that it cries, as it were, for vengeance and challenges God's justice to punish it.

Q. Are we ever answerable for the sins of others?

A. Yes; as often as we are the cause of their sins through our own fault.

Q. In how many ways may this happen?

A. In nine ways. 1. By counsel. 2. By command. 3. By consent. 4. By provocation. 5. By praise or flattery. 6. By concealment. 7. By participation. 8. By silence. 9. By defence of the ill done.

LESSON XXI.

VIRTUE AND CHRISTIAN PERFECTION.

Q. Should we have no other care than to avoid mortal sins?

A. We should also be very careful to acquire the virtues suitable to our state of life.

Q. What is Christian virtue?

A. It is the firmness of the will to do, under all circumstances, what is pleasing in the sight of God.

Q. How do we become virtuous?

A. By the grace of God and our constant exertions to comply with all our Christian duties.

Q. How are Christian virtues divided?

A. Into Theological and Moral virtues.

Q. How many theological virtues are there?

A. Three: Faith, Hope, and Charity.

Q. Why are they called theological?

A. Because they relate immediately to God.

Q. Make short acts of faith, hope, and charity.

A. O my God, I believe all that Thou teachest me by the Catholic Church, because Thou art Eternal Truth.

O my God, I hope in Thee, because Thou art infinitely merciful.

O my God, I love Thee above all things, because Thou art infinitely good.

Q. When should we make acts of faith, hope, and charity?

A. We should make them very often, but especially when we are tempted against these virtues, and in the hour of death.

Q. Which are the chief moral virtues?

A. The four cardinal virtues: 1. Prudence. 2. Justice. 3. Fortitude. 4. Temperance.

Q. Why are they called cardinal virtues?

A. Because they are the foundations of all good works, or, as it were, the hinges on which the whole moral life of a Christian must constantly move.

Q. What is prudence?

A. Prudence is a virtue which makes us distinguish between what is truly good and pleasing to God, and what only appears to be so.

Q. What is justice?

A. Justice is a virtue which makes us always do what is right, and give every one his due.

Q. What is fortitude?

A. Fortitude is a virtue enabling us to endure any hardship or persecution, rather than fail in our duty.

Q. What is temperance?

A. Temperance is a virtue restraining our sensual inclinations and desires, especially our inordinate appetite for eating and drinking.

Q. What virtues are contrary to the seven capital sins?

A. 1. Humility. 2. Liberality. 3. Chastity. 4. Meekness. 5. Temperance. 6. Brotherly Love. 7. Diligence.

Q. What is humility?

A. Humility is a virtue which makes us acknowledge our own meanness, weakness, and sinfulness, and look upon all good as coming from God.

Q. What is liberality?

A. It is a virtue which inclines us to use our property for the relief of the needy, or for other praiseworthy purposes.

Q. What is chastity?

A. Chastity is a virtue which makes us hate all unclean inclinations and desires by which this virtue is violated.

Q. What is meekness?

A. Meekness is a virtue which makes us suppress all desire of revenge, and any unjust anger and displeasure.

Q. What is brotherly love?

A. Brotherly love is a virtue which makes us wish every one well, and sincerely condole with our neighbor in his distress.

Q. What is diligence?

A. Diligence is a virtue which makes us serve God readily and cheerfully, promote His honor to the best of our power, and faithfully perform all our duties.

Q. Why must we endeavor every day to become better and holier?

A. Because Jesus Christ says to all: "Be ye perfect, as also your heavenly Father is perfect." Matt. v. 48.

Q. For what other reason should we endeavor to become holier every day?

A. Because our happiness in heaven will be in proportion to the efforts we make on earth to become holy.

Q. Is there any other weighty reason which should impel us to advance in perfection every day?

A. Not to become better is to become worse, and to fall at last into everlasting ruin.

Q. When are we perfect?

A. We are perfect when we are free from all inordinate love of the world and of ourselves, and love God above all, and all in God.

Q. How shall we reach this perfection?

A. By imitating Jesus Christ.

Q. What particular means have been pointed out by Jesus Christ to reach perfection?

A. Those three which are called the Evangelical Counsels, that is, voluntary poverty, perpetual chastity, and entire obedience to a spiritual superior.

Q. What is voluntary poverty?

A. It is a free surrender of the independent use of all temporal things, in order to find less hindrance in striving for those goods that are everlasting.

Q. What is perpetual chastity?

A. It is a free and perpetual renunciation, not only of all impure pleasure, but even of marriage, in order to be able to give ourselves up entirely to the service of God.

Q. What is entire obedience?

A. It is a free renunciation of one's own will, in order to do the will of God more surely under a superior who keeps the place of God.

Q. Who are bound to keep the Evangelical Counsels?

A. All religious, and all those who have bound themselves by vow to keep them.

Q. Can people in the world who are not priests or religious also lead a holy life?

A. Yes, if they do not live after the spirit and maxims of the world; but according to the spirit and sayings of Jesus Christ.

Q. Is then the spirit of the world at variance with the spirit of Jesus Christ?

A. Most undoubtedly, as we clearly see from those sentences of Jesus, which are called the "Eight Beatitudes."

Q. Which are the Eight Beatitudes?

A. 1. "Blessed are the poor in spirit; for theirs is the Kingdom of Heaven."

2. "Blessed are the meek; for they shall possess the land."

3. "Blessed are they that mourn; for they shall be comforted."

4. "Blessed are they that hunger; for they shall be filled."

5. "Blessed are the merciful; for they shall obtain mercy."

6. "Blessed are the clean of heart; for they shall see God."

7. "Blessed are the peace-makers; for they shall be called the children of God."

8. "Blessed are they that suffer persecution for justice sake; for theirs is the Kingdom of Heaven." Matt. v. 3–10.

Q. How does it appear from these beatitudes that the spirit of Jesus Christ is at variance with the spirit of the world?

A. Because worldly-minded people esteem those very persons miserable and foolish, whom Jesus Christ called blessed.

Q. What means must a Christiàn use, be his condition what it may, in order to become perfect?

A. He must love prayer, often hear the Word of God, and receive the holy Sacraments.

Q. What else must he do?

A. He should watch over his senses, and control all his irregular affections and passions, and perform his daily actions in the state of grace, and with the intention of pleasing God.

Q. What should we do to make more sure of easily avoiding unlawful things?

A. We should refuse ourselves many things that are lawful, dear, and agreeable to us.

Q. Is it lawful to take recreation?

A. We may take proper recreation in due time; we should, however, sanctify it by a good intention, and by the remembrance of God, and keep within the bounds of modesty.

Q. What should be our intercourse with our neighbor?

A. It should be kind and affable, so as not to offend any one, and prudent, so as not to be misled by evil.

Q. How should we act when under afflictions and trials?

A. We should firmly believe that God sends them for our good, and His own glory, and beg of Him the necessary grace to bear them with entire resignation to His holy will.

FAMILIAR EXPLANATION

OF

CHRISTIAN DOCTRINE.

PART IV.

THE MEANS OF GRACE.

LESSON I.

ON THE GRACE OF GOD.

Q. Can we keep the commandments and be saved by our own natural strength?

A. No; without the grace of God we can neither begin, continue, nor accomplish the least good work towards our salvation.

Q. How do we know this?

A. From the words of Jesus Christ, and His apostle St. Paul.

Q. What are the words of Jesus Christ?

A. "Without me, you can do nothing." John xv. 5.

Q. What are the words of St. Paul?

A. "It is God, who worketh in you, both to will and to accomplish, according to his good will." Philip. ii. 13.

Q. Did God declare the same thing long before?

A. He did so by the prophet Ezechiel, saying: "I will cause you to walk in my commandments, and to keep my judgments, and do them." Chap. xxxvi. 27.

Q. What are we to understand from these passages?

A. That man works only so much good as God, by His grace, enables him to work.

Q. Is this the solemn declaration of the Catholic Church?

A. Yes; it is an article of our holy faith, that no one can do the least work conducive to salvation without God's particular assistance.

Q. How does the grace of God assist us?

A. It enlightens the understanding and strengthens the will to avoid evil and to will and to do what is pleasing to God.

Q. Why is grace so necessary to everything that relates to salvation?

A. Because eternal salvation or the enjoyment of God is so great a supernatural good, that we can obtain it only by supernatural means, that is, by God's help and grace.

Q. What is this help or grace called?

A. The grace of assistance, *i. e.* actually helping grace, and transient grace, acting as it does transiently upon the soul.

Q. Does God give His grace to all men?

A. Yes; God gives to all men sufficient grace, to do His will and be saved.

Q. What is this sufficient grace?

A. It is the grace of prayer, that is, God gives to every man grace enough to pray, and thus to obtain, by prayer, all graces necessary for salvation.

Q. How do we know that God gives to every man the grace of prayer?

A. God commands all men to pray to Him, and ask for His graces, which command He could not give them if He did not give them the grace to pray.

Q. But are there not many men who say that they cannot pray? How can they have sufficient grace to pray?

A. It may be that they are not able to perform a fervent prayer, to which God grants those graces necessary for salvation, but if they ask and continue to ask of God the grace to pray better, He will hear them.

Q. What are the words of St. Alphonsus on this subject?

A. "As God, in the natural order, ordained that man should be born naked, and in want of many of the necessaries of life, and as at the same time He has given him hands and understanding to provide for all his wants, so also, in the supernatural order, man is born incapable of obtaining salvation by his own strength; but God, in His infinite goodness, grants to every man the grace of prayer, and wishes that all should make constant use of this grace, in order thereby to obtain all other necessary graces."

Q. What do the Fathers of the Council of Trent say on this subject?

A. "God does not command impossibilities, but, when commanding, He admonishes us to do what we are able, and pray for what we are not able to do, and He then aids us that we may be able." Council of Trent, Sess. 6, chap. xi.

Q. Is it then certain that God will give all the

graces necessary for salvation to every man if he sincerely asks for them, and continues to ask for them?

A. This is as certain as that there is a God.

Q. How do we know this?

A. Because God has most solemnly promised to give to all men, without exception, all that they ask of Him.

Q. What are His words?

A. "Amen, amen, I say to you, if you ask the Father anything in my name, he will give it to you." John xvi. 23; and, "Every one who asks shall receive." Matt. vii. 7.

Q. What do we learn from these words of our Lord?

A. That the grace of prayer is a universal means by which every grace necessary to bring us to eternal life may be obtained with certainty, since the Son of God cannot lie.

Q. Why do you call prayer a universal means of salvation?

A. 1. Because this means of grace is given to all without exception; and, 2. Because, to this means only God has promised all the efficacious helps or graces of assistance necessary for our salvation.

Q. But, are not the sacraments necessary means of salvation?

A. They are; but they are only particular means, each producing and procuring particular graces: baptism produces one, penance another, and so with the other sacraments, or means of salvation; but to none of these, nor to all put together, without prayer, has God promised all the graces necessary for eternal life.

Q. On what, then, does our salvation depend?

A. On making a good use of the grace of prayer. By making use of this grace the worst sinner, as well as the greatest saint, may obtain every efficacious grace necessary for his salvation; for Jesus Christ has promised to hear the prayers of all, and He cannot break His promise.

Q. What are we to learn from this?

A. That no one can excuse himself before God by saying that his salvation is impossible on account of the difficulties and obstacles which he meets in the way of salvation.

Q. Why can no one excuse himself thus?

A. Because God will answer—If you have not light and strength and courage enough to overcome all obstacles in the way of your salvation, why do you not ask me to come to your assistance?

Q. Whose fault is it if a sinner is damned?

A. It is his own fault, because he did not profit by the grace of prayer.

Q. What happens to the sinner when he prays in all sincerity to God to save him, and continues to make this prayer?

A. 1. God enlightens the sinner so as to understand the misery and danger of his state. 2. He inspires the heart of the sinner with confidence in His mercy to make him firmly hope for the forgiveness of all his sins. 3. God strengthens the will of the sinner so as to induce him to amend his life and receive the Sacrament of Baptism or (if baptized) the Sacrament of Penance as the means of reconciliation.

Q. Does the grace of God, then, force our free will to do good?

A. By no means; it not only leaves it perfectly free, but even increases considerably the liberty of the will.

Q. How so?

A. Because grace so powerfully assists our will as to make us do what leads to salvation, and avoid what leads to damnation. Now to be able to avoid evil and to do good is to be truly free; but not to be able to do so, is to be a child of sin and misery, a slave of the passions and of the devil.

LESSON II.

THE GRACE OF JUSTIFICATION.

Q. What does the sinner become by receiving the sacrament of baptism or penance?

A. He becomes a child of God, a temple of the Holy Ghost, an heir of heaven, and capable of performing good works towards his salvation.

Q. What is this great grace called?

A. Sanctifying grace, or the grace of justification.

Q. Why is it thus called?

A. Because it makes the soul just or holy in the sight of God.

Q. How long does this sanctifying grace remain in the soul of the justified man?

A. It remains as long as he does not commit mortal sin.

Q. Can the sinner merit sanctifying or justifying grace?

A. No; he cannot.

Q. Why can he not?

A. Because all good works performed in the state of mortal sin, are dead works, and of too little value to merit so great a grace.

Q. Is it an article of our holy faith that a sinner cannot, whilst in the state of mortal sin, merit the grace of justification?

A. It is.

Q. What does the Church teach on this subject?

A. That "whatever precedes justification, whether faith or good works, is insufficient to merit the grace of justification." Council of Trent, Sess. 8. c. viii.

Q. How, then, is the justification of the sinner brought about?

A. It is brought about gratuitously, and through the pure mercy of God.

Q. In consideration of whom?

A. Not in consideration of his own merits, but in consideration of the merits of Jesus Christ.

Q. How so?

A. Jesus Christ is our only mediator, and by the price of His blood He has merited for us the grace of reconciliation with His Father.

Q. Is it then impossible for the sinner to obtain by his good works the grace of justification?

A. The sinner may, by his good works, avert many temporal punishments, dispose himself to receive the grace of conversion, and obtain it infallibly by prayer, but he can never merit it.

Q. What above all disposes the sinner for the grace of justification?

A. Faith in Jesus Christ our blessed Redeemer.

Q. Can any one be justified without this faith?

A. No, because it is impossible to please God, or to perform any good in the supernatural order without faith.

Q. Is faith alone sufficient to justify the sinner?

A. No; because, besides having faith, the sinner must fear and love God; he must be sorry for his sins, and make a firm resolution never to commit them again.

Q. Are all these necessary conditions, or are they works of merit?

A. They are not works of merit, but necessary conditions, without which it is impossible for the sinner to be received into the friendship of God.

Q. What is said in the fourth chapter of Deuteronomy, v. 29?

A. "You shall find God, if you seek him with all your heart."

Q. What says the prophet Ezechiel?

A. "If the impious man be converted and do penance, he shall live and shall not die." Chap. xviii. 21.

Q. What does our Saviour Himself say?

A. "You are my friends, if you do the things that I command you." John xv. 14.

Q. What do we learn from these passages?

A. That faith alone is not sufficient to justify the sinner.

Q. Does not St. John say: "He that believeth in the Son hath life everlasting"? (Chap. iii. 36.)

A. St. John speaks here of an efficacious faith, and means that he who believes in the Son of God in such a manner as to practise His doctrine, will have life everlasting.

Q. Does not St. Paul say: "We account a man to be justified by faith without the works of the law"? Rom. iii. 28.

A. St. Paul speaks here of works of the Jewish law, and not of works of the Christian law.

Q. How can you show that he does not speak of works of the Christian law?

A. Because St. Paul surely does not contradict St. James, who writes thus: "You see that by works a man is justified, and not by faith only." Nor does St. Paul contradict himself, and yet he says: "Not the hearers of the law are just before Christ, but the doers of the law shall be justified." Rom. ii. 13. Again he says: "In Jesus Christ neither circumcision availeth anything, nor uncircumcision, but faith which worketh by charity." Gal. v. 6.

Q. How is it, then, that the same Apostle says: "Therefore, being justified by faith, let us have peace with God"? Rom. v.

A. The Apostle speaks here of a living faith, which is animated by charity and fruitful in good works.

Q. What sacrament conveys the grace of justification to the soul?

A. Baptism or penance.

Q. Can we merit heaven whilst in the state of mortal sin?

A. We cannot, because all the good works performed in the state of mortal sin are dead works, for which we cannot get any reward in heaven.

Q. Can we merit heaven whilst we are in the state of the grace?

A. A just man, by his good works, merits an increase of glory, but it is impossible for him to merit the first degree of glory.

Q. To whom are we indebted for the right which we have to Paradise?

A. Solely to the mercy of God, and to the merits of Jesus Christ.

Q. How so?

A. Because it was Jesus Christ who, by His merits, obtained for us heaven as our inheritance.

Q. Why do you say that the just man merits by his good works an increase of glory?

A. Because heaven is held out to us in Scripture as a recompense, and a recompense cannot be obtained without merit.

Q. What are the words of our Saviour?

A. "Rejoice and be exceeding glad, because your reward is very great in heaven." St. Matt. v. 12.

Q. What says the Holy Ghost through the wise man?

A. "To him that soweth justice, there is a faithful reward."

Q. What says St. James?

A. "Blessed is the man that endureth

temptation, for he shall receive the crown of life." Chap. i. 12.

Q. What says St. Paul?

A. "I have finished my course—there is laid up for me a crown of justice, which the Lord, the just judge, will render to me at that day." 2 Tim. iv. 7, 8.

Q. What is it that gives value to our good works?

A. Sanctifying grace.

Q. Is it God who gives it to us or do we give it to ourselves?

A. It is a gift which we receive from the infinite liberality of God.

Q. What does St. Paul say, speaking of this sanctifying grace?

A. "The charity of God is poured out into our hearts, by the Holy Ghost, who is given to us." Rom. v. 5.

Q. To whom are we indebted for sanctifying or justifying grace?

A. We are indebted for it solely to the merits of Jesus Christ.

Q. What do we remark concerning the efficacy of the merits of Jesus Christ?

A. That Jesus Christ, not content with meriting heaven for us, has also obtained for us that grace, by means of which we may be enabled to merit still higher degrees of glory.

Q. But since our Saviour says: "When you shall have done all the things that are commanded you, say: We are unprofitable servants; we have done that which we ought to do"—Luke xvii. 10—how can we presume that we are able to merit anything?

A. We are, it is true, unprofitable servants with regard to God, but not so with regard to ourselves. We are unprofitable servants with regard to God, because, although we should not perform any good actions, God would not be the less happy on that account—whilst we are not unprofitable towards ourselves, since by our good works we are enabled to obtain that recompense which He has been pleased to promise us.

Q. Could God require of us the performance of good works, without promising us, at the same time, any recompense?

A. He certainly could.

Q. What do the Fathers of the Council of Trent say on this subject?

A. "The goodness of God towards man is so great, that He is desirous that His own gifts should be changed into merits for them." Sess. vi. 16.

Q. Are we all bound to do good works?

A. Yes; for "Every tree that doth not yield good fruit, shall be cut down and cast into the fire." Matt. iii. 10.

Q. What kind of good works should we perform before all others?

A. Those, the performance of which is commanded to all Christians by the commandments of God and of the Church; and, 2. Those which are necessary, or useful, to fulfil the duties of our state of life.

Q. Are there any other good works especially recommended to us in Holy Scripture?

A. Yes; prayer, fasting, and alms, that is, the works of devotion, mortification, and charity.

Q. What is it that God is particularly pleased with in our good works?

A. Our intention to please and honor Him by our good works.

Q. How may we make a good intention?

A. We may make it in the following manner: "O my God, I do this for the love of Thee," or, "My Jesus, all for Thy honor and glory."

Q. When should we make a good intention?

A. It is very useful to make it before and after each action, but we should make it especially in the morning.

Q. Have we any just reason to confide in the good works which we perform in the state of grace, and with the intention of pleasing and honoring God by them?

A. God forbid that a Christian should confide in himself, or glory in himself, and not in the Lord. "God forbid that I should glory but in the cross of our Lord Jesus Christ, by whom the world is crucified to me and I to the world." Galatians vi. 14.

LESSON III.

THE SACRAMENTS.

Q. What did Jesus Christ do to make us sure of receiving the graces which He merited for us by His Passion and Death?

A. He gave us certain outward signs as means to convey those graces to our souls.

Q. What do we call those outward signs?

A. We call them sacraments.

Q. What, then, is a sacrament?

A. A sacrament is an outward sign, ordained by Jesus Christ as a means to convey His grace to our souls.

Q. What grace do the sacraments convey ?

A. They convey or increase sanctifying grace, and each sacrament also bestows particular graces, according to the end for which it was ordained.

Q. How must the sacraments be received in order to convey these graces ?

A. We must receive them with due preparation.

Q. What sin is it to receive a sacrament unworthily ?

A. It is a mortal sin—a sacrilege.

Q. Do the sacraments give grace when administered even by unworthy priests ?

A. Yes, because the grace given by the sacraments does not proceed from him who administers them, but from our Lord Jesus Christ, Who ordained them.

Q. Were all the sacraments ordained by Jesus Christ ?

A. Yes; because God alone, the Author of grace, can attach to outward signs the power of giving grace and holiness.

Q. What follows from all this ?

A. That it is the sin of heresy for one to say that the sacraments serve only to signify grace.

Q. How many sacraments are there?

A. There are seven: Baptism, Confirmation, Holy Eucharist, Penance, Extreme Unction, Holy Orders, and Matrimony.

Q. How do we know that there are seven sacraments?

A. From the infallible teaching of the Church, which has, at all times, and in all countries, taught that there are seven sacraments.

Q. How are the seven sacraments divided?

A. Into sacraments of the *living*, and sacraments of the *dead*, and into such as can be received *only* once, and such as can be received *more* than once.

Q. Which are the sacraments of the living?

A. Confirmation, Holy Eucharist, Extreme Unction, Holy Orders, and Matrimony.

Q. Why are they called sacraments of the living?

A. Because, in order to receive them, we must be living in the state of grace.

Q. Which are the sacraments of the dead?

A. Baptism and Penance.

Q. Why are they called sacraments of the dead?

A. Because, when receiving them, we either are not, or need not be in the state of grace.

Q. Which sacraments can be received only once?

A. Baptism, Confirmation, and Holy Orders.

Q. Why can they be received but once?

A. Because they stamp upon our souls an indelible character or spiritual mark, which, in a special manner, consecrates us to the service of God, and will forever remain stamped on our souls, either for our greater glory in heaven, or greater misery in hell.

LESSON IV.

BAPTISM.

Q. Which is the first and most necessary of the sacraments?

A. Baptism.

Q. Why is baptism the first sacrament?

A. Because no other sacrament can be received before baptism.

Q. Why is baptism the most necessary sacrament?

A. Because without baptism no one can be saved.

Q. What is baptism?

A. Baptism is a sacrament which cleanses the soul from original sin, and also from the actual sins of which the person to be baptized may be guilty. It makes us Christians, children of God, and heirs to the kingdom of heaven.

Q. Is the punishment due to sin also remitted by baptism?

A. Yes; the temporal as well as the eternal punishment is remitted.

Q. Why, then, do we, after baptism, still experience several effects of original sin, such as death, concupiscence, and many other infirmities?

A. God permits us to experience these effects in order to make us better understand the great malice of sin, and to increase our merits for heaven by our combats and sufferings.

Q. Who may be baptized?

A. All the members of the human family of every age and sex.

Q. What must adults learn before they can be baptized?

A. They must know at least the principal

truths of the Catholic religion, and believe firmly in them.

Q. What else is required of them ?

A. They must be really *sorry* for their sins, purpose to live up to the teachings of the Church, and wish to be baptized.

Q. How do we know that infants also must be baptized ?

A. We know it from Scripture and tradition.

Q. What are the words of Holy Scripture ?

A. "Unless a man be born again of water and the Holy Ghost, he cannot enter into the Kingdom of God." John iii. 5.

Q. What do we learn from this passage ?

A. That God desires the salvation of all men without exception; that no one can be saved who has not received baptism; that therefore, it is God's will that every person should be baptized.

Q. What do we know from tradition about the baptizing of infants ?

A. It is a well-known fact that the baptism of infants was practised in the first ages of the Church, as an institution of the Apostles.

Q. What does Origen say on this subject ?

A. "The Church has been taught to give baptism even to infants."

Q. What says St. Irenæus ?

A. "Our Lord came to save all men—all, I say, who are regenerated through Him, as well newly born infants, as others." 2 Lib. adv. Heres. c. 39.

Q. What does St. John Chrysostom teach in his homily to the neophytes ?

A. "We baptize newly born infants, that they may be cleansed from sin, and may become the abode of the Holy Ghost."

Q. What says St. Cyprian ?

A. "If baptism is denied to no one, much less should it be withheld from infants, who are as yet stained by no other than original sin." 59th Epistle.

Q. What says St. Augustine ?

A. "The practice of the Church in baptizing infants is derived from the Apostles;" and, "since the baptism of infants has been constantly practised by the Church, what Christian will be so bold as to say that such baptism is of no avail." Lib. IV. de Bapt.

Q. What sin do parents commit by delaying, without a very grievous reason, the baptism of infants for more than ten or eleven days ?

A. They commit a mortal sin.

Q. How is baptism given?

A. By pouring water on the head of the person to be baptized, pronouncing at the same time the words ordained by Christ.

Q. What are the words to be said whilst pouring the water?

A. "I baptize thee in the name of the Father, and of the Son, and of the Holy Ghost." Matt. xxviii. 19.

Q. Who can baptize?

A. Priests are the ordinary ministers of baptism; but in cases of necessity, when a priest cannot be had, any person, man or woman or child, who has come to the use of reason, may lawfully give baptism.

Q. Is the baptism given by non-Catholics also valid?

A. It is valid if they strictly observe in it all that is necessary for baptism.

Q. Is it necessary to have holy or baptismal water in baptism?

A. No; any natural water will do.

Q. What intention must he have who baptizes?

A. He must have the intention to baptize indeed, that is, to do what the Church does, or what Christ has ordained.

Q. What name should be given to the child in baptism?

A. The name of some saint, in whom the child may have an intercessor with God, and an example for imitation.

Q. Of what should sponsors, or godfathers and god-mothers, be particularly mindful?

A. They should bear in mind that they become, as it were, the spiritual parents of the child that is baptized, and make in his name the profession of faith and the baptismal vows.

Q. What are the obligations of sponsors towards their godchild?

A. They must take care that the child be well instructed in the Catholic religion, if his parents should neglect, or be unable to perform this duty. Nor can they marry their godchild or his parents.

Q. Who can be godfather and godmother?

A. Only good practical Catholics should be taken as sponsors.

Q. How many godfathers and godmothers does the Church admit?

A. The Church generally admits but one godfather for a boy, and one godmother for a girl; or at most, one godfather and one godmother for one person to be baptized.

Q. Can the baptism of water never be supplied?

A. When it is impossible to have it, it may be supplied by the baptism of desire, or by the baptism of blood.

Q. What is the baptism of desire?

A. An earnest wish to receive baptism, or to do all that God requires of us for our salvation, together with a perfect contrition, or a perfect love of God.

Q. What is the baptism of blood?

A. Martyrdom for the sake of Christ.

LESSON V.

CEREMONIES OF BAPTISM.

Q. What are sacred ceremonies?

A. Sacred ceremonies are certain visible signs or actions, expressing something holy and divine.

Q. Did Christ ordain the special ceremonies attached to the administering of the sacraments?

A. No; these ceremonies or solemnities are ordained by the Church.

Q. Why does the Church make use of so many ceremonies in administering the sacraments, and in all other divine functions?

A. She does so in order to excite in us devotion and reverence for the holy mysteries of religion, and to indicate their meaning and explain their effects:

Q. But is there not something superstitious in these ceremonies ?

A. If it cannot be said that there was anything superstitious in the ceremonies of the Old Law, most of which were prescribed by God Himself—far less can it be said that there is anything superstitious in the ceremonies of the New Law.

Q. Have we the authority of the Scriptures for the use of ceremonies ?

A. St. Paul, writing to the Corinthians, says, that all things should be done with *order* and *decency.* Now, to preserve order and decency, ceremonies are almost indispensable.

Q. Why does the child, or person to be baptized, remain without, or at the entrance of the church before baptism ?

A. Because it is baptism alone that gives him the right to enter the church.

Q. What is the meaning of the priest breathing three times in his face ?

A. It signifies the new and spiritual life

the child receives by the grace of the Holy Ghost.

Q. What is the meaning of the sign of the cross made upon the child's forehead and upon his breast?

A. It signifies that he is becoming the property of his crucified Redeemer, whose doctrine he is to carry in his heart, and profess openly.

Q. What is the meaning of the blessed salt put into the child's mouth?

A. It is an emblem of Christian wisdom, and of preservation from the corruptión of sin.

Q. Why are the exorcisms repeated several times?

A. To free the child from the power of the devil, in the name of the Blessed Trinity.

Q. What is the meaning of the laying of the priest's hand upon the child?

A. It signifies the protection of God; and the stole that is laid upon the child, and by which he is led into the Church, is a sign of the power of the Church, by virtue of which the priest admits him into the Church.

Q. What is the meaning of the touching of the child's ears and nostrils with spittle in imitation of our Saviour? Mark vii. 30.

A. It signifies that, by the grace of this

sacrament, his spiritual senses are opened to the doctrine of Christ.

Q. What is the meaning of the anointing of the child with holy oil on the breast and between the shoulders?

A. It signifies that, as a champion of Christ, he has now manfully to fight against the devil and the world.

Q. Why must the person to be baptized renounce, before baptism, Satan, all his works, and all his pomps?

A. Because no one can belong to Christ, unless he renounce not only *Satan*, but also all his works, that is, sin, and his *pomps*—the spirit and vanities of the world, by which Satan blinds men and leads them to sin.

Q. What else does the person to be baptized promise?

A. He promises to believe in Christ and His doctrine, to avoid sin, and to lead a new life in conformity with the will of God.

Q. What does God, on His part, promise this person?

A. He promises His grace and life everlasting.

Q. What are these mutual promises called?

A. The covenant of baptism.

Q. Why does the priest place a white linen cloth upon the child's head after baptism?

A. To remind us that we should preserve the innocence we have received, pure and spotless until death.

Q. What does the priest say in putting this linen cloth on the child?

A. "Receive this white garment, and see thou carry it without stain before the judgment-seat of our Lord Jesus Christ, that thou mayest have eternal life."

Q. What is the meaning of the lighted candle, which is put into the child's hand after he is baptized?

A. That a Christian ought to shine by his faith and holy life before the whole world.

Q. Why is the child's head anointed with chrism after baptism?

A. To signify that he is now a Christian, an anointed of God.

LESSON VI.

CONFIRMATION.

Q. What is confirmation?

A. Confirmation is a sacrament by which we receive the Holy Ghost, in order to make us strong and perfect Christians and soldiers of Jesus Christ.

Q. What is the outward sign in this sacrament?

A. The holy chrism, and the imposition of the Bishop's hands.

Q. What is the invisible or inward grace which is bestowed upon the soul?

A. Confirmation increases sanctifying grace in us; it gives us the Holy Ghost, to enable us to profess our faith openly and live up to it, and it imprints a spiritual mark that is never effaced.

Q. Does Holy Scripture speak of the sacrament of confirmation?

A. In the Acts of the Apostles we read that the people of Samaria had already received baptism, but that they had not yet received the Holy Ghost, and for this reason St. Peter and St. John went to lay their hands upon them, and thus they received the Holy Ghost. Chap. viii.

Q. What do we learn from this passage?

A. That confirmation was given by the Apostles, St. Peter and St. Paul.

Q. How so?

A. The imposition of hands takes place only when the sacrament of holy orders, or of confirmation is given. Now, it is certain that the Apostles did not confer the order of priesthood on all the inhabitants of Samaria; therefore, it was the sacrament of confirmation which they administered.

Q. Are there any passages of the Fathers of the Church, to prove that confirmation was practised in the first ages of Christianity?

A. The Fathers are decisive on this point.

Q. What says St. Cyril?

A. "Whilst a visible unction is performed on the body, the soul finds itself sanctified by the inward working of the Holy Ghost."

Q. What are the words of St. Augustine on this subject?

A. "The sacrament of holy chrism is a sacrament just as holy as baptism."

Q. Who can give confirmation?

A. The Catholic Bishops only, as successors of the Apostles, have power to give confirmation. In urgent cases, however, the Pope can delegate this power to a priest.

Q. How is confirmation given?

A. The Bishop extends his hands over all those who are to receive confirmation, and prays for them all in general, that the Holy Ghost may come down upon them; then he lays his hand upon each one in particular, making the sign of the Cross with chrism on the forehead of the person to be confirmed, at the same time pronouncing the following words: "I sign thee with the sign of the Cross, and I confirm thee with the chrism of salvation, in the name of the Father, and of the Son, and of the Holy Ghost," after which he finishes by giving his blessing to all in common.

Q. Of what is the chrism, blessed by the Bishop on Maundy Thursday, made?

A. Of oil of olives, and balm.

Q. What does oil signify?

A. The inward strength which we receive to combat the enemies of our salvation.

Q. Why is fragrant balm mixed with the oil?

A. To signify, that he who is confirmed receives the grace to preserve himself from the wickedness of the world, and to send forth, by a holy life, the sweet odor of virtue.

Q. Why does the Bishop make the sign of the Cross on the forehead of him whom he confirms?

A. To give us to understand that a Christian must never be ashamed of the Cross, but boldly profess his faith in Jesus crucified.

Q. Why does the Bishop, after he has anointed him, give him a slight blow on the cheek?

A. To remind him that, being now strengthened, he ought to be prepared to suffer patiently any kind of affliction for the sake of Jesus.

Q. Is confirmation necessary to salvation?

A. Confirmation is not absolutely necessary to salvation; yet it would be a great sin not to receive it, through neglect or indifference.

Q. Who can receive confirmation?

A. All baptized persons.

Q. How often may a person be confirmed?

A. Only once.

Q. How is a person to prepare himself for receiving confirmation?

A. He must free himself from all mortal sins, know the principal truths of our faith, especially those concerning this sacrament; and he should have a great desire for the grace of the Holy Ghost, and promise Almighty God to live and die as a perfect Christian.

Q. What should we do after confirmation?

A. We should give humble thanks to God; spend that day in devotion and recollection; and make earnest efforts to become holy Christians.

Q. Why are sponsors, or godfathers and godmothers, admitted also in confirmation?

A. That they may present to the Bishop those who are to be confirmed, and afterwards assist them in leading a Christian life.

Q. What should the sponsor do whilst the Bishop lays his hand upon the person to be confirmed?

A. The sponsor should, at the same time, lay his hand on the right shoulder of the person to be confirmed; and thus he becomes the spiritual parent and guardian of his godchild, and contracts with him a spiritual relationship, which is the same impediment of marriage as in baptism.

Q. Who may be godfathers and godmothers of those who are to be confirmed?

A. Only good Catholics, who have been themselves confirmed. Parents cannot be the sponsors of their children, and the sponsor in baptism is not to be the sponsor in confirmation.

LESSON VII.

THE HOLY EUCHARIST.

Q. Did God ever promise to men to give them something especially and most wonderful?

A. From the early times God promised to

men to give them something most wonderful.

Q. Was it heaven that God said He would give us?

A. No; it was something far better even than heaven itself.

Q. What was it that God said He would give away to men?

A. He said he would give away to men—*Himself.*

Q. Could any one understand how God could be given to men?

A. Nobody could understand this mystery.

Q. Why could nobody understand it?

A. Because God kept it a secret to Himself.

Q. For how many years did God wait before He gave Himself to men?

A. For about four thousand years.

Q. Why did God wait so long before He gave Himself to men?

A. That men might better learn the unspeakable greatness of the gift.

Q. What great miracle took place when the world was about four thousand years old?

A. God, the Son, the second person of the Holy Trinity, became man, and lived for thirty-three years on earth.

Q. What did He do during the last three years of His life?

A. He did most wonderful things. He cured the sick, gave sight to the blind, hearing to the deaf, and raised the dead to life.

Q. Did many people follow Him?

A. The people came around Him in crowds to hear His blessed words, and to see Him do works which no one but God could do.

Q. How many people followed Him into the wilderness on one occasion?

A. Five thousand men, besides women and children.

Q. What great miracle did Jesus Christ perform for these people?

A. With only five loaves of bread and two fishes He fed all these people, and they ate as much as they liked.

Q. What happened after this great miracle?

A. After the people had eaten the bread which Jesus had given them so wonderfully, they followed Him still more eagerly.

Q. When our Divine Saviour saw how eagerly the people followed Him what did He say to them?

A. He said: "You follow me because you did eat of the bread I have given you and were filled. But I will give you other bread, much better than the bread you have just eaten."

Q. What did the Jews reply to this?

A. They asked our Saviour whether he would give them a bread better even than the beautiful manna which Moses gave to their fathers in the desert.

Q. What answer did Jesus make to this question?

A. He said: "Your fathers ate that bread, and yet your fathers are dead. But if any man eat of the bread that I shall give to you, he shall not die."

Q. What did the Jews say on hearing this?

A. They were very eager to get that wonderful bread, and asked our Lord to give it to them.

Q. What did our Lord do when he saw the Jews eager to get the wonderful bread of which He spoke?

A. He now, at last, told men the great secret which He had kept to Himself for four thousand years.

Q. And what was this great secret?

A. Our Lord now told men *how* He would give Himself away to them—that He would give them His own flesh to be their food.

Q. What are His words?

A. He said: "The bread that I will give is my flesh, for the life of the world." John vi.

Q. As soon as the words of Jesus reached the ears of the people and they knew what a wonderful thing He was going to do for them, what would you expect them to do?

A. I would expect them all to kneel down before the Son of God, and say, "O Jesus, we believe the word Thou hast spoken, because Thou hast the words of eternal life. We believe that Thou wilt give us Thy flesh to eat, and Thy blood to drink. We praise Thee and thank Thee for this blessed gift."

Q. Did many of these people speak thus?

A. No; instead of thanking our Lord, they began to talk and dispute about the meaning of His words.

Q. What did they say?

A. To the very face of Christ they spoke as do some who are not Catholics, nowadays, saying: "How is it possible for him to give us His flesh to eat? We do not believe it."

Q. When Jesus heard the people speak thus, what did He say to them?

A. He assured them most solemnly that they would not go to heaven unless they would eat His flesh and drink His blood.

Q. In what words did He assure them of this?

A. In these: "Amen, amen, I say to you, except you eat my flesh and drink my blood *you shall not have life in you.* For my flesh is meat indeed, and my blood is drink indeed." John vi.

Q. What happened when our Lord told the people so solemnly that they would not go to heaven unless they would eat His flesh and drink His blood.

A. Many of the disciples of Jesus left Him because they would not believe Him.

Q. Who were those who believed Jesus?

A. The Apostles.

Q. What did the Apostles answer when Jesus asked them: "Will you also go away?"

A. They said: "O Jesus, thou hast the words of eternal life. We believe what thou sayest. We believe that thou wilt give us thy flesh to eat and thy blood to drink."

Q. What did the Apostles expect from that time?

A. They expected that Jesus Christ would fulfil His promise to give them His sacred flesh and blood.

Q. When did Jesus fulfil His promise?

A. On Maundy Thursday.

Q. On what occasion?

A. At the Last Supper He ate with His Apostles.

Q. Where did He eat the Last Supper with His Apostles?

A. In a large dining-room in the city of Jerusalem.

Q. Entering that room the evening before Jesus died on the Cross, what should we have seen there?

A. Jesus, sitting at a table with His twelve Apostles—the Creator in the midst of His creatures.

Q. What else?

A. We should have seen how Jesus worked the greatest miracle that ever was, or will be worked.

Q. What was this wonderful miracle?

A. We should have seen how Jesus gave away Himself, how He gave His own most sacred body and blood to be the food of His creatures.

Q. By what power could He do this?

A. By the infinite power of the Godhead; because Jesus is God, who can do all things. He has but to speak the word, and whatever He wills is done, and done directly.

Q. Can you give an instance of this power of the word of God?

A. Yes; we know that at the creation God said: "Be light made, and light was made." Gen. i. 3.

Q. In what manner did Jesus Christ, at the Last Supper, give His own body to be the food of His creatures?

A. He spoke the word which changed bread into His body and wine into His blood.

Q. How was this done?

A. After Jesus had fully instructed His Apostles about the great miracle He was to perform, and the great gift He was to make them, He, first of all, took the bread into His holy and venerable hands, He lifted up His blessed eyes to heaven, and then He spoke these solemn words: "*Take ye and eat:* THIS IS MY BODY."

Q. As soon as Jesus had spoken those words, what became of the bread in His hands?

A. Quicker than a flash of lightning that bread was changed into His body; and the Apostles ate the sacred flesh of Jesus.

Q. How did Jesus give His own blood to be the drink of His creatures?

A. As He had taken bread, so He also took

the chalice with wine, and gave to His Apostles saying: "*Drink ye all of this:* FOR THIS IS MY BLOOD of the New Testament, which shall be shed for many unto the remission of sins." Matt. xxvi. 26.

Q. What became of the wine in the chalice as soon as these words of Jesus Christ were spoken?

A. As one day the winds and the sea obeyed the voice of Jesus, so also, on this occasion, Jesus was obeyed by the wine. In that moment the wine was changed into His sacred blood; and the Apostles drank of the most precious blood of Jesus Christ.

Q. What are the words "This is My Body. This is My Blood," called?

A. The "*words of Consecration.*"

Q. How do we know that, with these words: "This is My body, this is My blood," Jesus Christ gave His true Body, and His Blood, to the Apostles?

A. We know it, because Jesus Christ did not say *in* this bread, or *with* this bread, is my body, but He said: "This is my body."

Q. What follows from this?

A. That, after those words, the bread did not remain, because it is impossible that that which is *flesh,* should be at the same time *bread.* Now, Christ expressly declared that that which He held in His hand was His own *flesh ;* therefore it was no longer bread.

Q. Who, then, first received the body and blood of Jesus Christ, under the appearance of bread and wine ?

A. The twelve Apostles.

Q. Was no one else to share this blessing of blessings ?

A. It was the will of Jesus that, from this moment, all His poor creatures should freely eat His flesh, and drink His blood, to make them holy before God.

Q. But how could this be done, since Jesus knew that in about forty days He would be in heaven, and no longer on earth to give away His flesh and blood ?

A. Jesus left others on earth to change for Him bread and wine into His body and blood.

Q. What others did He leave on earth to do this for Him ?

A. He gave power to His Apostles to change bread and wine into His body and blood, and to give it to the people as He gave it to them.

Q. In what words did Jesus Christ give this power to His Apostles ?

A. He said to them, "Do this in remembrance of me."

Q. What did He mean by those words?

A. Jesus meant to say this: By My power I have changed bread and wine into My body and blood. I give you power to do the same. Take bread and wine into your hands, and speak over the bread—"This is my body," and over the wine—"This is my blood," and bread and wine will be instantly changed into My body and blood, and then give it to others for the good of their souls. And this power to change bread and wine into My body and blood give ye to others, who shall give it again to others, and so on to the end of the world, that all My people may know Me and receive Me, they in Me and I in them.

Q. How long were the body and blood of Jesus Christ to be given to men?

A. The body and blood of Jesus will be given by the priests of Jesus Christ to the people, till the end of the world.

Q. When does the priest make use of the power which he has received from Jesus Christ to change bread and wine into the body and blood of Christ?

A. About the middle of the Mass, the priest

takes bread and speaks over it the words: "THIS IS MY BODY."

Q. What becomes then of the bread?

A. By the power of God the bread is changed into the body of Jesus Christ.

Q. What does the priest do after this?

A. He speaks over the wine in the chalice the words: "THIS IS MY BLOOD."

Q. What becomes of the wine when these words are pronounced?

A. It is immediately changed into the blood of Jesus Christ.

Q. What is this change called?

A. *Transubstantiation,* which means a real change of the whole substance of the bread into the whole substance of the body of Christ our Lord, and of the whole substance of the wine into the whole substance of His blood.

Q. Has this always been the doctrine and belief of the Catholics of all times, and in all countries?

A. Yes; as all the Fathers testify.

Q. What says St. Ambrose?

A. "Before the consecration, there is bread alone—but after the words of consecration are pronounced, the bread is changed into the body of our Lord." Lib. IV., c. 4.

Q. What says St. Gregory of Nyssa?

A. "I firmly believe, that the bread is changed into the body of Christ." Cat., c. 37.

Q. But if the Holy Eucharist is the body of Christ, how can it still be called simply bread? for instance, St. Paul says: "The bread which we break is it not the partaking of the body of the Lord?" and again, "Whosoever shall eat this bread unworthily, etc." 1 Cor. x. 16.

A. The Holy Eucharist is called *bread*, not because it is so in reality, but because it was bread before it was consecrated.

Q. Can you give an instance of this manner of speaking?

A. In the Gospel of St. Matthew, it is said: "The blind see, the lame walk," chap. xi., which is to be understood of those who were before blind or lame.

Q. What other answer can you give?

A. The Eucharist is also called *bread*, because it has the appearance of bread.

Q. Give an example taken from Scripture?

A. The Scripture called the three angels who appeared to Abraham, three men, because they appeared under the shape of men; in like manner, the Scripture calls that *bread*, which has the appearance of bread.

Q. What do you mean by the species or appearances of bread and wine?

A. I mean that Jesus Christ leaves the shape, taste, smell, and color of the bread and wine, as they were before the bread and wine were changed into His body and blood.

Q. Why does not Jesus Christ also change the shape, taste, and color of the bread and wine?

A. Our blessed Saviour leaves these appearances of bread and wine, because He uses them to hide Himself under them.

Q. Why does He thus hide Himself?

A. Because if He were to show Himself in all His heavenly brightness and glory, every one would be afraid to go near Him, and receive Him.

Q. Is Jesus Christ present in the Eucharist at all times?

A. He is really present from the moment that the words of consecration are pronounced. For our Saviour said: "This is my body," and it is most certain that what Christ said, was true at the moment in which he said it.

Q. Can you explain more clearly what you have just said?

A. Christ does not say, this *will* be My body when you will eat it—He says: This *is* My body—and the word "*is*" marks present, and not future time.

Q. What says St. Ambrose on the words of consecration?

A. He says that the words of consecration are as powerful as those which God used in creating the world. Lib. IV., c. 4.

Q. What follows from this?

A. That the body of Jesus Christ is present immediately after the words of consecration, just as the world was created the moment after God had spoken the word which made it come forth from nothingness.

Q. What says St. Cyril in his epistle to Golosyrius?

A. He says, that it is the height of folly to assert that the consecrated Host ceases to be such some days after its consecration.

Q. How long does Jesus Christ remain present under the species?

A. He remains as long as the species last.

Q. What would happen to the body of our Saviour, if a host were, by accident, to fall into the fire or water?

A. The body of Jesus Christ would suffer nothing by it—the species only would be consumed.

Q. Is there under the appearance of bread, only the body, and under the appearance of wine, only the blood of Jesus Christ present?

A. No; under each species, Christ is present entire and undivided, as He is entire and undivided in heaven.

Q. When the priest breaks or divides the Sacred Host, does he also break the body of Christ?

A. No; he breaks or divides only the species or appearances, the body of Christ itself is present in each part entire and living, in a true, though mysterious manner.

Q. What do we call Jesus Christ present under the appearances of bread and wine?

A. The Holy Eucharist, or the Blessed Sacrament, or the Sacrament of the Altar, or the Sacred Host, or Viaticum.

Q. What, then, is the Holy Eucharist?

A. The Holy Eucharist is the body and blood of our Lord Jesus Christ, who is truly, really, and substantially present, under the appearances of bread and wine.

Q. Why is it called "Eucharist"?

A. From the Greek word "Eucharistia," which means "Good Grace," because it contains Jesus Christ, our Lord, the source of all gifts and graces.

Q. Why is it also called "Blessed or Most Holy Sacrament"?

A. Because it contains Jesus Christ himself, the author of all the sacraments, and of all holiness.

Q. Why is it also called "The Sacrament of the Altar"?

A. Because it is offered and preserved on the altar.

Q. Why is it called "Sacred Host"?

A. Because it contains Jesus Christ, the true Host, or Victim, immolated for us.

Q. Why is it called "Viaticum"?

A. Because Viaticum means provision for a journey, and Jesus Christ in this sacrament is the spiritual food, by which we are strengthened during our pilgrimage on earth, and especially in the hour of our death, when we pass to eternal happiness and glory.

Q. What is the outward sign of this sacrament?

A. The appearances of bread and wine.

Q. What is the inward grace it conveys to the soul?

A. Jesus Christ himself, the Author and Giver of all graces.

Q. Is Jesus Christ to be adored in the Blessed Sacrament?

A. Most assuredly, since He is truly God. St. Paul says that all angels adore him—He requires not less from men.

Q. Is it, then, a duty for us to kneel down before the Blessed Sacrament?

A. It is, for as St. Augustine says: "It is a sin *not* to adore Him in this sacrament." (In Psalm 98.)

Q. What says St. Ambrose on this subject?

A. "We adore the flesh of Jesus Christ during the celebration of the Sacred Mysteries." (Lib. III. De Spirit Sanct.)

Q. What does the Real Presence of Jesus Christ, in the Blessed Sacrament, require us to do?

A. To visit Him often, and to adore Him with the deepest humility possible, and with the most ardent love and gratitude.

Q. How does the Church induce us to show due honor to Jesus Christ in the Blessed Sacrament?

A. She often exposes the Blessed Sacrament for public adoration, gives benediction with it, carries it reverently about in solemn procession, has established Feasts and Confraternities of the Blessed Sacrament, and of the Sacred Heart of Jesus, and has ordered that a lamp, as an emblem of adoration and love, be kept burning day and night before the altar where the Blessed Sacrament is kept in the Tabernacle.

Q. Why did Jesus Christ institute the Blessed Sacrament?

A. That He might continue to offer Himself to His Heavenly Father for us in the *Holy Sacrifice of the Mass,* and give Himself, in Holy Communion, as food to our souls.

LESSON VIII.

THE SACRIFICE BEFORE THE COMING OF CHRIST.

Q. Does a great lord of this world wish to be honored by his servants?

A. He does.

Q. How much should he be honored by his servants?

A. As much as he deserves.

Q. In what manner does he wish his servants to honor him?

A. By obeying all his commands.

Q. Which of all lords deserves to be honored most?

A. God, Who is the Lord of heaven and earth.

Q. Are men His servants?

A. Yes; because He is their Supreme Lord and God.

Q. What honor did God, at all times, require men to give Him?

A. The honor of adoration.

Q. What do you mean by the honor of adoration?

A. We give God the honor of adoration if we worship Him as the Supreme Lord of heaven and earth, and acknowledge His supreme dominion over all His creatures.

Q. How can we show best that we give this honor to God?

A. By doing all that He commands.

Q. Did our first parents, Adam and Eve, show in this manner that they acknowledged and honored God as the Supreme Lord and Master of heaven and earth?

A. No; they offered a very great insult to God by disobeying His command.

Q. What became of them in that moment?

A. They became the enemies of God.

Q. Could they, as enemies of God, again do anything by which to appease and please God?

A. As enemies of God they could no longer please Him in anything they did.

Q. Did they remain enemies of God?

A. No; God showed mercy to them.

Q. How did God show mercy to them?

A. He gave them the grace to be very sorry

for their sin of disobedience. They asked His pardon, and were ready even to lay down their lives to repair the injury they had offered to God by the sin of their disobedience.

Q. What did God give them to understand?

A. God gave our first parents to understand that all the penances and good works they could perform, together with the sacrifice of their lives, would not be enough to cancel their great debt.

Q. How did He console them?

A. He consoled them by the promise of a Redeemer who would live and die in perfect obedience to His holy will in order to blot out their sin, and who, by His obedience, would honor Him far more than he had been or could be dishonored by them or by their whole posterity.

Q. What did Adam and Eve do after this consoling promise?

A. They firmly resolved always to honor and worship God as their Supreme Lord by living up to His holy will for the remainder of their life, and hoped, by so doing, to obtain forgiveness and life everlasting, through the merits of the Redeemer to come.

Q. But had not our first parents become much inclined to evil; was not their will greatly weakened on account of their sin; were they not very apt to forget themselves, break their good resolutions, even so far as to neglect to give God the honor of adoration?

A. Yes; they were very apt to neglect this most sacred and essential duty towards their most merciful Creator.

Q. What, then, did God do to strengthen the resolve of our first parents always to give Him the due honor and homage of adoration?

A. He gave them a positive command to offer Him sacrifice, that is to say, such outward acts of divine worship as would fittingly express the sentiments of their heart.

Q. How did God give this command?

A. He instructed our first parents to offer Him, instead of their life, other sensible objects; to destroy or otherwise change the same, in order to declare and acknowledge by this destruction or change of sensible things, that He was the Supreme Lord of the Universe, the Sovereign Master of life and death; that, were He to require it, they would be willing even to sacrifice their own life in order thus to render Him an honor and homage of which He alone was worthy and well deserving.

Q. What else did God give our first parents to understand?

A. He also gave them to understand that these sacrifices were to remind them of the Redeemer to come, and of the sacrifice which He would make to take away their sin; that these sacrifices of theirs, as figures of the sacrifice of the Redeemer to come, would be pleasing to Him if made in the proper manner, and with the proper dispositions of the heart.

Q. In what manner, then, was the offering of a visible thing to be made to God?

A. The visible thing offered had to be destroyed or changed:—animals, for instance, were slain, other sensible objects were burned or poured out, such as wine, oil, and the like.

Q. With what intention, or disposition of the heart, should these offerings be made to God?

A. With the intention thus to give God supreme honor—the honor of adoration, and to show their hope in the merits of the sacrifice of the Redeemer to come.

Q. In what, then, consisted the character or essence of sacrifice?

A. The character or essence of sacrifice was

always held to consist in the *destruction, or change of the thing offered,* as without this destruction or change it seemed that man did not fittingly express his inward acknowledgment that God was the Supreme Lord of the Universe, the Sovereign Master of life and death, and as such worthy even of being honored by the sacrifice of man's life, were He to require it.

Q. What follows from this ?

A. From this it is easy to understand how it never came to pass that sacrifices were offered to any one except God, they having always been considered the highest act of worship, an act which could not be rendered to any creature.

Q. Were also sacrifices made to God for other purposes than merely to give God the honor of adoration ?

A. Yes; sacrifices were also made to thank God for graces received, or to obtain particular favors, or to appease God after having offended him.

Q. Did not this original revelation or command of God concerning sacrifice become very much corrupted in the course of time ?

A. Yes; men, supposing that that which

they loved and prized the most would be the most pleasing to God, at last came to sacrifice their fellow-men, nay, even their own children, and thus, instead of honoring God by sacrifice, they only dishonored Him in the highest degree.

LESSON IX.

Q. What did God do in order that sacrifices might always be made to Him in the manner and with the intention which He had taught our first parents?

A. He chose a particular people to whom He gave particular laws about the sacrifices they were to offer.

Q. What particular people was this?

A. The Jewish nation.

Q. What did God's laws to the Jewish nation ordain?

A. They ordained: 1. What things should be offered to God in sacrifice.

2. For what intention sacrifices should be offered.

3. Who were to be the priests to offer sacrifice.

4. The manner in which sacrifices should be offered.

Q. What did the Jews offer to God in sacrifice?

A. They offered certain animals, bread, salt, fruits, wine, oil, etc.

Q. Whom did God choose as priests to offer sacrifice to Him?

A. Aaron and his sons and their descendants.

Q. In what manner were sacrifices to be made?

A. The things offered were, as God ordained in the beginning of the world, either to be destroyed by fire, or otherwise changed and rendered useless.

Q. What were the people to declare by this destruction or change of the things offered?

A. That they wished to give to God the supreme honor of adoration, and to acknowledge that He was the Supreme Lord of heaven and earth, the Sovereign Master of life and death.

Q. What else were the people fittingly to express by this destruction or change of the things offered to God?

A. They were also to express and acknowledge thereby, that on account of their sins they had deserved everlasting destruction.

Q. What were these sacrifices called?

A. Burnt-offerings or holocausts.

Q. Were such sacrifices also made for other intentions?

A. Yes;- sacrifices were also made with the intention of thanking God for blessings received, or of appeasing Him after having offended Him, or of obtaining particular favors.

Q. Why were sacrifices ordained to thank God for certain favors received?

A. To remind the people of their duty of acknowledging God as the Author and Giver of all blessings.

Q. What were these sacrifices called?

A. Thank-offerings.

Q. Why were sacrifices ordained to appease God after having offended Him?

A. To remind the people of their guilt before the Lord, and of the hope they should place in the Redeemer to come, by the merits of whom alone they would be pardoned, and received again into the friendship of God.

Q. What were these sacrifices called?

A. Sin-offerings.

Q. Why were sacrifices ordained to obtain certain graces and blessings?

A. To remind the people of the necessity

of praying to God, in order to obtain the graces necessary to live and die in His friendship.

Q. What were these sacrifices called?

A. Sacrifices of impetration.

LESSON X.

HOLY MASS—THE SACRIFICE OF THE NEW LAW.

Q. Since sacrifice was instituted by God Himself in the very beginning of the world, for the most sacred ends, how long was it to last?

A. Sacrifice was never to cease so long as human beings remained on earth.

Q. How can this be, since the sacrifices of the Old Law are no longer offered to God?

A. The reason why the sacrifices of the Old Law are no longer offered is because Jesus Christ, our Blessed Saviour, abolished them.

Q. Why did He abolish them?

A. Because they were imperfect, and to last only for a time, and then to give way to the perfect sacrifice that was to succeed them.

Q. How could they be imperfect, since God Himself ordained them?

A. God ordained them only as emblems,

figures, and representations of that undefiled oblation which was to succeed them.

Q. Could not the sacrifices of the Old Law take away sin?

A. Those sacrifices were good in themselves because appointed by God, "but it is impossible," says St. Paul, "that sin should be taken away with the blood of oxen and goats." Heb. x. 4.

Q. How do we know that those sacrifices were to last only for a time, and then to give way to the perfect sacrifice that was to succeed them?

A. God Himself foretold by His prophet that those sacrifices would be abolished and succeeded by a perfect one.

Q. In what words did God foretell this?

A. In these: "I have no pleasure in you (Jews), and I will not receive a gift from your hand. For, from the rising to the setting of the sun, my name is great among the heathens, and in every place there is a sacrifice, and there is offered to my name a clean oblation." Malachy i. 10.

Q. How do we learn from this prophecy that the Jewish sacrifices would be rejected?

A. Because God expressly says: "I will receive no gift from your hand."

Q. How do we learn by this prophecy that another sacrifice would be substituted for the Jewish sacrifices?

A. Because God plainly declares that "in every place there is a sacrifice offered to my name."

Q. How do we learn by this prophecy that a perfect sacrifice was to succeed the Jewish sacrifices?

A. Because God calls the new sacrifice "*a clean oblation,*" a pure sacrifice.

Q. What else does God foretell by the prophet Malachy?

A. That the new sacrifice, or clean oblation, will be offered to Him "*from the rising to the setting of the sun.*"

LESSON XI.

Q. When Jesus Christ abolished the Jewish sacrifices because they were no longer pleasing to His Heavenly Father, as had been foretold by the prophet Malachy, did He not, at the same time, abolish the law of sacrifice altogether?

A. By no means. Our Divine Saviour came on earth, not to destroy the law of sacrifice, but to fulfil it, to make it perfect; whatever was essential to the right worship of God in the Old Law, in the Jewish religion, remained essential also in the New Law, the Christian religion. Sacrifice, then, which was the very essence of the Jewish religion, remained also the essence of the Christian religion.

Q. How did our Saviour fulfil the law of sacrifice and render it perfect?

A. He substituted a perfect victim for the victims offered up in the Old Law—for sheep, oxen, lambs, and the like.

Q. Who is this perfect victim or clean oblation?

A. Jesus Christ, the Son of God, Himself.

Q. How did He become our victim?

A. The Son of God is equal to His Father in all things. He, therefore, deserves the same honor and worship as His Father, and cannot give Him the honor of adoration, or thank Him for us, or appease Him for our sins, or obtain favors from Him for us. So He became man, and as man He adored and worshipped His Father for us, thanked Him, appeased Him, and prayed to him for us.

Q. Was the honor of adoration which Jesus Christ gave to His Heavenly Father for us, was

the offering which He made of Himself for our sins, were the prayers and thanksgivings which He offered for us, more pleasing to His Heavenly Father than all the sacrifices which were offered in the Old Law to honor God, to thank Him, appease Him, and obtain favors from Him ?

A. They were, indeed, infinitely more pleasing to Him.

Q. Why so ?

A. Because whatever Jesus Christ did as man, is attributed to His Divine Person, who is infinite. Therefore, all that He has done for us is of an infinite nature. The honor of adoration which He paid on earth to His Heavenly Father for us, is infinite; His atonement for our sins is infinite ; His thanksgivings are infinite, and His prayers are infinite in merit and in value.

Q. When did Jesus Christ more particularly honor and worship His Father for us, thank Him, appease Him for our sins, and pray for us ?

A. When about to die on the Cross. He then offered to His Heavenly Father, in our behalf, His life and death, together with all He had done for us on earth during thirty-three years, exclaiming in a loud voice: "*It is consummated.*"

Q. What did our Blessed Saviour mean by these words, "It is consummated"?

A. He meant to say that He had done all that was necessary—1. To honor His Heavenly Father for us, and repair the insults offered to Him by our sins. 2. To appease Him for our sins. 3. To thank Him for all His benefits and blessings. 4. To obtain for us all possible spiritual and temporal benefits and blessings.

Q. What do we call the offering which Jesus Christ made of Himself to His Heavenly Father on the Cross in our behalf?

A. We call it *the visible, bloody sacrifice, or offering of Jesus Christ on the Cross,* because He shed His blood for us in a visible manner.

Q. When was this bloody sacrifice perfected, or entirely accomplished?

A. We have seen above that the true character, or essence of sacrifice, consists in the destruction or the change of the thing offered to God. So the bloody sacrifice of Jesus Christ was perfected, or entirely accomplished at the same instant that the separation of His blood from the body caused His death.

LESSON XII.

Q. Did Jesus Christ wish to offer Himself for us every day even to the end of the world for those intentions for which He offered Himself on the Cross in a visible and bloody manner?

A. He did, indeed, for He knew that He was *that clean oblation* foretold by the prophet Malachy, to be offered to the Heavenly Father "*in every place, from the rising to the setting of the sun.*"

Q. But how could this be done, since our Blessed Saviour knew that after His resurrection He could die no more, and that forty days after, He was to be in heaven, and not on earth to offer Himself in sacrifice for us to His Heavenly Father?

A. His love for the honor of His Father, and His charity for us, found an easy means to sacrifice Himself every day and everywhere to the end of the world, but not in a visible and bloody manner as on the Cross, but in an *invisible* and *unbloody* manner.

Q. How could Jesus sacrifice Himself in an invisible and unbloody manner?

A. He did so at the Last Supper, when—1. He took and offered bread and wine. 2. Changed the same into His body and blood, and, under the appearance of bread and wine, offered Himself for us to His Heavenly Father for the four intentions just mentioned; and then, 3. Received His own body and blood, and gave the same also to His Apostles, as St. Thomas Aquinas (de Humanit. Christi, Artic. xvii.), St. Jerome and many others teach.

Q. What do we call this?

A. We call it the *unbloody or Eucharistic sacrifice* of Jesus Christ, or the *Holy Mass.*

Q. Did Jesus Christ, then, at the Last Supper, really offer His body and blood for us to His Father?

A. Yes; He offered His body and blood for us not only whilst He was upon the Cross, but also when He celebrated the Last Supper.

Q. How does this appear?

A. This appears clearly from these words of Jesus Christ: "This is my body, which is *given* for you." Luke xxii. 19. Here our Saviour does not say—"This is my body, which *will* be given for you," but He says, which *is given* for you *now,* at the moment in which I am speaking.

Q. Does not this appear still more clearly from the words which Jesus Christ pronounced when holding the chalice?

A. Yes; for the Greek text says: "This is the chalice, which *is shed* for you."

Q. What follows from these words?

A. The chalice was not shed for us on the Cross, therefore it was shed for us at the Last Supper.

Q. Is there any difference between the bloody sacrifice of Jesus Christ on the Cross, and His unbloody sacrifice at the Last Supper?

A. There is no essential difference. The only difference is in the manner in which Jesus Christ offered Himself on those two occasions. At the Last Supper the manner in which He offered Himself was *unbloody* and *invisible*, whilst on the Cross it was bloody and visible. In each instance, the priest was the same, and the victim offered was also the same —Jesus Christ Himself.

Q. But was it not said above, that the true character or essence of sacrifice consists in the destruction or change of the thing offered in sacrifice, and that, therefore, the sacrifice of Jesus Christ on the Cross was perfect, or entirely accomplished, only at the moment of His death? But since His resurrection, Jesus Christ can die no more. How then, can He be a perfect sacrifice under the appearances of bread and wine, since a sacrifice cannot be perfect without the loss of life?

A. Jesus Christ, it is true, can no more die or lose the glorious life which He possesses in heaven. But under the appearances of bread and wine, He possesses a kind of life—called His sacramental, or Mystic Life—which He can lose and does lose as soon as the appearances of bread and wine cease to exist.

Q. In what, then, consisted the essence of this unbloody or Eucharistic sacrifice?

A. The essence of this sacrifice consisted in rendering present by the words of consecration, the holy Victim—His sacred body under the two species, and in the oblation which He made of it.

Q. In what words did Jesus Christ make the oblation of His body to His heavenly Father?

A. The same words which rendered the body of Christ present under the two species, served also to make the oblation thereof.

Q. When was the unbloody sacrifice of Jesus Christ entirely accomplished?

A. At the very instant that He lost His sacramental or mystic life.

Q. When did He lose this life?

A. Soon after He and the Apostles had received His body and blood.

Q. Of how many parts did the unbloody sacrifice of Jesus Christ consist?

A. Principally of these: 1. The offering of bread and wine. 2. The change of bread and wine into the body and blood of Jesus Christ; and 3. The eating of the flesh and drinking of the blood of our Saviour.

Q. Who, then, first celebrated the first Mass on earth?

A. Our Lord Jesus Christ Himself at the Last Supper.

Q. Can you now tell what the Mass really is?

A. The Mass is the unbloody sacrifice of the body and blood of Jesus Christ under the appearances of bread and wine.

LESSON XIII.

Q. How could Jesus Christ offer Himself in Mass "in every place from the rising to the setting of the sun" after His ascension into heaven?

A. By instituting a new and perfect order of priesthood to offer up the *unbloody sacrifice* in every place of the world.

Q. How many classes of the priesthood were there in the Old Law?

A. There were two distinct classes: One, the priesthood of Aaron, who offered the blood of animals; the other, the priesthood of Melchisedech, who offered bread and wine.

Q. Did our Blessed Saviour unite in His own divine person both of these classes of the priesthood?

A. He did, as was foretold by the royal prophet David, who called Jesus Christ a "*Priest forever according to the order of Melchisedech.*" Ps. cix.

Q. Why is He called a priest "according to the order of Melchisedech"?

A. Because, at the Last Supper, He used bread and wine, according to the rite of Melchisedech.

Q. How was Jesus Christ a priest according to the rite of Aaron?

A. Because on the day after the Last Supper He offered up *Himself* in a bloody manner as the victim of our sins, according to the rite of Aaron.

Q. Did Jesus Christ also unite the two kinds of sacrifice of the Old Law—the bloody, or the sacrifice of animals, and the unbloody, or the sacrifice of bread and wine, of the fruits of the earth?

A. He united both kinds of sacrifice in the

one adorable sacrifice of His body and blood, which He offered up under the appearances of bread and wine.

Q. But how is the bloody sacrifice of Jesus Christ, or His death on the Cross caused by the separation of the blood from the body, particularly represented in His unbloody sacrifice—in Holy Mass?

A. The death of Christ, which was caused by the separation of the blood from the body, is strikingly represented by the two distinct consecrations.

Q. How do you explain this?

A. By virtue of the words which the priest pronounces, the *body* of Christ becomes present under the appearance of bread, and *His blood* under the appearance of wine; and both these appearances being visibly *separated* from each other—the separation of the blood in the chalice from the body under the appearance of bread, represents the bloody death on the Cross in an unbloody mystical manner.

Q. Why is Jesus Christ called by David a priest forever?

A. Because He continues to the end of the world to offer up the unbloody sacrifice of His body and blood by the hands of the new and perfect order of priests which He instituted at the Last Supper.

Q. How did Jesus Christ institute a new and perfect priesthood?

A. After He had sacrificed His body and blood in an invisible and unbloody manner at the Last Supper, He, at that very time, empowered and commanded the Apostles to do the same, and thus instituted the new and perfect order of priests.

Q. In what words did Jesus Christ give this power and command to the Apostles?

A. In these: "Do this in commemoration of me."

Q. What is the meaning of these words?

A. Our Saviour meant to be thus understood: I took bread and brake, and gave to you, saying, this is My body, and really and substantially made it My body, which is given for you—I took the chalice, gave thanks, and said: This is My blood, and really and substantially made it My blood, which shall be shed for many. I thus offered to My Heavenly Father in a mystic and unbloody manner, My real body and blood, that same victim which is to be immolated on the

Cross in a visible and bloody manner. So do you, take bread, and blessing it, make it My body; and taking wine, bless it, and make it My blood; and thus continually present to My Father, in an unbloody manner, not a different, but the self-same sacrifice which shall be offered up in a bloody manner once upon the Cross: Do this for a commemoration of Me, for as often as you shall eat this bread, and drink this chalice, you shall show the death of the Lord until He come.

Q. Did the Apostles obey the command of Jesus Christ to offer up the unbloody sacrifice?

A. They did, as we can clearly see from the Acts of the Apostles (chapter xiii. 2), where St. Luke informs us that as the Apostles were ministering, that is to say, as they were sacrificing to the Lord, the Holy Ghost said to them: "Separate me Saul and Barnabas." The same sacrifice which the Evangelist distinguishes by the term "ministration," we Catholics, at the present day, call the "Mass." St. Matthew, the Apostle, as history informs us, was pierced with a lance whilst celebrating the holy sacrifice of the Mass.

Q. How long has the holy sacrifice of the Mass been offered?

A. It has been offered from the time of the Apostles up to the present day, and will so continue to be offered to the end of the world.

Q. Where, then, do we see fulfilled the prophecy of Malachy, that "from the rising of the sun to the going down, there is offered to my name a clean oblation"? Chap. i.

A. Only in the Catholic Church, whose priests daily offer the holy sacrifice of the Mass, the clean oblation for the living and the dead.

Q. What says St. Augustine of the sacrifice of the Mass?

A. "This sacrifice," he says, "was established as a substitute for all the sacrifices of the Old Law." De Civit., lib. 17.

Q. What says St. Irenæus?

A. "The Apostles received the sacrifice from Jesus Christ, and the Church having received it from the Apostles, celebrates it at the present day throughout the world, according to the prophecy of Malachias." Lib. iv. c. 32.

Q. Has any enemy of the Catholic religion ever

been able to prove that a Pope or Bishop introduced the Sacrifice of the Mass?

A. No; not one of all the enemies of our holy religion could ever prove that the Mass was introduced by a Pope or Bishop.

Q. What follows from all this?

A. It follows that we have received the sacrifice of the Mass from Jesus Christ, through the Apostles. For, when a custom prevails universally in the Church, and it is impossible to show what Pope, or Bishop, or Council introduced it, we are certain that it is derived from the Apostles.

Q. Did Jesus Christ institute Mass in the manner in which it is celebrated at the present day?

A. He instituted only the principal parts of the Mass, the accessory part comes from the holy Catholic Church.

Q. What do you call the principal parts of the Mass?

A. The principal parts of the Mass are: 1. *Offertory;* 2. *Consecration;* and 3. *Communion.*

Q. What takes place at the Offertory?

A. The priest offers bread and wine.

Q. What takes place at the Consecration?

A. The priest pronounces, in the name of

Jesus, the sacred *words of consecration,* by which the bread and wine are changed into the body and blood of Jesus Christ.

Q. What takes place at the Communion?

A. The priest consumes the body and blood of our Lord.

Q. What do you call the accessory part?

A. The accessory part is composed of all the ceremonies of the Mass.

LESSON XIV.

Q. If, as you said, the Sacrifice of the Mass and the Sacrifice of the Cross are but one and the same sacrifice, why, then, is the same sacrifice daily renewed; was not the Sacrifice of the Cross sufficient for the redemption of the whole world?

A. The Sacrifice of the Cross is indeed of infinite value, and more than sufficient for the redemption of all mankind, but to be of profit to us, we must make use of the means necessary to apply it to our souls, and these means are the Sacrifice of the Mass, the sacraments, prayer, and good works.

Q. How, then, must we consider the Sacrifice of the Mass?

A. As an efficient means by which the merit of the Sacrifice of the Cross is, in a special manner, applied to our souls.

Q. For what intentions, then, should we hear and offer up the Sacrifice of the Mass?

A. We should hear and offer up Mass as a sacrifice of adoration and praise, of thanksgiving, of propitiation, and impetration.

Q. Who, in Mass, praises and honors the Heavenly Father for us, thanks Him for all the blessings bestowed upon us, appeases Him for our sins, and offers His prayers to Him to obtain for us all spiritual and temporal blessings?

A. It is Jesus Christ Himself, who, under the appearances of bread and wine, offers Himself to His Heavenly Father, through the hands of the priest.

Q. What must be your principal intention in hearing Mass?

A. To honor the Heavenly Father with the honor of adoration with which Jesus Christ, His Son, honored Him for us on earth, and which He offers to Him in every Mass.

Q. Why should this be your chief intention in hearing Mass?

A. Because the most essential duty of man is to pay to God the honor of adoration and acknowledge His supreme dominion over all creatures.

Q. How much does God deserve this honor of adoration?

A. He deserves it in an infinite degree.

Q. But how can we offer to God an infinite honor of adoration since we are but finite creatures?

A. Jesus Christ has given us an easy means to do so.

Q. How so?

A. Being an infinite Person as He is, all the honor of adoration which Jesus Christ paid to His Father, was infinite, and as He offered this honor to His Father for us, it is ours, especially at Mass, where He again offers for us to His Father all the acts of adoration of His life on earth. Therefore we offer to God an infinite honor of adoration if, at Mass, we offer to Him the infinite acts of adoration of His well-beloved Son, Jesus Christ.

Q. For what other intentions should we hear Mass?

A. To thank God for all His graces and blessings, spiritual and temporal.

Q. How do you hear Mass for this intention?

A. By offering up to God the infinite acts of

thanksgiving which Jesus Christ offered to Him on earth, and again offers for us in Mass.

Q. For what other intention should we hear Mass?

A. To atone thereby for our own sins and for the sins of all the living and dead.

Q. In what sense is Mass a sacrifice of propitiation or atonement for the sins of the living?

A. It is a sacrifice of propitiation for the living, because it obtains for them the spirit of true sorrow for their sins, and the grace to do penance for them, and it is also a sacrifice of propitiation because it remits the temporal punishments which the just still owe to the Divine Justice, on account of certain sins.

Q. In what sense is it a sacrifice of propitiation for the dead?

A. In this, that it contributes to the remission of the temporal punishments of the souls in Purgatory.

Q. How do you prove Mass to be a sacrifice of propitiation?

A. From these words of our Saviour: "This is my blood which shall be shed for many for the remission of sins." Matt. xxvi. 28.

Q. What says the Apostle St. Paul?

A. "Every high priest is appointed for men in the things that appertain to God, that he may offer up gifts and sacrifices for *sins*." Heb. v. 1.

Q. What conclusion do you draw from this text?

A. That since we have pontiffs and priests, they must necessarily offer up sacrifice for *our sins*.

Q. Is there, then, more than one sacrifice of propitiation? Was it not the Sacrifice of the Cross alone which atoned for our sins?

A. The Sacrifice of the Cross and the Sacrifice of the Mass are but one and the same sacrifice.

Q. Why so?

A. Because in both it is the same High Priest who offers, and the same Victim who is offered, namely, Jesus Christ our Lord,—the priest acting only in the name of Christ.

Q. What, then, does Jesus Christ do for us at Mass to atone for our sins?

A. He offers to His heavenly Father all the infinite acts of atonement of His whole life, but especially that great act of atonement which He offered for our sins on the Cross by shedding His most precious blood.

Q. What is the power of this act of atonement offered by Jesus Christ at Mass to His Heavenly Father?

A. It appeases the Heavenly Father, Who grants to sinners the grace of true repentance, and to the just on earth, and to the souls in purgatory, the remission of temporal punishments still due on account of their sins.

Q. Was the Sacrifice of the Mass offered for the dead in the first ages of Christianity?

A. It was, as may easily be shown from the testimony of the Fathers.

Q. What says St. Jerome?

A. He says that by every Mass, not only one, but several souls are delivered from purgatory. Apud Bern. de Busto, Serm. 3 de Missa.

Q. What says St. Augustine?

A. It is not to be doubted, that the dead are aided by alms, prayers, and by *the salutary sacrifice.* T. V. Serm. 172, n. 2, 3, col. 1196.

Q. Is there still any other intention for which we should hear Mass?

A. We should also hear Mass with the intention of obtaining all possible graces and favors, spiritual and temporal, especially the grace to *live* and *die* in the holy fear and love of God.

Q. In what sense is Mass a sacrifice of impetration, a source of all possible blessings to us?

A. In this: Jesus Christ offers in Mass to His Father all those prayers which He offered to Him with abundant tears on earth during his life of thirty-three years, and especially when hanging on the Cross, to obtain for us all those graces and favors which He knew we needed in this world, to enable us to lead a holy life, and die in His holy fear and love.

Q. How powerful are these prayers and tears of Jesus Christ with His heavenly Father?

A. They are of such a power that if we offer them at Mass to the heavenly Father He grants us whatsoever we ask of Him in the name of His beloved Son.

Q. What follows from all this?

A. That we cannot offer to God greater praise and honor, or more acceptable thanksgivings for graces received, or acts of atonement for our sins, or more powerful prayers, than by hearing Mass with recollection and devotion.

Q. What else follows?

A. It also follows that we are bound to assist at the Holy Sacrifice of the Mass.

Q. How does this follow?

A. If God, for four thousand years, required men to give Him by special, though imperfect sacrifices, the honor of adoration, and to thank and appease Him, and obtain from Him the necessary graces to live and die in His holy fear and love, how much more does He not require Christians to offer to Him that clean and perfect oblation of the body and blood of His Son Jesus Christ, in honor of His divine Majesty, in thanksgiving, in atonement for their sins, and to obtain all necessary graces for their spiritual and temporal welfare!

Q. How may Mass be heard for these intentions by those not using a prayer-book?

A. This may be done in the following manner: Let them say during Mass the Rosary of the Blessed Virgin Mary. Let them say the ten Hail Marys of the first decade in the following manner: "Hail Mary, full of grace, the Lord is with thee, blessed art thou among women, and blessed is the fruit of thy womb, Jesus, *whom I offer to God in honor of His*

Divine Majesty." Holy Mary, Mother of God, pray for us sinners, now, and at the hour of our death. Amen.

In the Hail Marys of the second decade, add after the word Jesus, "*Whom I offer to God in thanksgiving for all His benefits.*" Holy Mary, Mother, etc.

In the Hail Marys of the third decade, add after the word Jesus, "*Whom I offer to God in satisfaction for all my sins, and for those of all the living and the dead.*" Holy Mary, Mother, etc.

In the Hail Marys of the fourth and fifth decade, add after the word Jesus, "*Whom I offer to God to obtain all the graces necessary to live and die in His friendship.*"

Q. What do you say at the elevation of the Sacred Host?

A. I say: "*O my God, for the love of this Thy Son, forgive me my sins, and let me live and die in Thy grace.*"

Q. What do you say at the elevation of the blood of Jesus Christ in the chalice?

A. I say: "*O my God, through the blood of Jesus Christ make me love Thee more and more, and grant me a happy death.*"

Q. What do you say when the priest receives communion?

A. I say: "*O my Jesus, I love Thee and wish to receive Thee. I embrace Thee, let me never more be separated from Thee.*"

Q. In what spirit should we assist at Mass?

A. When at Mass, we should remember that as we are associated with the priest of Christ in offering the adorable Victim to God, so should we be associated with the Divine Victim, in the spirit of self-sacrifice; we should offer ourselves with Him; we should lay on the altar the oblation of our soul and body, our memory, will, and understanding; our thoughts, words, actions, and intentions of the day; our life, death, and whole being, that all may be sanctified by union with Him who is immolated for the love of us. We should offer all generously to God, with self-renunciation, that the mystic death of Jesus in His temple may produce in our souls a similar death—the death of our evil inclinations to worldly pleasures and allurements, but above all, the death of our self-will, in order thus to become a fit holocaust in the sight of God, of which He may dispose according to His good pleasure, for His greater glory and for the good of our own soul and of our fellow-men.

Q. What does one show by neglecting to comply with his essential duty of hearing Mass, especially on Sundays and holy-days of obligation?

A. He shows either an utter ignorance of his most essential duty towards God, or an abominable want of faith, an ingratitude towards God of the blackest kind, and a fearful want of charity towards himself.

Q. To whom are the fruits of the Mass applied?

A. The fruits of the Mass are partly applied to all mankind, but more especially to the whole Church, both militant and suffering; but they are more particularly applied: 1. To the priest who celebrates it; 2. To those for whom in particular he offers it up; and 3. To all those who assist at it with devotion.

Q. To whom do we offer the Sacrifice of the Mass?

A. We offer it principally to God alone, but we also celebrate in it the memory of the Saints, especially of the Blessed Mother of God.

Q. How do we celebrate the memory of the Saints in the Mass?

A. We offer up the Mass to God in thanksgiving for all the graces bestowed upon them in this life, and we ask them to pray for us.

LESSON XV.

Q. What is signified by the vestments which the priest wears at Mass ?

A. They represent the different circumstances of the Passion of our Saviour.

Q. What does the Amice represent, which the priest wears around his neck ?

A. It represents the linen which covered the face of our Saviour.

Q. What does the Alb represent ?

A. The white garment, with which Herod, in derision, clothed our Saviour.

Q. What does the Chasuble represent ?

A. The purple cloak which was thrown on our Saviour through mockery.

Q. What does the Cross traced on the Chasuble represent ?

A. The Cross which our Saviour dragged through the streets of Jerusalem.

Q. What do the veil of the Chalice and the corporal represent ?

A. The linen which covered the body of

our Saviour when it was placed in the sepulchre.

Q. What does the Altar represent ?

A. The Calvary on which our Saviour was crucified.

Q. Why is the Missal carried from the left to the right side of the Altar ?

A. To represent that the Gospel passed over to the Gentiles from the Jews, who rejected it.

Q. Why do all stand whilst the Gospel is read ?

A. To show our readiness to do all that the Son of God has commanded us to do.

Q. Why does the priest, at the Offertory, mingle some water with the wine ?

A. To represent the union of the Divine with the human nature.

Q. Why does the priest, at the Consecration, elevate the Sacred Host ?

A. To represent to us how Jesus Christ was elevated on the Cross.

Q. Why does he divide the host into three parts, letting one of them fall into the Chalice ?

A. To represent the separation of the soul of Jesus Christ from the body, and to signify that the soul descended into Limbo.

Q. Why does the priest pray sometimes in a loud and sometimes in a low voice ?

A. He does so in order to imitate our Saviour, Who prayed thus on the Cross.

Q. Why does the priest give a blessing at the end of Mass?

A. To represent the blessing which Jesus Christ gave to His disciples before His ascension into heaven.

Q. Why is the Mass said in Latin?

A. 1. In order that the service of God may be everywhere uniform; 2. In order that by always using the same words and the same prayers, the changes to which languages are subject, may be avoided; and 3. That being obliged to learn the Latin language, all the priests of the world may be able to communicate with one another.

Q. But is it not an injury to the people to hear Mass said in a tongue which they do not understand?

A. Not at all; for the Almighty receives all prayers in whatever language they are said, and the people may, if they wish, read the prayers said at Mass, which they will find translated in every prayer-book.

Q. But does not the Apostle say: "In the Church I had rather speak five words with my understanding, than ten thousand words in a strange tongue"? Cor. xiv. 19.

A. The Apostle speaks here of instruction, for he immediately adds: "That I may instruct others also."

Q. Does not the same Apostle say: "If I pray in a tongue my spirit prayeth, but my understanding is without fruit"? Chap. xiv. 14.

A. The Apostle here speaks of those who had the gift of tongues, and requires of them to offer up public prayers in a language understood by the people.

Q. Why so?

A. Because, if public prayers were made in an unknown tongue, those who assist at them would not know whether or not the prayers were proper, nor could they answer, Amen.

Q. Are not Catholics under the same inconvenience when hearing Mass?

A. No; for many understand Latin, and those who do not, soon learn the sense of the the prayers of the Mass, because the Church requires her pastors to explain the Mass to the people.

LESSON XVI.

HOLY COMMUNION.

Q. When the people go to Holy Communion, you see the priest at the altar, holding in his hand something which looks like white bread—Is it bread?

A. No, it is not bread; it is the body of Jesus Christ, as truly and really as there is a living God—that body which was nailed to the Cross, and is sitting at the right hand of God in heaven.

Q. What do we say of those who have received the body and blood of Jesus Christ?

A. We say, that they received or went to "Holy Communion."

Q. What, then, is Holy Communion?

A. It is the receiving of the body and blood, the soul and divinity of Jesus Christ, under the appearance of bread and wine.

Q. Who may receive Holy Communion?

A. Only baptized persons who know what Communion is, and who are in the grace and friendship of God.

Q. Are we bound to receive Holy Communion?

A. Yes, we are bound to receive it, for Jesus Christ says: "Amen, amen, I say unto you: except you eat the flesh of the Son of man, and drink his blood, you shall not have life in you." John vi. 54.

Q. Is it also necessary to drink the chalice, in order to receive the blood of Christ?

A. No; because we receive Jesus Christ whole and entire, under each kind.

Q. Is the blood, then, contained under the appearance of bread?

A. It is, and so also is the body contained under the appearance of wine.

Q. Does not the priest receive more than the laity?

A. He does not.

Q. Why do priests confine the use of the chalice to themselves; is it because they have a better right to it than the people?

A. No, for when a Pope, Bishop, or priest receives communion without saying Mass, he receives only under the appearance of bread.

Q. What is the reason that priests never dispense with the chalice when saying Mass?

A. The reason is, that Jesus Christ instituted the Holy Eucharist, not only as a sacrament, but also as a sacrifice, for which both kinds are required.

Q. Why does the Catholic Church give Holy Communion to the faithful in one kind only, namely, under the appearance of bread?

A. 1. To prevent the sacred blood from being profaned, since, under the appearance of wine, it might easily be spilled, and could not well be preserved.

2. To make it easy for all to receive our Lord, since many feel a disgust at drinking out of the same chalice.

3. To declare thereby against the heretics, that Christ is present whole and entire under each kind.

4. Because we receive as much under one kind as we receive under both.

5. Because Jesus Christ promises eternal life to those who receive Him under one kind, as well as to those who receive Him under both. John vi. 50, 52, 58, 59.

Q. But did not Pope Gelasius command all Catholics to receive the chalice?

A. He did, but only on account of the Manicheans.

Q. What were the errors of the Manicheans?

A. Amongst other things they believed that wine was a creature of the devil.

Q. What means were adopted by Gelasius to hinder those heretics from going to Communion with Catholics?

A. He commanded the Catholics to receive the chalice, knowing well that the Manicheans, from the horror in which they held wine, would not approach the Holy Table.

Q. What follows from this?

A. That, previous to this order of the Pope, which made it impossible for the Manicheans to associate with Catholics, it was customary to receive our Lord only under the species of bread.

Q. But did not our Saviour say: "Drink ye all of this"?

A. He did, but only to the Apostles.

Q. But if the command to "drink" was here given only to the Apostles, may we not say with equal propriety, that the command to "eat" was also given only to them?

A. The command both to *eat* and *drink* was given on this occasion only to the Apostles and their successors in the priesthood.

Q. How do you prove this?

A. Our Saviour said: "Eat and drink," to

those only to whom He said: "Do this in remembrance of me." Now He addressed these last words, "do this in remembrance of me," only to the Apostles and their successors in the priesthood.

Q. How do you show that these last words were addressed only to the Apostles?

A. In these words, Christ gave the power of consecrating and of distributing the Holy Eucharist. It is clear that this power was given only to the Apostles and their successors.

Q. How can you show that both kinds are not essential to the sacrament?

A. If both species of bread and wine were necessary for the sacrament, Jesus Christ would not surely have promised as much to those who receive only one, as to those who receive both. And again, if the two kinds were necessary for the sacrament, the Church of the first ages would not have administered the one without the other; but that she did so frequently we have the most abundant proof.

Q. In what words does Jesus Christ tell us that Communion under one kind is sufficient for salvation?

A. In these: "Whoever eateth of this bread shall live for ever." John vi. 50, 52, 58, 59.

Q. How do we know that Jesus Christ has a most ardent desire to be received in Holy Communion?

A. We know it from these words of our Lord: "With desire I have desired to eat this Pasch with you."

Q. What does Jesus Christ promise to those who receive Him worthily in Holy Communion?

A. He promises them life everlasting.

Q. With what does He threaten those who will not receive Him?

A. He threatens them with everlasting punishment.

Q. What follows from this promise and threat of Jesus Christ?

A. They prove the unutterable desire of Jesus Christ to unite Himself to us in Holy Communion.

Q. Why has He so great a desire to come to us in Holy Communion?

A. Because His desire to save us is so unutterably great, and because He knows that without receiving Him we shall not be able to lead a holy life.

Q. When Jesus Christ has come in Holy Communion into a soul that has made a good confession, what does he give to that soul?

A. Jesus Christ enriches that soul with his graces and gifts. He blesses it, and makes it happy and beautiful like an angel of God.

Q. What else does Jesus Christ do to that soul?

A. He unites Himself to it in a most intimate manner. He increases its faith, hope, and charity.

Q. What other blessing does Jesus bestow upon that soul?

A. He makes the soul hate sin and love the holy will of God.

Q. Does Jesus Christ bestow upon that soul any other blessing?

A. Yes; He also makes the soul strong to resist the temptations of the devil, bad example, and its own inclinations to evil.

Q. Is it, then, a great blessing to receive Holy Communion?

A. To receive Holy Communion is the greatest of blessings.

Q. What reward has Jesus Christ promised to those who often receive him worthily in Holy Communion?

A. He has promised them heaven, and that he will raise them up at the last day.

Q. In what words did He promise all those blessings?

A. In these: "He that eateth my flesh and drinketh my blood, abideth in me, and I in him. As the living Father hath sent me, and I live by the Father, so he that eateth me, the same also shall live by me. He that eateth my flesh and drinketh my blood has everlasting life and I will raise him up in the last day." John vi.

Q. Does Jesus Christ bestow these blessings upon all who receive Him in Holy Communion?

A. Jesus Christ bestows these blessings only upon those who receive Him worthily, that is, on those who are free from mortal sin.

Q. Who receive Communion unworthily?

A. Unworthy communicants are—1. All those who knowingly are in mortal sin, and who go to Communion after having been refused absolution.

2. All those who have wilfully concealed a mortal sin in confession.

3. All those who, though they have confessed their grievous sins, have, nevertheless, no true sorrow for them all, and no firm purpose of amendment.

Q. Who have no true sorrow for their sins?

A. 1. All those who do not intend to keep the promise they made in confession to avoid mortal sin.

2. All those who are not willing to forgive their enemies.

3. All those who have no intention to restore ill-gotten goods, or the good name of their neighbor after having injured him.

4. All those who are not fully determined to keep away from taverns, grogshops, and snch places as have always proved occasions of sin to them; and, 5. All those who will not break off sinful company.

Q. What sin is committed by unworthy communicants?

A. They commit, like Judas, a great sacrilege, and make themselves guilty of the body and blood of our Lord.

Q. Who has assured us of this?

A. The Apostle St. Paul, in these words: "Whosoever shall eat this bread or drink the chalice of the Lord unworthily, shall be guilty of the body and of the blood of the Lord. He eateth and drinketh judgment to himself." 1 Cor. xi. 27, 29.

Q. What are often the evil effects of an unworthy Communion even in this life?

A. Blindness of the understanding, hardening of the heart, apostasy from the faith, and sometimes a sudden death, and other temporal punishments.

Q. What must we do after we have committed a mortal sin?

A. We must make a good confession before we receive Communion.

Q. What else should we do?

A. We should also endeavor to cleanse our soul from venial sin, and excite in ourselves sentiments of fervor and devotion.

Q. Do venial sins render our Communions unworthy?

A. Venial sins do not render our Communions unworthy, but Jesus Christ, on account of them, withholds from us many graces which otherwise He would give us.

Q. What else is required before Holy Communion?

A. We must be fasting from midnight.

Q. Who are not obliged to be fasting?

A. Those who are dangerously ill, and receive Jesus Christ by way of Viaticum, that is, as a preparation for their passage into eternity.

Q. Which are the best exercises before Holy Communion?

A. The acts of Faith, Hope, and Love; acts of Humility, heartfelt Sorrow, and great Desire.

Q. In what manner should we go to Holy Communion ?

A. With the greatest reverence, with hands joined, and eyes modestly cast down.

Q. If Holy Communion stops on the roof of the mouth should it be removed with the fingers ?

A. No; but with the tongue.

Q. What should we do after Communion ?

A. We should return with great modesty to our place and spend at least a quarter of an hour in thanking Jesus Christ for so great a blessing.

Q. What else should we do ?

A. We should also ask Him to make us love Him in time and in eternity, so that we may never do anything by which He would be forced to leave us, and cast us into the torments of hell.

Q. How should we spend the day of Communion ?

A. We should spend it as much as possible in pious recollection, and avoid worldly amusements.

LESSON XVII.
PENANCE.

Q. What is the sacrament of penance?

A. Penance is a sacrament by which the sins, committed after baptism, are forgiven.

Q. When did our Lord institute this sacrament?

A. When He breathed on the Apostles and said: "Whose sins you shall forgive, they are forgiven them, and whose sins you shall retain, they are retained." John xx. 23.

Q. How is this forgiveness conveyed to our souls?

A. By the absolution of the priest, joined with contrition, confession, and the purpose of rendering satisfaction on the part of the penitent.

Q. What is absolution?

A. It is the form of words used by the priest: "I absolve thee from thy sins, in the name of the Father, and of the Son, and of the Holy Ghost."

Q. In whose name does the priest forgive sins?

A. In the name of God.

Q. What priests can give absolution?

A. Only those who are authorized to do so by the Pope or the Bishop of the diocese.

Q. Did Christ give this power to the Apostles only?

A. No; He gave it also to all who were to succeed the Apostles in the priesthood, as the Church has always believed and taught.

Q. Why was the power of forgiving sins to pass from the Apostles to their successors?

A. Because Christ instituted the means of salvation for all times, and for all men who are in need of them.

Q. Does the priest truly forgive the sins, or does he only declare that they are forgiven?

A. Keys are not given to a person that he may *declare* the gate to be open, but that he may have the power either to open or shut it. Thus also the power of forgiving sins is not given to priests, in order that they may *declare* sins to be forgiven, but that they may really and truly forgive or retain them.

Q. Can all sins be forgiven by the sacrament of penance?

A. Yes; all the sins which we have committed after baptism, if we confess them with the necessary sentiments of contrition.

Q. But why must we confess our sins in order to obtain the forgiveness of them?

A. Because Christ so ordained it when He instituted the sacrament of penance.

Q. How do we know that Christ ordained confession?

A. That Christ ordained confession is clear from His own words to the Apostles: "Whose sins you shall forgive, they are forgiven them, and whose sins you shall retain, they are retained."

Q. How does it clearly follow from these words of Christ that we are bound to confess our sins to the priest?

A. Because the priests cannot make a distinction between the sins that are to be forgiven, and those that are not to be forgiven, unless sins are confessed to them. And being appointed judges by Jesus Christ, they must have a knowledge of the case, before they can pronounce sentence.

Q. Did the first Christians confess their sins?

A. Yes; as is clear from Holy Scripture testifying that "Many of them that believed, came confessing and declaring their deeds." Acts xix. 18.

Q. Has private confession always been practised in the Church?

A. There never was a time, nor a country,

in which Catholics were not obliged to confess their sins, as may be easily proved from the testimony of the Fathers.

Q. What says St. Cyprian in his sermon about those who had fallen into sin ?

A. "My dear brethren," says he, "let each one confess his sins whilst he yet enjoys life, and has the opportunity of being helped by the priest." (Sermon de Lapsis.)

Q. What says St. Basil ?

A. "It is necessary that we confess our sins to those to whom the dispensation of the Sacred Mysteries has been confided." (Rule 229).

Q. What says St. Ambrose in his second book on Penance, chap. 6 ?

A. "If you wish to obtain grace, confess your sins, for an humble confession dissolves all the bonds of sin."

Q. But would not God forgive our sins if we were to confess them to Him alone ?

A. By no means, as otherwise the full power which Christ gave to the priests, of forgiving and retaining sins, would be vain and useless.

Q. What says St. Augustine on this subject ?

A. "Let no one say: I do penance privately before God; God, Who knows me, sees what is going on in my heart. Was it then said in vain: 'Whatsoever ye shall loose on earth, it shall be loosed in heaven'?—were then the keys given in vain to the Church of God?" Hom. xlix. chap. 3.

Q. Is, then, the sacrament of penance necessary for salvation to all those who have grievously sinned after baptism?

A. It is, as is clear from Christ's words "Whose sins you retain they are retained."

Q. Can the sacrament of penance never be supplied?

A. If the sacrament of penance cannot be received it can be supplied by perfect contrition, with a firm resolution to confess our sins as soon as possible.

Q. What graces does the sacrament of penance convey to the soul?

A. 1. It remits the sins committed after baptism, together with the eternal punishment and at least a part of the temporal punishment due to our sins. 2. It restores sanctifying grace, or increases it if not lost; and, 3. It also gives particular graces which enable us to lead a holy life.

Q. What must we do in order to receive the sacrament of penance worthily?

A. We must—1. Examine our conscience. 2. Have true sorrow or contrition for our sins. 3. Firmly purpose amendment of life. 4. Confess our sins; and, 5. Render satisfaction, or do the penance which the priest gives us in confession.

Q. What is meant by examining our conscience?

A. To examine our conscience means to reflect carefully on the commandments of God and the Church, and the duties of our state of life, in order to know how often we have sinned against those commandments, by thought, word, deed, and omission.

Q. How do we begin the examination of conscience?

A. By asking the Holy Ghost to give us the grace rightly to know our sins, to be truly sorry for them, and to confess them sincerely.

Q. What should we do after this?

A. We should try to remember the time when we made our last confession, and then go carefully over the commandments to find out our sins.

Q. What faults are to be avoided in the examination of conscience?

A. We should not be too hasty and superficial, nor too scrupulous in making it.

Q. How much time should be spent in the examination ?

A. The more carelessly we have lived, and the longer we have staid away from confession, the more time and care ought we to employ in examining ourselves.

Q. How can we render this examination easy ?

A. By examining our conscience every day, and by going often to confession.

Q. What is contrition ?

A. Contrition is a hearty sorrow for our sins, and a true detestation of those sins.

Q. What are the qualities of a good contrition ?

A. Contrition must be—1. *Interior*, that is, it must come from the heart.

2. It must be *supernatural*, that is, we must be sorry for our sins, either on account of their deformity, or because by them we have offended the infinite goodness of God, and on that account forfeited heaven and deserved hell.

3. It must be *sovereign*, that is, our sorrow for having offended God must be greater than our sorrow for any other cause.

4. It must be *universal*, that is, we

must be sorry for *all* our sins, at least for *all* our mortal sins.

Q. Is the confession of a person good if he has no sorrow for his venial sins ?

A. If a person has only venial sins to confess, and is not truly sorry for *any* of them, his confession is not good; but if he is sorry at least for one of them and purposes not to commit it again, his confession is good.

Q. What should a person do who has only venial sins to confess, and doubts whether he has true sorrow for at least one of them ?

A. Such a person should be sorry for some grievous sin of his past life, and confess it again, saying at the end of his accusation: "For these and all my other sins, which I cannot at present call to my remembrance, and also for the sins of my past life, especially (here he should tell a sin of his past life) I am heartily sorry," etc.

Q. What should a person do who is not sure of having wilfully committed a sin since his last confession, and yet wishes to receive the sacrament of penance ?

A. Such a one should also accuse himself of a sin of his past life, and make again an act of contrition for it.

Q. Would God forgive a person who confesses his sins and is sorry for them, only because his sins caused him to lose his health, property, good name, and the like?

A. No; God would not forgive the sins of that person, because the sorrow for them is only natural sorrow, which is of no avail.

Q. How may we obtain supernatural contrition?

A. We must earnestly beg it of God, and make use of such reflections as may move us to it.

Q. How many kinds of supernatural contrition are there?

A. Two; perfect contrition and imperfect contrition.

Q. When is contrition perfect?

A. Contrition is perfect when it arises from the best motive of sorrow, that is, sorrow for God's sake, from the love of God, Who is infinitely good in Himself and also so good to us.

Q. When is contrition imperfect?

A. Our contrition is imperfect when we are sorry for our sins only because by them we have offended God, and on that account have lost heaven and deserved hell.

Q. Will God forgive the sins of a person who

confesses his sins and has only imperfect contrition for them?

A. He will, because the sacrament supplies what is wanting to his sorrow.

Q. But should we not endeavor as much as possible to obtain perfect contrition?

A. Yes, we should, because the greater our sorrow is, the surer is the forgiveness of our sins.

Q. Should we make the act of contrition before or after confession?

A. We should make it before confession, or at least before the priest gives us absolution.

Q. On what other occasions should we make acts of perfect contrition?

A. In danger of death, and as often as we have the misfortune to commit a mortal sin and cannot immediately go to confession.

Q. Can nothing else besides contrition ever obtain forgiveness for sins?

A. No; contrition is so necessary to obtain forgiveness, that its place cannot be supplied by anything, or in any case.

Q. What is meant by purpose of amendment?

A. Purpose of amendment is a firm resolution, by the grace of God—1. To avoid not only all mortal sins; but 2. Also the proximate or next occasions of sin; 3. To make use of the necessary means of amendment; 4. To make due satisfaction for our sins; and, 5. To repair whatever injury we may have done to our neighbor.

Q. What is meant by proximate occasion of sin?

A. By the proximate occasion of sin is meant a person,. a place, an amusement, that will probably lead us into sin.

Q. Are we strictly bound to avoid the proximate occasion of sin?

A. Yes, whenever it is possible, for he who is not willing to avoid the occasion of sin, does not sincerely purpose to avoid sin itself.

Q. What should a person consider who is not really willing to avoid the occasion of sin or give up his evil habit of sinning?

A. He should consider that the priest cannot give him absolution, or if he gives it, it is of no avail before God, but renders the receiver still more guilty before the Lord.

Q. What is confession?

A. Confession is the accusation made to a priest of all our sins which we can remember, in order to obtain absolution of them.

Q. What are the necessary qualities of confession?

A. Confession must be—1. Entire; 2. Sincere; and 3. Clear.

Q. When is confession entire?

A. When we confess, at least, all grievous sins which we remember, together with their number and necessary circumstances.

Q. What must we do if we do not recollect the exact number of our sins?

A. We must give it as nearly as possible, saying, for instance, I have committed this sin about —— times a day, week, or month.

Q. What kind of circumstances must we confess?

A. We should especially confess those circumstances which change the nature, or considerably aggravate the guilt of our sins; for instance, to steal something from the Church is not only a sin of theft, but also a sin of sacrilege, and should be so confessed.

Q. What should we avoid in declaring those circumstances?

A. We must avoid as much as possible making known any person who may be concerned in our sins, leave out all useless tales, and express ourselves in as modest a manner as the nature of the sin allows.

Q. Are we also bound to confess venial sins?

A. We are not bound to confess venial sins, yet it is very good and advisable to do so.

Q. But if we do not know whether something we have done is a mortal sin or a venial sin, what are we to do?

A. We should confess it, because many people mistake mortal sins for venial sins.

Q. When is confession sincere?

A. When we accuse ourselves just as we find ourselves guilty before God, without concealing, or disguising, or excusing our sins.

Q. What sin would we commit by wilfully concealing a mortal sin in confession?

A. We would commit the great sin of sacrilege, and make ourselves guilty of eternal damnation.

Q. What must we do if we have left out something in confession which we were obliged to tell?

A. If we forgot to tell it, all that is necessary is to mention it in our next confession; but, if we left it out through shame, we must also say in how many confessions we left it out, and then make over again all those sacrilegious confessions.

Q. When is confession clear?

A. When we express ourselves so as to let the confessor clearly see the state of our conscience.

Q. What is a general confession?

A. A general confession is one in which we repeat all, or some of our former confessions.

Q. When is a general confession necessary?

A. As often as our former confessions were sacrilegious, either through want of sincerity, or of sorrow and purpose of amendment; or through a very culpable negligence in the examination of our conscience.

Q. When is a general confession chiefly useful and advisable?

A. 1. Before first communion; 2. Before entering upon a state of life; 3. In dangerous illness; 4. At the time of a Jubilee, a Mission, etc.

Q. How do you make your confession?

A. When I see the priest ready to hear me, I say: "Bless me, father, for I have sinned;" I then repeat half the "I confess, etc.," as far as "through my fault," after which I say, "Since my last confession, which was a week, or month, or year ago (telling how long since), when I received absolution (or did not receive absolution), I accuse myself of"—here, I tell each of my sins and how many times I committed them, as well as I can, at least, how many times a day, or week, or month. When I have confessed my sins, I say: "For these and all my other sins, which I cannot remember, I am heartily sorry; I purpose amendment, and humbly beg pardon of God, and penance and absolution of you, my ghostly father." I then repeat the other half of the "I confess."

Q. What should be done after the confession is made?

A. We should listen while the priest tells us what is good for our soul, and receive the penance which he gives us.

Q. What should we do whilst the priest is giving us absolution?

A. We should renew our act of contrition with all the fervor of which we are capable.

Q. What are we to do if we should not receive absolution?

A. We should humbly go by the advice of the priest, by true amendment render ourselves worthy of absolution, and return to the priest at the appointed time.

Q. What should we do after confession?

A. We should go and kneel down again, and thank God for His great mercy to us.

LESSON XVIII.

SATISFACTION.

Q. What is satisfaction in the sacrament of penance?

A. It is the performance of the penance which the priest gives us in confession.

Q. Why does the priest give us a penance to perform after confession?

A. He gives it for the expiation of the temporal punishment due for sin, and also for the amendment of our life.

Q. Can a man, then, render satisfaction for his sins?

A. No; Jesus Christ alone has satisfied for our sins, but with the help of His grace, we may apply His satisfaction to our souls.

Q. In what manner is the satisfaction of Jesus Christ applied to our souls?

A. In two ways, it either removes the entire punishments due for our sins, or else only a part of them.

Q. On what occasion does it remove all punishments?

A. At baptism.

Q. When does it remove but a part of them?

A. Commonly in the sacrament of penance.

Q. Is not, then, the whole punishment remitted with the guilt ?

A. No; for it often happens that God when He pardons a sin changes the eternal punishment due to the sinner, into a temporal one.

Q. What did the Prophet Nathan say to David, who had already repented for his sin ?

A. "The Lord hath taken away thy sin, nevertheless, the child that is born to thee shall surely die." 2 Kings xii.

Q. Can the sinner obtain the remission of the temporal punishments still due to the divine justice ?

A. He can, with the grace of God, and the Scriptures exhort him to obtain the remission of those punishments.

Q. What says the Prophet Daniel ?

A. "Redeem thy sins with alms." C. 4.

Q. Why does not God always remit the temporal punishments due to sin, together with the eternal ?

A. 1. Because His justice demands that, by enduring such temporal punishments we should make some kind of reparation for the injury done to Him; and, 2. Because God wishes that the fear of such punishment should render us more cautious, and protect us from relapsing into sin.

Q. What sin is it not to perform the penance given in confession?

A. It is commonly a venial sin not to perform at all, through our own fault, the penance given in confession for venial sins, and it is a mortal sin not to perform a great penance given for a mortal sin.

Q. What should we do if we know that we are not able to perform the penance which the priest has given us?

A. We should respectfully request him to give us another which we are able to perform.

Q. Should we not perform any other penance than that which is given us in confession?

A. We should also endeavor, to the best of our power, to satisfy the Divine Justice by the voluntary works of penance, and by patience in our sufferings.

Q. What will await us in the world to come if we neglect to make due satisfaction to divine justice?

A. We shall have so much the more to suffer in purgatory without any merit for heaven.

Q. Under what other obligation are we after confession?

A. We must also, to the best of our ability,

repair the scandal given by our sins, and the injury we have unjustly done to our neighbor, and make use of the means necessary not to fall back into sin, and to amend our life.

Q. What should those think who always fall back into the same grievous sins?

A. They have reason to fear that their confessions are bad.

Q. What means should we especially use in order not to fall back into sin?

A. We should—1. Strictly follow the instructions and directions of our confessor. 2. Carefully avoid the occasions of sin. 3. Daily examine our conscience. 4. Be assiduous in prayer, in hearing the word of God, and receiving the Sacraments of Penance and of the Holy Eucharist; and, 5. Often meditate on the eternal truths.

LESSON XIX.

INDULGENCES.

Q. What means does the Church offer us to cancel the temporal punishments due to our sins?

A. She grants us indulgences.

Q. What is an indulgence?

A. An indulgence is the remission of some temporal punishment.

Q. Are sins remitted by an indulgence?

A. No; sins are remitted in the sacrament of penance, and not by indulgences.

Q. Has the Church power to remit temporal punishments?

A. The Church has power to remove such obstacles as hinder our entrance into heaven. Temporal punishment is an obstacle that hinders our entrance into heaven. Therefore the Church has power to remit temporal punishment.

Q. From whom has the Church the power of granting indulgences?

A. From Jesus Christ, Who made no exception when He said: "Whatsoever thou shalt loose on earth, it shall be loosed also in heaven." Matt. xvi. 19, and xviii. 18.

Q. How does the Church remit the temporal punishment due to our sins?

A. By making to divine justice compensation for us from the inexhaustible treasure of the merits of Christ and His saints.

Q. When did the Church begin to grant indulgences?

A. Ever since the commencement of Christianity.

Q. Did the Apostles grant indulgences?

A. St. Paul remitted to the incestuous man of Corinth, the punishment imposed upon him.

Q. What are his words?

A. "If I have forgiven anything, for your sakes have I done it in the person of Christ." 2 Cor. ii. 10.

Q. What is generally required to gain an indulgence?

A. We must be in the state of grace, and perform the good works prescribed for gaining the indulgence.

Q. What are we bound to believe concerning indulgences?

A. These two articles of faith—1. That God has given to His Church the power of granting indulgences. 2. That the use of indulgences is salutary to the Christian.

Q. Who has the right to grant indulgences?

A. This right belongs especially to our Holy Father, the Pope, who, as successor of St. Peter, has received from Christ the keys of the kingdom of heaven; the bishops have also power to grant partial indulgences.

Q. Why are indulgences very salutary?

A. 1. Because we cancel by them our temporal punishment; at least, to a certain extent.

2. They induce us to do true penance and amend our life, since without penance and amendment of life they cannot be gained.

3. They urge us to receive often the sacraments of Penance and Holy Eucharist, and to perform good works.

4. They console us in our fear of the judgment of God.

Q. Is it not true, then, that the Church, by granting indulgences, frees us from the obligation of doing penance?

A. No; she does not free us from the obligation of doing penance, for the greater our spirit of penance and love for God are the more certain we are of gaining indulgences. The Church wishes to assist us in our efforts to expiate in this life all temporal punishments, in order thus to effect what in ancient times she endeavored to attain by rigorous penitential canons.

Q. How many kinds of indulgences are there?

A. Two. *Plenary Indulgence*, which is the

full remission of all temporal punishment; and *Partial Indulgence,* which is the remission of but a part of the temporal punishment.

Q. What is meant by an indulgence of forty days or seven years?

A. The remission of such a debt of temporal punishment as a person would discharge if he did penance for forty days or seven years, according to the ancient canons of the Church.

Q. What is meant by a Jubilee?

A. A Jubilee is a Plenary Indulgence which the Pope grants every twenty-five years, or upon extraordinary occasions, during which time, in order to increase the spirit of penance in the faithful, confessors have a special power to commute private vows into other works of piety, and absolve in all reserved cases.

Q. Can an indulgence also be rendered available to the souls in Purgatory?

A. Yes, all those which the Pope has expressly declared to be applicable to them.

LESSON XX.

EXTREME UNCTION.

Q. What is Extreme Unction?

A. A sacrament instituted chiefly for the spiritual strength and comfort of those who are in danger of death by sickness.

Q. How do we know that Jesus Christ instituted this sacrament?

A. We know it from Holy Scripture, and the constant, infallible teaching of the Church.

Q. What are the words of Holy Scripture concerning this sacrament?

A. The Apostle St. James writes: "Is any man sick among you, let him bring in the priests of the church, and let them pray over him, anointing him with oil in the name of the Lord; and the prayer of faith shall save the sick man, and the Lord shall raise him up, and if he be in sin, they shall be forgiven him." Chap. v. 14, 15.

Q. Who can receive Extreme Unction?

A. Every Catholic who has come to the use of reason and is in danger of death by sickness.

Q. Is Extreme Unction necessary to salvation?

A. Extreme Unction is not absolutely necessary to salvation: yet it would be a great sin not to receive it through neglect or indifference.

Q. How is this sacrament given?

A. The priest anoints the different senses of the sick person with holy oil, and uses at each anointing, this form of prayer: "Through this holy unction, and His most tender mercy, may the Lord forgive thee whatever sins thou hast committed by thy sight, by thy hearing," etc.

Q. What are the effects of Extreme Unction?

A. Extreme unction—1: Increases sanctifying grace; 2. It remits venial sins and also those mortal sins which the sick person can no more confess; 3. It remits the temporal punishments due to sin; 4. It frees the soul from the darkness of the understanding, the hardness of heart, and from affections to sensible things; 5. It encourages and strengthens the soul in her sufferings and temptations, and gives her great confidence in the mercy of God.

Q. Does this sacrament produce any other effects?

A. Yes; it often relieves the pains of sickness, and sometimes restores perfect health.

Q. How do we know this?

A. From St. James, who says: "The prayer of faith shall save the sick man, and the Lord shall raise him up."

Q. When does Extreme Unction restore health?

A. When it is received in due time and the restoration of health is not hurtful to the soul.

Q. How soon, then, should sick persons be anointed?

A. As soon as their sickness is considered dangerous.

Q. Why should they not put off being anointed till there is no hope of recovery?

A. Because when sick persons are as yet in a state of being cured by natural means, the virtue of the sacrament of Extreme Unction will obtain for them bodily health if their recovery be conducive to their spiritual welfare.

Q. What follows from this?

A. That it is very unreasonable for a sick person to delay being anointed till there is no hope of recovery, because it is then impossible for him, in the natural course of things, to be restored to health by the virtue of Extreme Unction.

Q. What is necessary for sick persons to receive all the graces of this sacrament?

A. They must receive it in the state of grace.

Q. How should they prepare for Extreme Unction?

A. They should previously confess their sins, or at least make an act of contrition, and then receive holy Viaticum, for such is the perpetual practice of the Church.

Q. How often can Extreme Unction be received?

A. In every dangerous illness it can be received *once;* it can, however, be repeated, in the event of a relapse, after the first dangerous crisis has passed.

Q. What should be in the room of a dying person?

A. 1. A crucifix, blessed and indulgenced.

2. A picture of the blessed Virgin Mary.

3. Holy water.

4. A table, covered with a white cloth, and two blessed candles.

5. The Rosary.

LESSON XXI.

HOLY ORDERS.

Q. On whom did Christ confer the priesthood?

A. On His Apostles.

Q. Was the priesthood to end with the death of the Apostles ?

A. No; no more than the Church was to end with them.

Q. How was the priesthood continued ?

A. By the Sacrament of Holy Orders.

Q. What is Holy Orders ?

A. Holy Orders is the sacrament which bestows upon those who receive it the full powers of priesthood, together with a special grace to discharge faithfully their sacred duties.

Q. What is the chief power of priesthood ?

A. The power to change bread and wine into the body and blood of Jesus Christ.

Q. When did Jesus Christ give this power to the Apostles and their successors ?

A. At the Last Supper, when he said: "Do this for a commemoration of me."

Q. Does this sacrament bestow any other power ?

A. Yes; it gives to the receiver also the power of forgiving sins, and of performing other divine functions.

Q. Are there, in Holy Orders, any visible signs by which the communication of the invisible power and grace is indicated ?

A. Yes, there are several; as, the imposition

of hands, and the prayer of the bishop, the delivery of the chalice with wine, and of the paten with bread.

Q. Are the imposition of hands and prayer also mentioned in Holy Scripture?

A. Yes, they are; for St. Paul writes to Bishop Timothy: "I admonish thee that thou stir up the grace of God, which is in thee by the imposition of my hands," 2 Tim. i. 6; and by prayer and imposition of hands, Paul and Barnabas were also ordained: "Then they, fasting and praying, and imposing their hands upon them, sent them away." Acts xiii. 3.

Q. Does not St. Peter, when he writes: "You are a kingly priesthood," teach us that all Christians are priests?

A. From these words of St. Peter, it follows no more that all Christians are true priests, than that all are true kings.

Q. What is the precise meaning of this passage?

A. That all Christians are both priests and kings only in a spiritual sense: they are priests to offer to God sacrifices of faith, hope, and charity, of prayer and mortification, they are kings to rule over their own souls, and to subject their passions to the law of the Gospel.

Q. To whom belongs the power of ordaining priests?

A. To Bishops, and to them alone, as may be shown, both from Scripture and tradition.

Q. How do you prove this from Scripture?

A. St. Paul writing to Bishop Titus, says: "I left thee in Crete, that thou shouldst ordain priests in every city." C. i. 5.

Q. How do you show from tradition, that priests can be ordained by Bishops only?

A. From the beginning of Christianity up to the present time, there cannot be named a single priest that was not ordained by a bishop.

Q. What says St. Epiphanius against Arius?

A. He says that the seventy-fifth heresy is, to say with Arius, that priests and Bishops have an equal power.

Q. What says St. Jerome, writing to Evagrius?

A. He says, that priests do almost the same things as Bishops, but they do not *ordain* priests.

Q. Cannot also civil authorities, or Christian communities, confer spiritual powers?

A. They cannot, for the simple reason that they have no spiritual powers.

Q. Can a priest be deprived of his ordination?

A. No; because ordination, like baptism, imprints an invisible character upon the soul.

Q. Are there any other orders besides those of priests and Bishops?

A. Yes; there are others, which are preparatory degrees to the priesthood.

Q. Which are these orders?

A. 1. The four *minor orders*, by which those who receive them are qualified for various offices connected with the divine service.

2. The order of *sub-deacon*, conferred on him who has to assist the deacon when serving at the altar; and,

3. The order of *deacon*, conferred on him who immediately assists the priest at the altar, and helps him also in baptizing, preaching, and giving Holy Communion.

Q. Who can, and ought to become a priest?

A. He only who is called by God to the holy state of the priesthood.

Q. What should the faithful do in order to obtain worthy priests?

A. They should often pray with fervor to God for so great a gift, and render themselves worthy of it by their love of the Church, and respect for the priesthood.

LESSON XXII.

MATRIMONY.

Q. Who instituted matrimony?

A. God Himself.

Q. When did God institute matrimony?

A. When He gave to Adam in Paradise Eve for his wife.

Q. What life were they to lead?

A. They were to lead a godly life and live together in conjugal fidelity and love.

Q. Was matrimony always respected as a holy institution?

A. The greater part of mankind disregarded the sanctity of matrimony in the same proportion as they forgot God and His holy law.

Q. Who restored matrimony to its original state?

A. Jesus Christ, our blessed Redeemer.

Q. How did He do it?

A. By raising matrimony to the dignity of a sacrament, and by ordaining that marriage should subsist between one man and one woman only, and last until the husband or wife is dead.

Q. What are the words of our Saviour on this subject?

A. "I say to you, that whosoever shall put away his wife, and shall marry another, committeth adultery; and he that shall marry her that is put away, committeth adultery," Matt. xix. 9; and "What God has joined together, let no man put asunder," v. 6.

Q. Why can the bond of marriage never be dissolved?

A. Because Jesus Christ never gave the power either to any ecclesiastical or civil authority to dissolve the bond of marriage.

Q. Are the husband and wife, then, always bound to live together?

A. For grave reasons they may obtain permission from ecclesiastical superiors to live separated from each other. They remain, however, always married until the death of either the husband or the wife.

Q. What follows from this?

A. That neither of them can validly contract a second marriage whilst the other party is alive.

Q. What does St. Paul write on this subject?

A. "To them that are married, not I, but the Lord, commandeth that the wife depart not from her husband. And if she depart, that she remain unmarried, or be reconciled to her husband. And let not the husband put away his wife." 1 Cor. vii. 10, 11

Q. How do we know that matrimony is a sacrament?

A. We know this—1. From St. Paul, who calls matrimony in the Church "a great sacrament." Eph. v. 32.

2. From the infallible teaching of the Church, which has always held that matrimony is a sacrament.

Q. What, then, is matrimony in the Church of Jesus Christ?

A. It is a sacrament by which two single persons, man and woman, are married to each other, and receive grace from God to comply faithfully with the duties of their state until death.

Q. How is this sacrament received?

A. The bridegroom and the bride declare before their pastor and two witnesses, that they take each other for wife and husband, whereupon the priest blesses their union.

Q. What are the duties of married people?

A. 1. They should always live together in peace and conjugal fidelity.

2. They should assist each other in leading holy lives.

3. They should bring up their children in the fear and love of God, and not have such servants in the house as might endanger their innocence.

4. The husband should be kind to his wife, support and cherish her. The wife should obey her husband in all that is just and honorable, and conscientiously manage the domestic concerns.

Q. What are the words of St. Paul on this subject?

A. "As the church is subject to Christ, so also let the wives be to their husbands in all things," that is, in all things that are just and honorable. "Husbands, love your wives, as Christ also loved the church and delivered himself up for it. For no man ever hated his own flesh, but nourisheth and cherisheth it, as also Christ doth the church." Ephes. v. 24–29.

Q. What should married people bear in mind when they are tempted to break their conjugal fidelity?

A. 1. That by adultery they break the

solemn contract they have made in the presence of God and of the Church.

2. That they break the most sacred bond by which human society is united and kept together.

3. That they disturb domestic peace, hinder the good education of their children, and destroy the happiness of the whole family.

4. That they expose themselves to the danger of falling into disgrace and misery, and all kinds of sins and vices, and even of being severely chastised, and at last rejected by God Himself.

Q. What should those bear in mind who intend to enter into the married state?

A. 1. They should not thoughtlessly make the promise of marriage.

2. They should be properly instructed and be free from impediments.

3. They should live innocently previous to their wedding.

4. They should enter the married state with a pure and holy intention.

5. Before they marry they should make a good confession.

6. If possible there should be celebrated for

them the nuptial Mass, during which they receive Holy Communion and the nuptial blessing.

Q. Who make the promise of marriage thoughtlessly?

A. 1. All those who neglect to have previously recourse to God, and disregard His will, the advice of their confessor and of their parents, and the salvation of their own soul in the matter.

2. Those who in their choice care less for religion and virtue, than for temporal advantages; and, 3. Those who do not first consider whether they will be able to fulfil the weighty duties of the married state.

Q. Who will generally prove to be a bad husband?

A. 1. He who cannot support his wife and children.

2. He who is a free-thinker and a member of a secret society; and, 3. He who is addicted to gambling, drinking, cursing, and has no respect for his parents, brothers, and sisters.

Q. Who will generally turn out to be a bad wife and mother?

A. 1. She who is full of vanity and caprice, and is extravagant in dress.

2. She who is not pious, modest, industrious, and economical, and has not the requisite virtue, intelligence, and learning in religious matters in order to be able to give her children a Christian education.

Q. Are people bound to keep their promise of marriage?

A. Yes, they are; unless both parties voluntarily retract it; for either of them, for grave reasons, has a right to retract.

Q. What sin do those commit who receive the sacrament of matrimony with an unholy intention, or in the state of mortal sin?

A. They commit the sin of sacrilege, and, therefore render themselves unworthy of all the Divine graces and blessings.

Q. How many kinds of impediments to matrimony are there?

A. There are two kinds:

1. Such as render marriage *null;* for instance, consanguinity and affinity to the fourth degree, inclusively: spiritual relationship; a solemn vow of chastity; the fact of one of the parties not being baptized; likewise (in those places where the decree of the Council of Trent has been published) the fact of the marriage not being contracted in

the presence of a priest duly authorized and of two witnesses, at least; and others.

2. Such impediments as render marriage *unlawful*, as, for instance, the forbidden times, the simple vow of chastity, a promise of marriage to another person, mixed marriage, etc.

Q. What is understood by the forbidden times?

A. 1. The time between the first Sunday in Advent and the Epiphany of our Lord; and

2. The time between Ash-Wednesday and Low Sunday; within which times the Church forbids the *solemnizing of marriage*, because they have been set apart for penance and prayer.

Q. Can the impediments of marriage ever be dispensed with?

A. The Church can dispense with some, when there are sufficient reasons, but not with all; on this subject the parties must consult their pastor.

Q. What should we think of mixed marriages, that is, of marriages which are contracted between Catholics and non-Catholics?

A. That the Church has always disapproved of such marriages, and never permits them, except on certain conditions.

Q. Why does the Church disapprove of such marriages?

A. 1. Because the Catholic party is exposed to great danger of either losing, or becoming indifferent to the faith.

2. Because the Catholic education of the children is generally deficient, and often even impossible.

3. Because the non-Catholic party does not acknowedge matrimony, either as a sacrament or as indissoluble, and will, therefore, easily apply for a divorce, and marry again, leaving the Catholic party in misery and distress.

4. Because, for that very reason, such a marriage never is a true emblem of the indissoluble union of Christ with His Church, which union should be represented in each Christian marriage.

5. Because the happiness of conjugal union depends, above all, on unity of faith.

Q. On what conditions does the Church permit mixed marriages?

A. On these—1. That the Catholic party be allowed the free exercise of his or her religion.

2. That he or she earnestly endeavor to

gain, by persuasion, the non-Catholic consort to the true Church.

3. That all the children be brought up in the Catholic religion. (Briefs of Pius VIII., and Gregory XVI.)

4. A grave reason for contracting such a marriage.

Q. Is the Church obliged to make such conditions?

A. Yes, for otherwise she would either be indifferent to the eternal welfare of her children, or deny that she alone is the true saving Church.

Q. Can, then, a person never be permitted to contract a mixed marriage unless the Catholic education of the children be previously secured?

A. No; for such a marriage would be a grievous sin against the Catholic Church and the spiritual welfare of the children that may be born; wherefore the Church can, in no case, give her consent to it.

Q. Can parties consent to such a marriage?

A. By no means; and the parents who consent to such a marriage of their child, render themselves guilty of the same sin as the child, and incur a severe responsibility before God.

Q. What should one do in the choice of a state of life?

A. He should, above all things, consult God and the salvation of his soul. If, after mature deliberation, he thinks himself called to the marriage state, let him prepare for it by prayer, good works, and especially by a good general confession, and be careful not to follow those who, by sin and vice, draw the curse of God upon their heads.

Q. Are all men obliged to marry?

A. Not at all; else, why should the Apostle say: "I say to the unmarried, it is good for them if they so continue, even as I." 1 Cor. vii. 8.

Q. Does not the same Apostle say, that, in order to avoid all lewdness, every man should have a wife, and every woman a husband?

A. He only wishes to say, that it is lawful for every man to have *one* wife, and not more, or else, he would not have added: "Art thou loosed from a wife, seek not a wife."

Q. The same Apostle writing to Timothy, says: "It behoveth a Bishop to be the husband of one wife."

A. The Apostle means to say that a widower

who has been married more than once, ought not to be chosen Bishop.

Q. Does not God say to Adam and Eve, and in them to the whole Christian race, "increase and multiply"?

A. These words contain no command, but rather a blessing to render them fruitful.

Q. Does the Catholic Church hinder any one from marrying?

A. No; she leaves every one free in this matter.

Q. Does not the Church forbid priests to marry?

A. She does; but she obliges no one to become a priest.

Q. What does the Church require of those who receive Holy Orders?

A. She requires them to observe the vow of chastity, which they voluntarily make to God.

Q. Why does the Church require the vow of chastity from those who enter into Holy Orders?

A. She does so, in order that her priests may acquit themselves of the functions of the sacred ministry with greater decorum and liberty.

Q. What says St. Paul on this subject?

A. "He that is without a wife, is solicitous for the things that belong to the Lord, how he may please God. But he that is with a wife, is solicitous for the things of the world, how he may please his wife; and he is divided." 1 Cor. vii. 32, 33.

Q. Do we know of any faithful priest or Bishop who, in the primitive ages of the Church, married, after having received Holy Orders ?

A. The enemies of our religion cannot mention one.

Q. What are the words of the sacred canon of the second Council of Carthage ?

A. "We find it proper, that Bishops or priests, and all who are entrusted with the administration of the sacraments, should observe continence."

Q. Why did the council make this regulation ?

A. "In order," says the council, "to observe what was taught by the Apostles, and what has always been practised by the Church."

LESSON XXIII.

SACRAMENTALS.

Q. What are sacramentals?

A. Sacramentals are those things which the Church blesses or consecrates for the divine service, or for our own pious use; as, holy water, salt, oil, ashes, palms, bread, wine, etc.

Q. Why are such things called sacramentals?

A. Because they resemble sacraments.

Q. What is the difference between the sacraments and the sacramentals?

A. 1. The sacraments are instituted by Jesus Christ, and the sacramentals by His Church.

2. The sacraments operate by the efficacy which Jesus Christ gives them; the sacramentals, on the contrary, owe their effects to the prayers and blessings of the Church.

3. The sacraments produce an *infallible* effect, unless we put an obstacle in their way; but the effect of the sacramentals depends principally on the pious intention of the person who makes use of them.

4. The sacraments operate immediate, inward sanctification, but the sacramentals impart but subordinate graces.

5. The sacraments are necessary means of grace, ordained by Jesus Christ, but the sacramentals are only recommended by the Church as useful and pious practices.

Q. Why does the Church bless or consecrate the things belonging to the divine service?

A. In order to sanctify and dedicate them in a particular manner to the divine service, and render them more venerable and salutary to us.

Q. Why does the Church bless also bread, wine, fruits, and the like?

A. To imitate the example of Jesus Christ, Who blessed loaves and fishes; and also in order to pour out God's blessings over all His creatures cursed by the sin of Adam.

Q. What says St. Paul on this subject?

A. "Every creature is sanctified by the word of God and prayer." 1 Tim. iv. 5.

Q. Why are candles blessed on the Feast of the Purification?

A. Because it was on that day that our Saviour, Who is the *Light* of the world, first appeared in the Temple.

Q. Why are ashes distributed on the first day of Lent?

A. In order to remind us that we shall all again return unto the dust and ashes from which our bodies came.

Q. Why are palms blessed a week before Easter?

A. To commemorate the triumphant entry of our Saviour into Jerusalem.

Q. Why is our food blessed?

A. In order to implore God to bestow His blessings upon those who partake of it.

Q. What are exorcisms?

A. Exorcisms are the rites and prayers instituted by the Church for the casting out of devils, or restraining them from hurting persons, or abusing any of God's creatures to their harm.

Q. What are Agnus Deis?

A. Virgin wax, stamped with the image of the Lamb of God, blessed by the Pope with solemn prayers, and anointed with the holy chrism.

Q. What is the scapular?

A. The scapular is a badge of devotion to the Blessed Virgin, which was revealed to blessed Simon Stock, Superior of the Carmelites, in the twelfth century.

Q. What did the Blessed Virgin promise to Simon Stock?

A. She promised to obtain for those who constantly wear the scapular, and endeavor to lead a Christian life, extraordinary graces, and especially the grace of a happy death, and a speedy deliverance from Purgatory.

Q. Why should we make a devout use of the sacramentals?

A. Because, through them, we share in the prayers and blessing of the Church, in whose name the priest consecrates and blesses them.

Q. Has, then, the prayer of the Church a particular efficacy?

A. Yes, because she is the body of Christ, animated and guided by His spirit, and her prayer is always united with the prayer of Jesus Christ and His saints.

Q. For what does the Church usually pray when she consecrates or blesses anything?

A. She prays for protection against the devil, for peace, blessing, well-being of soul and body, and for the averting of God's judgments.

Q. What is the prayer of the Church when the priest blesses water?

A. She prays that by the power of the Holy

Ghost the snares of the wicked spirit may become harmless for those who use holy water.

Q. How long has holy water been in use ?

A. From the beginning of Christianity, as St. Cyprian, St. Cyril, St. Augustine, and many other Fathers testify.

Q. How should we use holy water ?

A. A good Christian sprinkles himself with holy water, not only when he enters or leaves the church, but also when he enters or leaves his house, when he rises in the morning or retires at night, and on other occasions, begging of God at the same time, that, through the blood of Jesus Christ, he may be more and more purified and protected from all dangers of soul and body.

LESSON XXIV.

PRAYER.

Q. What is prayer ?

A. Prayer is the elevation of the mind and heart to God.

Q. How do we raise our mind and heart to God ?

A. By thinking of God, by adoring, praising, and thanking Him, and by begging of Him blessings for soul and body.

Q. What is to praise God?

A. It is to rejoice at His greatness, goodness, and other perfections, and to adore and glorify Him because of them.

Q. Are we bound to praise God?

A. Certainly we are. God created us solely for that end, that we might glorify and praise Him in time and for all eternity.

Q. Ought we also to thank God for His gifts and blessings?

A. Yes, because ingratitude is a detestable vice, whereas gratitude is the best means to obtain new blessings.

Q. Must we also ask God for His gifts and blessings?

A. Yes, because Jesus Christ has commanded us to do so.

Q. What are His words?

A. He says: "Ask, and it shall be given you; seek, and you shall find; knock, and it shall be opened to you." Luke xi. 9.

Q. Is prayer necessary for salvation?

A. God has made prayer a necessary means of salvation, both for sinners and the just.

Q. Why is prayer necessary for sinners?

A. Because, without prayer they cannot recover the grace of God and be saved.

Q. Why is prayer necessary for the just?

A. Because, without prayer, the just cannot persevere in the grace of God to the end.

Q. But does not God know of what we stand in need?

A. God knows, indeed, all our wants; but we do not pray to God to make known to Him what we need, but to acknowledge that we depend on Him as the Giver of all blessings.

Q. Does God hear our prayer?

A. God hears our prayer whenever we ask of Him anything that may tend to our salvation.

Q. Who has assured us of this?

A. Jesus Christ, Himself, in these words: "Amen, amen, I say to you, if you ask the Father anything in my name, he will give it you." John xvi. 23.

Q. But does not this promise apply only to the just?

A. No; Jesus Christ, who said, "Whatsoever you ask, you shall receive" (Matt. xxi. 22), has also said: "Every one who asks, shall receive." Matt. vii. 7.

Q. What are the chief effects of prayer?

A. Prayer restores sinners to the grace of God; it keeps the just united to God by faith, hope, and charity; it detaches them from this world, and strengthens them against the attacks of their enemies: in a word, it obtains from God every grace, especially the grace of perseverance.

Q. How must we pray to obtain whatever we ask of God?

A. We must pray—1. For a lawful object. 2. With humility. 3. With devotion and fervor. 4. Our prayer must be followed by amendment of life. 5. It must be united with forgiveness of injuries. 6. It must be confident. 7. Our prayer must be persevering.

Q. When is the object of our prayer lawful?

A. When we pray for something that tends to our salvation.

Q. When is the object of our prayer unlawful?

A. When we pray for something that is hurtful to our salvation, or when we pray for deliverance from certain evils, which God knows to be useful to our advancement in humility, and other virtues; or when we pray for something from motives of ambition, or from indiscreet zeal and the like.

Q. When do we pray with humility?

A. We pray with humility if we pray with the consciousness of our own unworthiness, and with a sincere acknowledgment of our own weakness and misery.

Q. When do we pray with devotion and fervor?

A. When we think of what we say to God in prayer, and to whom we say it, and are in earnest to obtain what we ask.

Q. Why must our prayers be followed by amendment of life?

A. Because God cannot hear our prayer for salvation if we have not the desire to abandon sin, and the occasions of sin.

Q. What must we do if we have not this desire?

A. We must earnestly ask it of God, and He will give it to us.

Q. Why must our prayer be united with forgiveness of injuries?

A. Because Jesus Christ has assured us that our prayer will not be heard if we do not forgive our enemies.

Q. When do we pray with confidence?

A. When we firmly hope that God will hear our prayer if we pray for something that tends to His honor and our own salvation.

Q. What should encourage us to pray with unwavering confidence?

A. 1. The unbounded yearning of God, our Father, to communicate to us Himself, and all His gifts. 2. The fact that all the graces we can ask have been merited for us by Jesus Christ. 3. The solemn assurance of Jesus Christ that His Heavenly Father will give us whatever we ask, for the sake of His merits.

Q. Why must we pray with perseverance?

A. Although Jesus Christ has promised to give us everything we ask of Him, yet He has not promised to hear our prayers immediately; therefore we must continue to pray until He graciously grants our prayer.

Q. Why does God often delay hearing our prayer?

A. God delays hearing our prayer for several reasons:

1. That He may try our confidence in Him.

2. That we may long more ardently for His gifts and hold them in higher esteem.

3. That He may keep us near Him and give us occasion to pray with greater fervor and earnestness.

4. By delaying, He wishes to unite Himself more closely to us.

5. God often delays granting our prayer, if what we ask for be not profitable to us at the time, but would be so only at a later period.

Q. How often must we pray?

A. Jesus Christ says that "we ought always to pray, and not to faint." Luke xviii. 1. It is, therefore, considered a mortal sin to neglect prayer for a whole month.

Q. How is it possible for us to pray always?

A. It will be easy for us to pray always if we have a great love for prayer or for conversation with God.

Q. How so?

A. Because this love will make us think often of God's presence, and of frequently raising up our hearts to Him in short aspirations and loving affections.

Q. What should we do in order to learn how to pray well?

A. To know how to pray well is a great gift of the Holy Ghost. Therefore we should incessantly ask God to bestow this gift upon us.

Q. When are we under particular obligation to pray?

A. We must pray whenever we are tempted to sin; in times of private and public calamities; before and after meals, and more especially on rising in the morning, and before going to bed at night.

Q. Where should we pray?

A. We should pray everywhere, but especially in the church, before Jesus Christ in the Blessed Sacrament.

Q. For whom should we pray?

A. We should pray for all men. For the living and the dead; for friends and enemies; especially for our parents, brothers, and sisters, benefactors, spiritual and temporal superiors, and for the conversion of heretics and infidels.

Q. How many kinds of prayer are there?

A. There are two kinds of prayer—Vocal prayer, and mental prayer, called meditation.

Q. What prayer is called vocal?

A. That which is said in distinct words.

Q. When do we perform mental prayer or meditation?

A. When we reflect upon the life and sufferings of Jesus Christ, as we do, for instance, when making the Way of the Cross, or when we reflect upon the perfections of God, or other truths of our religion, in order to excite in our souls pious sentiments and firm resolutions to lead a holy life.

LESSON XXV.

OUR LORD'S PRAYER.

Q. Which is the best of all prayers?

A. The Lord's Prayer, or the "Our Father."

Q. Why is the Our Father called the Lord's Prayer?

A. Because Jesus Christ, our Lord, has taught it to us and commanded us to say it. Matt. vi. 9–13.

Q. Why is this prayer called the best of all prayers?

A. Because in this prayer we ask for all those graces and blessings of which we chiefly stand in need.

Q. Of what does the Lord's Prayer consist?

A. It consists of an invocation and seven petitions.

Q. What is the invocation ?

A. " Our Father, who art in heaven."

Q. Why does Jesus Christ teach us to pray Our " Father," and not Our " Lord or God," who art in heaven ?

A. He wishes to remind us that God is our Father, who, as such, has an unbounded yearning to bestow on us both Himself and all his goods, and that therefore we should pray to Him with an unlimited confidence.

Q. Why do we say our Father, and not my Father ?

A. Because God is the Father of all men, and we are all his children, and therefore we should love one another as brothers, and pray for one another.

Q. Why did Jesus Christ add the words, " who art in heaven " ?

A. To remind us that heaven is our true country, for the sake of which we should be willing to undergo every trouble and hardship.

Q. What do we pray for when we say " Hallowed be thy name " ?

A. We pray that God may be known, praised, loved, and served by all men.

Q. Why is this the first petition ?

A. Because we should esteem the honor and glory of God first before all things.

Q. What do we pray for when we say "Thy kingdom come"?

A. We pray that the kingdom of God—the Catholic Church—may be more and more extended, and that God may come and reign in our hearts by His grace and may admit us hereafter to His heavenly kingdom.

Q. What do we pray for when we say "Thy will be done on earth as it is in heaven"?

A. We pray that God may enable us by His grace, to do His will in all things as faithfully as the blessed do in heaven.

Q. What do we pray for when we say "Give us this day our daily bread"?

A. We pray that God may give us daily all that is necessary for our souls and bodies.

Q. What do we pray for when we say "Forgive us our trespasses as we forgive them that trespass against us"?

A. We pray that God may forgive us our sins, as we forgive others the injuries they do us.

Q. What do we pray for when we say "Lead us not into temptation"?

A. We pray God that He may give us grace not to yield to temptation.

Q. What is temptation?

A. Temptation is any thought, or desire, or word, or action that may lead us to sin.

Q. Who tempts us to sin?

A. Our own corrupt nature, the world, and the devil.

Q. Why does God permit us to be tempted to sin?

A. To keep us humble, to try our faithfulness, or to punish us for our unfaithfulness, to increase our zeal for virtue, and to add to our merits.

Q. Is it a sin to be tempted to sin?

A. To be tempted to sin is no sin as yet; but to expose ourselves without a sufficient reason to temptation, or to yield to it, is a sin.

Q. What must we do whenever we are tempted to sin?

A. We must immediately pray to God to give us grace to overcome the temptation.

Q. What do we pray for when we say "But deliver us from evil"?

A. We pray that God may free us from all evil of soul and body.

Q. What do we express by the word "Amen," at the end of the Our Father?

A. "So be it," that is, may God grant these our petitions.

LESSON XXVI.

THE ANGELIC SALUTATION, OR HAIL MARY.

Q. Of what is the Hail Mary composed?

A. Of a prayer of praise and a prayer of petition.

Q. Of what is the prayer of praise composed?

A. Of the words of the archangel Gabriel and St. Elizabeth.

Q. Which are the words of the archangel Gabriel?

A. "*Hail* (Mary), full of grace, the Lord is with thee, blessed art thou among women." Luke, i. 28.

Q. When did the archangel speak thus to Mary?

A. When he announced to her that she would become the mother of God.

Q. Which are the words of St. Elizabeth?

A. "And blessed is the fruit of thy womb," Luke i. 42, to which we add the name of Jesus.

Q. On what occasion did St. Elizabeth speak those words to Mary?

A. When the Blessed Virgin Mary visited her.

Q. What is the meaning of the word "Hail"?

A. It means rejoice, or be glad.

Q. What is the meaning of the word "Mary"?

A. It means Star of the Sea.

Q. Why do we call Mary "Full of grace"?

A. Because, from the very first moment of her life she was filled with grace and always increased in grace, and because of her was born our Saviour Jesus Christ, the Author of all graces.

Q. Why do we say "The Lord is with thee"?

A. Because God always was with Mary in a most special manner, by reason of which she is justly called the chosen daughter of the Heavenly Father, the true mother of the Divine Son, and the immaculate spouse of the Holy Ghost.

Q. Why do we say "Blessed art thou among women"?

A. Because Mary alone among all women was chosen to be the Mother of God, while she remained at the same time a virgin.

Q. Why do we add the words "Blessed is the fruit of thy womb, Jesus"?

A. To show that the veneration of Mary is inseparable from the veneration of Christ, and that we praise the mother for the sake of her Son.

Q. Of what is the prayer of petition composed?

A. Of the words added by the Church: "Holy Mary, Mother of God, pray for us sinners, now, and at the hour of our death. Amen."

Q. Why were those words added by the Church?

A. That we might profess before the whole world that Mary is truly the Mother of God, and that we might often implore the help of her prayers in all our necessities, and obtain, through her intercession, the grace of a happy death.

Q. Is it a great grace to die a happy death?

A. It is a grace so great that we cannot merit it by anything whatsoever; but God gives it to those who daily pray for it.

Q. By what means shall we die a happy death?

A. 1. By leading a good life.

2. By performing many good works.

3. By being charitable to the poor.

4. By being devout to the Blessed Virgin.

5. By praying often for the grace of a happy death.

Q. Who are the patrons of a happy death?

A. 1. Our dear mother, the Blessed Virgin Mary.

2. St. Joseph.

3. The saints whose names we have received in baptism or confirmation.

4. Our Guardian Angel.

5. St. Michael, the Archangel.

6. St. Barbara.

7. The Holy Innocents.

8. Any saints or angels to whom we may have a particular devotion.

Q. Why do we say the Hail Mary after the Our Father ?

A. In order to beg the mother of God to add to our prayers her own most powerful intercession with her Divine Son.

Q. Why do we so often say the Hail Mary ?

A. To put us in mind of the Incarnation of the Son of God, and to honor His blessed mother.

Q. Are the prayers of the Mother of God very powerful ?

A. They are more powerful than the prayers of all the saints united, so that it was never heard that any one who had recourse to Mary, and with true devotion implored her intercession, was abandoned by God.

Q. What prayer do we say in the morning, at

noon, and at night, when the bell is rung for the "Angelus"?

A. We pray: "The Angel of the Lord declared unto Mary. And she conceived of the Holy Ghost. Hail Mary," etc.

"Behold the handmaid of the Lord. Be it done unto me according to thy word. Hail, Mary," etc.

"And the word was made flesh. And dwelt among us. Hail, Mary," etc.

"Pray for us, O holy mother of God!

"That we may be made worthy of the promises of Christ."

"Let us pray.

"Pour forth, we beseech Thee, O Lord, Thy grace into our hearts, that we to whom the Incarnation of Christ, thy Son, was made known by the message of an angel, may, by His Passion and Cross, be brought to the glory of His resurrection, through the same Christ, our Lord. Amen."

Q. Why do we say this prayer, commonly called the "Angelus"?

A. To thank God for the Incarnation of Christ, to honor the Blessed Virgin, and to recommend ourselves to her protection.

Q. What is the Rosary?

A. It is a very easy and most useful form of prayer, which was revealed to St. Dominic, in 1206, by the blessed Virgin Mary.

Q. Why was the Rosary revealed to St. Dominic and introduced by him?

A. In order that the people might learn to meditate on the sacred mysteries of our redemption, while they were occupied in the prayers which they counted on their beads.

Q. What were the effects of this method of meditation and prayer?

A. This method of meditation and prayer was attended by the special blessing of God, and has everywhere produced the most abundant fruits of grace.

Q. What has the Church done in order to encourage the practice of saying the Rosary?

A. Several Popes have attached very ample indulgences to the beads used in this devotion.

Q. Of what is the Rosary composed?

A. Of the Apostles' Creed, the Our Father, the Hail Mary, and the Glory be to the Father, etc.

Q. How many subjects of meditation does the Rosary contain?

A. The Rosary contains fifteen subjects of meditation, and these meditations are called mysteries, taken from the lives of our Lord and of His blessed mother.

Q. How are these mysteries divided?

A. They are divided into three distinct parts, called the *joyful*, the *sorrowful*, and the *glorious* mysteries.

Q. What do the joyful mysteries represent?

A. The Incarnation, the Birth, and the Infancy of our Blessed Redeemer.

Q. What do the sorrowful mysteries represent?

A. Our Lord's Passion and Death.

Q. What do the glorious mysteries represent?

A. The Risen Life of our Lord, and His triumphant Ascension into Heaven.

Q. Which are the five joyful mysteries?

A. 1. The Annunciation of our Lady, when the Son of God was conceived.

2. The Visitation to St. Elizabeth.

3. The Nativity of our Lord Jesus Christ.

4. The Presentation of our Lord in the Temple.

5. The finding of our Lord in the Temple among the Doctors.

Q. Which are the five sorrowful mysteries?

A. 1. The Agony of our Lord in the Garden.

2. The scourging of our Lord at the Pillar.

3. The crowning of our Lord with thorns.

4. His carrying of the Cross to Mount Calvary.

5. His Crucifixion and Death on the Cross.

Q. Which are the five glorious mysteries?

A. 1. The Resurrection of our Lord.

2. His Ascension into heaven.

3. The coming of the Holy Ghost.

4. The Assumption of our Lady into heaven.

5. Her coronation above all angels and saints in heaven.

Q. Give a short and easy method of saying the beads with the mysteries without a book?

A. Begin as usual:—

1. With the sign of the Cross.

2. Say the Creed, the Our Father, and three Hail Marys, and the Glory be to the Father, for an increase of faith, hope, and charity.

3. Then go on with the recitation of the decades as follows:

When you choose for your devotion the *joyful mysteries*, say the Hail Marys of the first decade in this manner: "Hail Mary, full of grace, the Lord is with thee, blessed art thou amongst women, and blessed is the fruit of thy womb, Jesus, *Whom thou didst conceive at the message of an angel:* Holy Mary, Mother of God, pray for us sinners, now, and at the hour of our death. Amen."

In the second decade, instead of the words "*Whom thou didst conceive,*" say: "*Whom thou didst carry in thy womb on thy visit to Elizabeth.*" Holy Mary, Mother of God, etc.

In the third decade, after the word Jesus, say: "*Who was born of thee at Bethlehem.*"

In the fourth decade: "*Whom thou didst present in the temple.*"

In the fifth: "*Whom thou didst find in the temple.*"

Having thus recited the five decades, end with the following

PRAYER.

O God! whose only begotten Son, by His life, death, and resurrection, has purchased for us the rewards of eternal life: grant, we beseech Thee, that, while we meditate upon these mysteries in the most holy Rosary of the Blessed Virgin Mary, we may imitate what they contain, and obtain what they promise: through the same Christ, our Lord. Amen.

When you select for your devotion the *sorrowful mysteries*, in the first decade, after the word Jesus, in the Hail Mary, say: "*Who sweat blood for us in the garden.*"

In the second decade: "*Who was scourged for us.*"

In the third: "*Who was crowned with thorns for us.*"

In the fourth: "*Who has carried His Cross for us.*"

In the fifth: "*Who was crucified for us.*"

For the glorious mysteries:

In the first decade, say: "*Who arose from the dead.*"

In the second: "*Who ascended into heaven.*"

In the third: "*Who sent the Holy Ghost.*"

In the fourth: "*Who took thee up into heaven.*"

In the fifth: "*Who crowned thee Queen of heaven.*"

Q. What is the Living Rosary?

A. The Living Rosary is the union of fifteen persons who say the whole Rosary, or fifteen decades every day, each person saying one decade.

Q. Why is it called Living?

A. Because, if a member dies, another takes his place, and thus the devotion is constantly kept up.

Q. What Pope approved of the Living Rosary?

A. Pope Gregory XVI. in his Brief of Jan. 27, 1832, and Feb. 2, 1832.

Q. What are Confraternities?

A. They are pious associations, generally approved of by the Popes, and established for the spiritual welfare of their members.

Q. How is the spiritual welfare promoted in Confraternities?

A. The members of Confraternities frequently pray for, and encourage one another in the performance of good works, and the frequenting of the sacraments; while God assists and protects them in a more particular manner, and the Church, too, grants them many spiritual privileges.

Q. What says St. Alphonsus, concerning those who do not belong to any Confraternity?

A. He says: There are found more sins in a man who does not belong to Confraternities, than in twenty who frequent them.

ADDITIONAL QUESTIONS AND ANSWERS.

For page 37.

Q. Give some instances?

A. The Council of Ephesus, in forming its judgment against Nestorius, said that it did so, "following the Canons and the Epistle of the Pope." The same Council also ratified, without any farther examination, the Papal condemnation of Pelagianism.

At Chalcedon, the Council, in drawing up its decisions on the point of controversy, did not appeal to the Synod which had been held at Constantinople under Flavian, but only to the decree of the Pontiff.

In the judgment upon Eutyches, Cecropius, Bishop of Sebaste, declared, in the name of all his brethren, that the Bishop of Rome had sent to them a formulary; that they all followed him, and subscribed his Epistle.

The Sixth General Council, in like manner, declared that it adhered to the dogmatic Epistle of Pope Agatho, and by it condemned the heresy.

For page 38.

Q. Has it always been acknowledged to be the prerogative of the first See in the Christian world that the Bishop of Rome could be judged by no man?

A. It was never heard of that the Head of the Church should be placed in judgment before his own subjects.

Q. Were the decisions of the Catholic Bishops assembled in a General Council ever binding on conscience as teachings of the Holy Ghost, before the Pope had declared and confirmed them as such?

A. They were not.

Q. Give an instance.

A. The Fifth General Council, for instance, held in 381, acquired the authority of an Œcumenical Council only by the subsequent acceptance and confirmation of the Pope.

APPENDIX.

A RULE OF LIFE

FOR THOSE WHO, LIVING IN THE WORLD, ASPIRE AFTER PERFECTION.

IN THE MORNING.

1. Rise at a fixed hour, for example, six o'clock; do not remain longer in bed without a reasonable motive.

2. As soon as you awake, offer your heart to God, make the sign of the Cross, and dress yourself quickly and modestly. Then, on your knees, say three "Hail Marys," in honor of the Immaculate Heart of the Blessed Virgin Mary, to obtain a great purity of body and soul.

3. Say your morning prayers, and make a meditation during half, or at least a quarter of an hour. It is better to say short prayers—"Our Father" and "Hail Mary,"—or to say your prayers going to or at your work, than to say no prayers at all.

4. Hear Mass, if it is possible.

DURING THE COURSE OF THE DAY.

5. Read a spiritual book for at least a quarter of an hour.

6. Say your beads, if possible, with the rest of the household.

7. Pay a visit to the Blessed Sacrament, and to the Blessed Virgin Mary, in the church if you can do so.

N. B.—For these three last exercises you can choose whatever time will least interfere with your daily occupations.

8. Frequently make short ejaculatory prayers, above all at the beginning and end of your actions. Employ chiefly acts of the love of God, such as these: *My dear Jesus, I love Thee....I wish very much to love Thee .... make me love Thee more and more, etc.*

9. Practise the mortification of the eyes, of the ears, and of the tongue, by sometimes refraining from looking, hearing, or saying things, which, though not dangerous, are useless, in order to be able more easily to abstain from what is dangerous, or even bad.

10. Seize carefully every opportunity of suffering any little pain, contradiction, or humiliation, for the love of God. In every such occasion submit yourself to the will of God, saying: *O my God, this is Thy Will; may Thy holy Will be done!*

11. At your meals deprive yourself in part or entirely of some little thing you are fond of; and never completely satisfy your appetite.

12. Do not eat between meals without necessity.

13. Fly idleness, bad company, and every occasion of sin, especially those in which chastity is in danger.

14. In temptations, especially those of impurity, make the sign of the Cross, if you are alone ; and say in your heart, *Jesus and Mary, help me.* If the temptation still continues, do not be troubled, but pray with greater earnestness, saying, *My dear Jesus, I would rather die than offend Thee.*

15. If you have the misfortune to commit a sin, do not give way to trouble, even though the sin be grievous, but make immediately a good act of contrition, with the firm purpose not to fall again, and to confess it as soon as possible.

IN THE EVENING.

16. At a fixed hour, for example, nine o'clock, say your night prayers, and make your examination of conscience ; recite the Litany of the Blessed Virgin, and then read over the subject of next morning's meditation.

17. Having said, on your knees, the three "Hail Marys," as in the morning, undress yourself with all modesty, and be careful to remain always decently covered in bed, and to preserve a modest posture.

18. Until you fall asleep, occupy your mind with the subject of the morrow's meditation, or with the remembrance of death, or some other pious thought.

19. Choose a good Confessor, in whom you have confidence ; open your heart to him without reserve, and be guided by his advice ; do not quit him without a strong reason.

20. Go to confession once a week, and receive the Holy Communion as often as your director judges proper.

21. Attend sermons and instructions as often as you can, endeavoring always to apply them to yourself, and to draw some practical resolution from them; enter some pious confraternity, with the sole view of attending to the interests of your soul.

22. If your health will permit, fast on every Saturday, and on the eves of the Feasts of the Blessed Virgin. At least perform in her honor some little act of mortification on those days, according to your state of health and your occupations. Nourish in your heart a tender devotion towards the Blessed Virgin, and address to her from time to time this fervent prayer: *My good Mother Mary, help me to love your divine Son Jesus with all my heart.* Wear the scapular, or at least the miraculous medal.

OBSERVATION.

As this rule of life does not of itself impose any obligation under pain of sin, no one must be alarmed if he cannot follow it in every thing. Let each one take that which is in accordance with the duties of his state of life, which ought always to be attended to in preference to any exercises of piety which are not of obligation.

Thus let each one do what he can, but cheerfully, and for the love of God.

A SHORT PRACTICAL METHOD OF MEDITATION.

In the preparation, say: 1. *My God, I believe that Thou art really present, and I adore Thee with all my heart* 2. *O Lord, I ought to be at this moment in hell; I am sorry for having offended Thee: grant me pardon.* 3. *O Eternal Father, for the love of Jesus and Mary, enlighten me.* Then recommend yourself to the most holy Virgin, to St. Joseph, to your Angel Guardian, and to your Patron Saint; for this purpose say a "Hail Mary," and then pass on to the meditation.

Read the meditation, and pause wherever you find food for reflection. After this, be careful to make affections of humility, gratitude, and, above all, of sorrow and love, resigning yourself in every thing to the divine will, and make an offering of yourself, saying: *O Lord, do with me whatever Thou pleasest, and tell me what Thou wilt have me to do, for I wish to do Thy will in all things.*

Be also very careful to ask for particular blessings and graces, as for example, begging of God the grace of holy perseverance, His divine Love, and the light and strength to do always the divine Will, and always to pray.

Before concluding your meditation, make a special resolution to avoid some defect, into which you fall most frequently; and then finish with an "Our Father" and "Hail Mary;" and remember always to recommend to God the souls in Purgatory, and poor sinners.

Live Jesus our Love
And Mary our Hope!

MORNING PRAYERS.

As soon as you awake, make the sign ✠ of the cross, saying:

GLORY be to the Father who hath created me. Glory be to the Son who hath redeemed me. Glory be to the Holy Ghost who hath sanctified me.

Blessed be the holy and undivided Trinity, now and forever. Amen.

On rising from your bed, say:

IN the name of our Lord Jesus Christ, I arise. May He bless, preserve and govern me and bring me to everlasting life. Amen.

While you are dressing, occupy yourself with pious thoughts. As soon as you are dressed, kneel down and say:

MY God, I adore Thee and love Thee with all my heart.

2. I thank Thee for all Thy benefits, and especially for having preserved me this night.

3. I offer Thee whatever I may do or suffer this day, in union with the actions and sufferings of Jesus and Mary, with the intention of gaining all the indulgences I can in favor of the souls in Purgatory.

4. I intend that every thought, word and work, and suffering shall be for Thy greater glory, and in honor of the Blessed Virgin Mary, of my Guardian Angel and of all my holy patrons.

5. I resolve to conform myself to Thy holy will, and particularly in those things which are contrary to my inclinations, saying always: May the most just, most high, most adorable will of God be in all things done, and praised, and for ever magnified.

6. I resolve to fly from all sin this day, and especially such a one (here mention the fault into which you fall the oftenest,) and I beg of Thee to give me perseverance for the love of Jesus Christ.

My Jesus, keep Thy hand over me this day! Most Holy Mary, take me beneath thy mantle! And do Thou, Eternal Father, help me for the love of Jesus and Mary!

Then say the following prayers:

The Lord's Prayer. The Hail Mary. The Creed.

Afterwards say three Hail Mary's in honor of the purity of the B. V. M.

HOW TO PASS THE DAY IN A HOLY MANNER.

When you are tempted to sin, say often:

Jesus and Mary.

When the bell rings for the Angelus, at morning, noon and evening, pray as follows:

THE Angel of the Lord declared unto Mary,
And she conceived of the Holy Ghost.
Hail Mary, etc.

Behold the handmaid of the Lord,
May it be done unto me according to thy word.
Hail Mary, etc.

And the Word was made flesh,
And dwelt among us.
Hail Mary, etc.

PRAYER.

POUR forth, we beseech Thee, O Lord, Thy grace into our hearts, that we to whom the incarnation of Christ, Thy Son, has been made known by the message of an angel, may, by his passion and cross, be brought to the glory of His resurrection, through the same Christ, our Lord. Amen.

Whoever says the Angelus daily for a whole month, and goes to confession and communion in the course of the same month, gains a plenary indulgence.—Benedict XIII.

Before meals, say:

BLESS us, O Lord, and these Thy gifts which we are about to receive from Thy bounty, through Christ our Lord. Amen.

After meals, say:

WE give Thee thanks, Almighty God, for all Thy benefits, who livest and reignest world without end. Amen.

May the souls of the faithful departed rest in peace! Amen.

When the clock strikes, say:

MY Jesus, I love Thee; never permit me to offend Thee again, and let me never be separated from Thee.

In adverse circumstances, say:

LORD, since Thou hast so willed it, I will it also.

When you know or doubt of some sin you have committed, say immediately:

MY God, I am sorry for having offended Thee; I will sin no more.

And if it was a grievous sin, confess it directly.

NIGHT PRAYERS.

In the name of the ✠ Father, and of the Son, and of the Holy Ghost. Amen.

COME, Holy Ghost, fill the hearts of Thy faithful, and enkindle in them the fire of Thy love.

V. Send forth Thy Spirit, and they shall be created,

R. And Thou shalt renew the face of the earth.

PRAYER.

O GOD, who hast taught the hearts of the faithful by the light of Thy Holy Spirit, grant us, by the same Spirit, to have a right judgment in all things, and evermore to rejoice in His consolation, through Jesus Christ, our Lord. Amen.

ACT OF THANKSGIVING.

I THANK Thee, O Lord, for all the graces and benefits which Thou hast bestowed upon me, especially for having given me

Jesus Christ for my redeemer, the Blessed Virgin for my mother, and for having called me to be a child of the only one true Catholic Church.

Ask yourself then seriously and carefully the following questions, by way of an

EXAMINATION OF CONSCIENCE.

Have I not sinned this day—

In thought? By willingly entertaining some unchaste, uncharitable, or covetous thoughts?

In word? By using immodest language—uttering oaths—curses—lies—passionate, slanderous, profane, or irreverent words? Have I given scandal so?

In action? By being idle?—slow or impatient about my work? Have I not been in evil or dangerous company? Done any immodest action? Been too free in my manners? Been rude, cross, or disobedient towards my parents or superiors? Been unkind, insolent, malicious, cruel or unjust towards my neighbor? Have I given any bad example to my children, my servants, my neighbors?

By omission? Have I refused or neglected to do any act of charity? Been watchful over my children, and others depending upon me, and careful for their salvation? Have I omitted my prayers, my penance, or some other duty?

Finally, examine whether you have kept the resolution you made in the morning. If not, consider well what was the cause of your fall, and seek out the means to preserve you from falling in future. For be assured that your whole Christian perfection depends upon the diligent examination of conscience.

Having finished this examination, make the following acts of Faith, Hope, Charity, and Contrition:

ACT OF FAITH.*

O MY God! who art the infallible Truth! I believe everything which the Holy Church commands me to believe, because Thou hast revealed it to her. I believe that Thou art the Creator of heaven and earth, that Thou dost reward the just in paradise,

* According to a concession of Pope Benedict XIV., granted in December, 1754, an indulgence of seven years and seven quarantines (280 days) may be gained by devoutly repeating these acts. If recited daily for a month, with confession and communion made in the course of the same month, a plenary indulgence is gained.

and punish the wicked eternally in hell. I believe that Thou art one divine essence in three persons, namely, the Father, the Son, and the Holy Ghost. I believe the carnation and the death of Jesus Christ. In a word, I believe all that the Holy Church believes. I thank Thee for having made me a Christian, and a Catholic, and I protest that I will live and die in this holy faith.

ACT OF HOPE.

O MY God! I confide in Thy promises, because Thou art faithful, powerful, and merciful, and hope, through the merits of Jesus Christ, for the pardon of my sins, final perseverance, and the everlasting glory of paradise.

ACT OF CHARITY.

O MY God! I love Thee with all my heart, and above all things, because Thou art infinitely good, and worthy of infinite love, and for love of Thee I love my neighbor as myself.

ACT OF CONTRITION.

O MY God! I am heartily sorry for all my sins, because by them I have lost heaven and deserved hell; but more than all because I have offended Thee, O my God, who art infinitely good, and worthy of all my love; but now I am firmly resolved, by the help of Thy grace, never to sin against Thee any more, and to avoid all the occasions of sin.

Then say, for the repose of the souls of the faithful departed:

One Our Father and one Hail Mary, with

V. Eternal rest give to them, O Lord.

R. And let everlasting light enlighten them.

V. May they rest in peace.

R. Amen.

Go to bed now, with holy thoughts, or repeating with your lips some short fervent ejaculations of love, and continue thus until you fall asleep. If you awake in the night, lift up your thoughts immediately to God, that no evil imaginations may enter your mind, and if they should, say promptly:

O JESUS! O Mary! No, no, let me die rather than do, or wish, or even think of such a thing. In the name of the Father, and of the Son, and of the Holy Ghost. Amen.

DEVOTION AT HOLY MASS.

HOW TO HEAR MASS WITH PROFIT.

To hear Mass with profit, we must hear it with attention, and for the intentions for which Jesus Christ offers Himself at Mass to His Heavenly Father. Now, Jesus Christ offers Himself to His Father—1. To honor Him for us; 2. To thank Him for us; 3. To satisfy Him for our sins; and 4. To obtain for us all kinds of blessings and graces. Mass may be heard for these intentions in the following manner:

FROM THE BEGINNING OF MASS TO THE GOSPEL.

Honor and praise the infinite Majesty of God, and acknowledge His supreme dominion over us by offering to Him the infinite acts of Divine praise and adoration of His Son and our Redeemer, Jesus Christ.

Prayer.

O my God, I adore Thee, and acknowledge Thee as the Lord and Master of my soul. All that I am, all that I have, I have from Thee. Thy infinite Majesty demands an infinite homage and worship. To acquit myself of this great debt, I offer Thee the humiliations and the homage which Jesus offers to Thee upon the altar. What Jesus does, I intend to do likewise, in union with Him. I humble and prostrate myself before Thy Majesty; I adore Thee, in union with the humiliations of Jesus. What a joy for me to know that the blessed Jesus offers up to Thee for me an infinite honor and worship.

Then say the Hail Mary ten times, in the following manner:

Hail Mary, full of grace, the Lord is with thee, blessed art thou among women, and blessed is the fruit of thy womb, Jesus, *whom I offer to God in honor of His Divine Majesty.* Holy Mary, Mother of God, pray for us sinners, now, and at the hour of our death. Amen.

FROM THE GOSPEL TO THE ELEVATION.

Offer to the Heavenly Father His Son, our Lord Jesus Christ, in satisfaction for your sins, by saying the following

PRAYER.

BEHOLD, O my God, the traitor who has so often rebelled against Thee! Alas, with sorrow I hate and detest, with all the affections of my heart, my most grievous sins; and I offer Thee in satisfaction for them the satisfaction which Jesus gives Thee upon the Altar. I offer Thee all the merits of Jesus, the Blood of Jesus; Jesus, God and Man, Who, as a Victim, is sacrificing Himself again for me. Since upon the Altar my Jesus is my Mediator and my Advocate, by His most precious Blood He is imploring pardon for me. I unite myself to the voice of that loving Blood; and I ask mercy for all my most grievous sins. The Blood of Jesus cries to Thee for mercy; my broken heart also cries to Thee for mercy. Ah, my beloved God, if my tears move Thee not, let the groans of my

Jesus move Thee; and that mercy which He obtained for all mankind upon the Cross, why should He not obtain it for me upon the Altar? Yes, I hope that, in virtue of that most precious Blood, Thou wilt pardon me all my sins, which I will never cease to lament even to the last moment of my life.

Then, say again the Hail Mary ten times, and add after the word Jesus, "*whom I offer to God in satisfaction for all my sins, and for those of all the living and dead.*" Holy Mary, Mother, etc.

FROM THE ELEVATION TO THE COMMUNION.

Ask all kinds of blessings and graces of your Heavenly Father, by offering to Him the prayers and sufferings of His well-beloved Son, our Lord and Redeemer, Jesus Christ.

PRAYER.

MY beloved God, I acknowledge myself quite unworthy of Thy favors; I confess my exceeding unworthiness, and that for my many grievous sins, I do not deserve to be heard by Thee. But how canst Thou refuse to listen to Thy Divine Son, who upon the

Altar offers to Thee for me His prayers, together with His Blood and His Life? Hear, I beseech Thee, my most beloved God, the prayers of this my great Advocate, and for His sake grant me all the graces Thou knowest to be necessary for me to accomplish the great affair of my eternal salvation. And now I make bold to ask of Thee a general pardon for all my sins, the grace of final perseverance; moreover, I beg of Thee, O my God, trusting in the prayers of my Jesus, all virtues in an heroic degree, and all those efficacious helps which I require to become a saint. I also ask of Thee the conversion of all unbelievers, and of all sinners, and particularly of those who are related to me, either by ties of kindred, or spiritually; I ask of Thee the deliverance, not of one soul only, but of all the souls in purgatory. Bring them all forth, so that by the efficacy of this Divine sacrifice that prison of purification may become empty. Convert all sinners to Thee. May this miserable world become a paradise of delights for Thee, from which, after having loved, served, and praised Thee during our life, we may all come at length to praise and bless Thee for all eternity in heaven. Amen.

The Hail Mary ten times, and add after the word Jesus, "*whom I offer to God to obtain all the graces necessary to live and die in His friendship.*" Holy Mary, Mother, etc.

FROM THE COMMUNION TO THE END OF MASS.

Thank Almighty God for all His blessings by offering to Him all the thanksgivings of our Blessed Redeemer.

PRAYER.

BEHOLD me, my most beloved God, laden with blessings, general and particular, which Thou hast bestowed upon me, and which Thou wilt still bestow upon me, in time and in eternity. I acknowledge that Thy mercies towards me have been, and are, infinite: I am ready to pay Thee for them, even to the last farthing; wherefore, in gratitude and in payment for them, behold this Divine Blood, this most precious Body, this innocent Victim, which I present to Thee by the hands of the priest. I am sure that this offering which

I present to Thee is sufficient to pay Thee for all the gifts Thou hast bestowed upon me. This gift of infinite value is of itself worth all the gifts which I have ever received, or ever shall receive from Thee. Ye holy angels, and all ye blessed saints of heaven, oh, help me to thank my God, and offer to Him, in thanksgiving for His blessings to me, not only this mass, but all the masses which are at this moment celebrated through the whole world; so that His most loving beneficence may receive a complete recompense for all the favors which He has shown me, and which He will confer upon me forever and ever. Amen.

Say the Hail Mary ten times, and add after the word Jesus, "*whom I offer to God in thanksgiving for all His benefits.*" Holy Mary, Mother, etc.

DEVOTIONS FOR CONFESSION.

HOW TO PREPARE FOR CONFESSION.

I. ASK GOD TO HELP YOU.

O MY God, help me to make a good confession, to know my sins, and to be truly sorry for them, because they have offended Thee. Keep me from sin for the time to come. Help me that I may sincerely and humbly confess all my sins, and that I may keep back nothing in my heart. Hail Mary, etc. My dear Angel Guardian, to your care I am given, watch over me and help me. Come, O Holy Spirit, etc.

You may say also a decade of the Rosary.

II. EXAMINE YOUR CONSCIENCE.

READ over the following examination of conscience, and when you come to any sin that you have done, especially if it is a great one, try to find out *how many times* you did it, at least how many times each day, or week, or month. Sometimes in one action there are more sins than one. If a child strikes its parent, there are two sins, one against the fourth Commandment, and another against the fifth.

Examination of Conscience.

First Commandment.—1. Did I neglect to learn the four great truths, the Apostles' Creed, the Commandments of God and the Church, the Sacraments, and the Our Father and the Hail Mary?

2. Did I neglect to say my morning and night prayers?

3. Did I go to sermons or prayers in Protestant churches or Sunday-schools? Did I give scandal by it, or join with them in worship? Did I read Protestant books or tracts?

4. Did I wilfully doubt, deny, or disbelieve the Catholic faith, or speak against it?

5. Did I despair of God's help, or expect it without doing what He commands me?

6. Was I uncharitable to the poor? Did I

lead others into sin? Did I ask fortune-tellers, or those who use charms, signs, toss cups, cut cards, read bad books, about such things?

7. Did I behave ill in church, or to any holy thing or person? Did I neglect saying my penance? Did I receive any sacrament with bad dispositions?

How often did I commit each sin?

Second Commandment.—1. Did I speak ill of God, or the Saints, or what is sacred?

2. Did I curse? Was it from my heart, or with God's name, or the name of Jesus Christ?

3. Did I take an oath, in a lie, or to do what is sinful? Am I accustomed to swear?

Third Commandment.—1. Did I work on Sundays or Holy-days of Obligation without necessity?

2. Did I lose Mass on Sundays or Holy-days by my own neglect, or by playing, or talking during Mass?

3. Did I stay away from Sunday-school, catechism, etc.

Fourth Commandment.—1. Did I love and help my parents?

2. Did I strike them, or show disrespect to them, especially in their presence? Did I curse them, or call them bad names, especially in their hearing?

3. Was I disobedient to them? Was I disobedient to them in a great thing, for example, by going to dangerous company, stopping from school, or being idle there?

Fifth Commandment.—1. Did I make evil wishes on myself or on others? Did I make such wishes from my heart?

2. Did I quarrel with my neighbor, or hate him, or entertain revengeful feelings for him?

3. Did I do harm to the life or health of myself or another? Did I get drunk?

Sixth and Ninth Commandments.—1. Did I wilfully dwell on immodest thoughts and desires?

2. Was I immodest in my words, looks, actions, alone or with others, or with anything?

3. Did I go to bad company, to bad dancing-houses, etc.?

4. Did I keep dangerous company with persons of the other sex? Did I read or keep bad books, papers, etc.?

Seventh and Tenth Commandments.—1. Did I steal? How much and how often? Was it from rich or poor people, or the Church?

2. Did I help others to steal? Did I receive stolen things? Did I cheat any person? Did I injure others in their goods, or in any way? Did I restore to another what was his? Did I pay my debts when able? Did I break any agreement without just reason?

Eighth Commandment.—1. Did I tell lies? Did they do great harm?

2. Did I speak of the faults of others, or say of them what was not true, form rash judgments, or entertain unjust suspicions?

3. Did I use bad language to others, or read their letters, or cause quarrels by tale-bearing?

Commandments of the Church.

1. Did I break the abstinence or fast?

2. Did I neglect the Sacraments, or my Easter duties?

3. Was I in secret or forbidden societies?

4. Did I wilfully conceal a great sin in confession through shame?

For Married Persons.—Invalid marriages with relations, etc.—marrying in any way against the regulations of the Church—cruelty or bad behavior to one another—giving their affections to another—leaving one another without just cause—wasteful spending of money—wife not taking care of the household—a wrong or improper use of marriage—wife not obeying her husband in the lawful duties of marriage—anything which might scandalize children.—*How often?*

For Parents.—Care before and after birth—allowing children to be brought up in a false religion—cruelty to, or cursing them—putting brothers and sisters in the same bed—not sending them to a good school, but to Protestant or other schools forbidden by the priest—neglect about their baptism, or their prayers—not sending them when seven years old to confession, mass, or catechism—letting them say bad words, read bad books, go into bad company, play about the streets with any one, or keep dangerous company with persons of the other sex—not letting them follow their vocation to be nuns, etc.—without just reason hindering their marriage, or forcing them to marry.—*How often?*

For Masters and Mistresses.—Ill-treatment of servants—over-working them—not giving them food enough—not paying their wages—breaking the agreement—allowing them to commit sin, or go into bad company, or asking them to do what is sinful—letting them neglect their religious duties, mass, or the Sacraments.—*How often?*

III. CONTRITION.

YOU must detest your sins and be sorry for them, because you offended God by them. Also you must make up your mind not to sin any more, and to keep away from the places or people who led you into sin before, as the burnt child keeps away from the fire. This is contrition. Say, then, the following Acts of Contrition, and tell God how sorry you are for having offended Him.

Acts of Contrition.—O my God! I am heartily sorry for having offended Thee; I detest my sins most sincerely, because they displease Thee, my God, who art so deserving of all my love, for Thy infinite goodness and most amiable perfections; and I firmly purpose, by Thy holy grace, never more to offend Thee, and carefully to avoid all the occasions of sin.

O my God, I am very sorry that I have sinned against Thee, because Thou art so good, and I will not sin again.

O Jesus, my Creator, my Redeemer! I remember how Thou wert nailed to the hard Cross—how Thy poor head was torn by the sharp thorns—how the holy blood came from Thy blessed body. And why didst Thou suffer all these cruel pains? O Jesus, Thy blessed heart speaks to me, and tells me that Thou didst die a bitter death on the Cross for the love of me, Thy poor child, to wash away my sins with Thy blood, and to save me from hell. Yes, it was my sins which nailed Thee to the Cross, and made thee die. O wicked sins, I hate and detest you. My good Jesus, I love Thee, and I am sorry with all my heart for sinning against Thee, because Thou art so good, and I promise Thee with a sincere heart that I will never sin again; let me die rather than sin again. Jesus, have pity on my poor soul—Thou didst not turn away Thy face from those who struck it and spit upon it; wilt Thou turn away from a soul that wants to love Thee? O Jesus, think how much it cost Thee to save my soul—how Thou didst buy it with Thy own blood, and die for it, and now, when Thou needest not die any more to save me—when Thou hast only to say the word—I forgive you—wilt Thou refuse to forgive Thy poor repenting child? Wilt Thou refuse to save a soul which Thou didst die to save? No, my Jesus, Thy heart is too kind and too good to refuse me pardon. I hope, I am sure, Thou wilt pardon me.

Dear Mary, Mother of Jesus, speak to Jesus, and ask Him to have pity on me, and forgive me.

IV. CONFESSION.

1. When the child has said the Acts of Contrition it goes to the confessional, where the priest is. It kneels down. Then the child, when it sees that the priest is ready to hear it, makes the sign of the cross, saying, "*Bless me, Father, for I have sinned.*"

2. After this it says: "I confess to Almighty God, to Blessed Mary, ever Virgin, to Blessed Michael the Archangel, to Blessed John the Baptist, to the holy Apostles Peter and Paul, and to all the Saints, that I have sinned exceedingly in thought, word, and deed—through my fault—through my most grievous fault."

3. Then the child says: "*Since my last confession, which was a week or a month since* (the child tells how long it is since), *when I received absolution* (*or did not receive absolution*), *I accuse myself of* ——;" here the child tells each of its sins against the commandments of God or the Church. If the child committed a mortal sin, it must tell how many times it committed the mortal sin.

4. When the child has confessed all its sins, it says: "*For these, and all my other sins, which I cannot at present remember, I am heartily sorry, purpose amendment, and humbly beg pardon and absolution of you, my ghostly Father.*"

5. Then the child says: "Therefore I beseech the Blessed Mary, ever Virgin, Blessed Michael the Archangel, Blessed John the Baptist, the holy Apostles Peter and Paul, and all the Saints, to pray to the Lord God for me."

6. After this the child listens attentively to the advice the priest gives to it. It takes great notice what penance the priest gives.

7. Then, while the priest is giving it absolution, it makes another Act of Contrition, saying, "O my God, I am very sorry for having sinned against Thee, because Thou art so good, and I will not sin again."

When the child has done its confession, it goes away and returns thanks to God, and takes care afterwards to say its penance as soon as it can.

An Act of Thanksgiving.

"O my God, I thank Thee for Thy great mercy to me, a poor sinner, and I beg of Thee to strengthen my weakness, that I may never sin any more." Hail, Mary, etc.; or a decade of the Rosary.

OR,

O Jesus, how worthy art Thou of my love, and what thanks do I not owe! I hope that through the merits of Thy blood, Thou hast forgiven me my sins. For this I thank Thee with my whole heart, and I burn with the desire to praise Thy mercy in heaven through all eternity. Until now, O my God, I have offended Thee often, but for the time to come, I will never offend Thee again. I am anxious to change my life. Thou dost merit all my love, and therefore I will love Thee truly and dearly. I will never again be separated from Thee. I have already promised Thee rather to die than offend Thee again. Once more I make this promise, and hope through Thy mercy to keep it.

I promise also to shun the occasions of sin, and to take the following means to keep me from falling again (*here name the means*). But thou knowest my weakness, O my God. Give me Thy grace, that I may remain true unto Thee until my death, and teach me, in the hour of temptation, to have recourse to Thee. Mary, help me! Thou art the Mother of perseverance, I place my hopes in thee.

FAULTS IN MAKING A CONFESSION.

1. Children often talk with one another while they are getting ready for confession.

2. Some children are in a hurry to get to confession, and do not wait till their turn comes.

3. Some are very slow in confessing their sins. They tell one sin, then a long stop—a second sin, then another long stop—and so on. Thus they make the priest lose much time.

4. Some people confess their good works instead of confessing their sins.

5. Some people confess other people's sins instead of their own sins.

6. Some people waste a great deal of time by saying many useless words, and telling long histories. Instead of saying, "I stole such a thing," they will tell the name of every street they went through on their road, and such like useless things.

7. Others say, "I stole," but they do not tell what they stole; or, "I broke the commandments," but they do not say which commandment they broke.

8. Some do not try to tell the number of their mortal sins, not even whether they were often or seldom.

9. There are others who, when the priest is speaking to them and giving them good advice, do not attend to him, but are thinking whether they have any more sins to confess, and they do the same when they are even making the Act of Contrition.

10. Some, instead of *accusing* themselves, *excuse* themselves. They say, "I committed

such a sin, but somebody put me up to it;" or, "I cursed, but they took the curse out of me;" or, "I said angry words, but could not help it."

11. Sometimes, when there is a real excuse, which ought to be told, people will not tell it. They say, "I lost Mass on Sunday;" they leave out, "because I was sick;" or, "I ate meat on Friday," leaving out, "because I forgot it was Friday."

12. Some seem to think that they must always be running back again to the priest for every little thing they forgot in confession.

13. Children sometimes forget to do their penance. But the worst thing of all is, the concealment of sins, through fear or shame.

14. It is wrong for a child to listen to what other children confess, and it is worse to speak of what it has heard.

15. Some children sometimes tell other children what they are going to confess or have confessed.

16. Some mark with a lead pencil, in the table of sins, those faults of which they are guilty.

PREPARATION FOR COMMUNION.

Before you receive the most holy Sacrament of the body and blood of Jesus Christ, you must cleanse your conscience from every mortal sin by the sacrament of penance. You must fast from the midnight before. When the time for Holy Communion is come, go up to the altar respectfully, kneel down there, take the cloth into your hands and hold it before your breast, do not wipe your mouth with it, let your head be raised up, the eyes shut, the mouth open, the tongue forward and resting on the under lip. Shut your mouth after receiving the blessed sacrament, and when it is a little moistened on your tongue, swallow it. If it stops on the roof of your mouth, do not remove it with your hand, but with your tongue.

PRAYERS BEFORE HOLY COMMUNION.

By St. Alphonsus.

My beloved Jesus, true Son of God, Who didst die for me on the Cross in a sea of sorrows and ignominy, I firmly believe that Thou art present in the most Holy Sacrament; and for this faith I am ready to give my life.

My dear Redeemer, I hope by Thy goodness, and through the merits of Thy blood, that when Thou dost come to me this morning, Thou wilt inflame me with Thy holy love, and wilt give me all those graces which I need to keep me obedient and faithful to Thee till death.

Ah, my God, true and only Lover of my soul, what couldst Thou do more to oblige me to love Thee? Thou wert not satisfied, my Love, with dying for me, but Thou wouldst also institute the most Holy Sacrament, making Thyself my food, and giving Thyself all to me; thus uniting Thyself most closely to such a miserable and ungrateful creature. Thou dost Thyself invite me to receive Thee, and dost greatly desire that I should receive Thee. O infinite Love! A God gives Himself all to me! O my God, O infinite Love, worthy of infinite love, I love Thee above all things; I love Thee with all my heart; I love Thee more than myself, more than my life; I love Thee because Thou art worthy of being loved; and I love Thee also to please Thee, since Thou dost desire my love! Depart from my soul, all ye earthly affections; to

Thee alone, my Jesus, my Treasure, my All, will I give all my love. This morning Thou dost give Thyself all to me, and I give myself all to Thee. Permit me to love Thee; for I desire none but Thee, and nothing but what is pleasing to Thee. I love Thee, O my Saviour, and I unite my poor love to the love of all the angels and saints, and of Thy Mother Mary, and the love of Thy Eternal Father! Oh, that I could see Thee loved by all! Oh, that I could make Thee loved by all men, and loved as much as Thou dost deserve!

Behold, O my Jesus, I am now about to draw near to feed on Thy most sacred Flesh! Ah, my God, who am I? and Who art Thou? Thou art a Lord of infinite goodness, and I am a loathsome worm, defiled by so many sins, and who have driven Thee out of my soul so often.

Domine, non sum dignus. Lord, I am not worthy to remain in thy presence; I should be in hell for ever, far away, and abandoned by Thee. But out of Thy goodness Thou callest me to receive Thee: behold, I come, I come humbled and in confusion for the great displeasure I have given Thee, but trusting entirely to Thy mercy and to the love Thou hast for me. I am exceedingly sorry, O my loving Redeemer, for having so often offended Thee in time past! Thou didst even give Thy life for me; and I have so often despised Thy grace and Thy love, and have exchanged Thee for nothing. I repent, and am sorry with all my heart for every offence which I have offered Thee, whether grievous or light, because it was an offence against Thee, Who art infinite goodness. I hope Thou hast already pardoned me; but if Thou hast not yet forgiven me, pardon me, my Jesus, before I receive Thee. Ah, receive me quickly into Thy grace, since it is Thy will soon to come and dwell within me.

Come, then, my Jesus, come into my soul, which sighs after Thee. My only and infinite Good, my Life, my Love, my All, I would desire to receive Thee this morning with the same love with which those souls who love Thee most have received Thee, and with the same fervor with which Thy most holy Mother received Thee; to her communions I wish to unite this one of mine. O Blessed Virgin, and my Mother Mary, give me Thy Son;

I intend to receive Him from Thy hands! Tell Him that I am Thy servant, and thus will He press me more lovingly to His heart, now that He is coming to me.

PRAYERS AFTER COMMUNION.

By St. Alphonsus.

The time after communion is a precious time for gaining treasures of grace, because the acts and prayers made whilst the soul is thus united to Jesus Christ have more merit, and are of more value, than when they are made at any other time. St. Teresa says, that our Lord then dwells in the soul enthroned as on a mercy-seat, and speaks to it in these words: My child, ask of Me what you will; for this end am I come to you to do you good. Oh, what great favors do those receive who converse with Jesus Christ after communion! The Ven. F. Avila never omitted to remain two hours in prayer after communion; and St. Aloysius Gonzaga continued his thanksgiving for three days. Let the communicant, then, make the following acts, and try, during the rest of the day to go on making acts of love and prayer, in order to keep himself united to Jesus Christ, Whom he has received in the morning.

Behold, my Jesus, Thou art come, Thou

art now within me, and hast made Thyself all mine. Be Thou welcome, my beloved Redeemer. I adore Thee, and cast myself at Thy feet; I embrace Thee, I press Thee to my heart, and thank Thee for that Thou hast deigned to enter into my breast. O Mary, O my patron saints, O my guardian angel, do you all thank Him for me! Since, then, O my divine King, Thou art come to visit me with so much love, I give Thee my will, my liberty, and my whole self. Thou hast given Thyself all to me, I will give myself all to Thee; I will no longer belong to myself; from this day forward I will be Thine, and altogether Thine. I desire that my soul, my body, my faculties, my senses, should be all Thine, that they may be employed in serving and pleasing Thee. To Thee I consecrate all my thoughts, my desires, my affections, and all my life. I have offended Thee enough, my Jesus; I desire to spend the remainder of my life in loving Thee, Who hast loved me so much.

Accept, O God of my soul, the sacrifice which I, a miserable sinner, make to Thee, and who desires only to love and please Thee. Work Thou in me, and dispose of me, and of all things belonging to me, as Thou pleasest. May Thy love destroy in me all those affections which are displeasing to Thee, that I may be all Thine, and may live only to please Thee!

PRAYER TO BE SAID EVERY DAY, TO OBTAIN THE GRACES NECESSARY FOR SALVATION.

ETERNAL Father, Thy Son has promised that Thou wilt grant us all the graces which we ask Thee for in His name. In the name, therefore, and by the merits of Jesus Christ, I ask the following graces for myself and for all mankind. And first, I pray Thee to give me a lively faith in all that the holy Roman Church teaches me. Enlighten me also, that I may know the vanity of the goods of this world, and the immensity of the infinite good that Thou art; make me also see the deformity of the sins I have committed, that I may humble myself and detest them as I ought; and, on the other hand, show me how worthy Thou art by reason of Thy goodness, that I should love Thee with all my heart. Make me know also the love Thou hast borne me, that from this day forward I may try to be grateful for so much goodness. Secondly, give me a firm confidence in Thy mercy of receiving the pardon of my sins, holy perseverance, and finally, the glory of paradise, through the merits of Jesus Christ and the intercession of Mary. Thirdly, give me a great love towards Thee, which shall detach me from the love of this world and of myself, so that I may love none other but Thee, and that I may neither do nor desire anything else but what is for Thy glory. Fourthly, I beg of Thee a perfect resignation to Thy will, in accepting with tranquillity sorrows, infirmities, contempt, persecutions, aridity of spirit, loss of property, of esteem, of relations, and every other cross which shall come to me from Thy hands. I offer myself entirely to Thee, that Thou mayest do with me and all that belongs to me what Thou pleasest; do Thou only give me light and strength to do

Thy will; and especially at the hour of death help me to sacrifice my life to Thee with all the affection I am capable of, in union with the sacrifice which Thy Son Jesus Christ made of His life on the Cross on Calvary. Fifthly, I beg of Thee a great sorrow for my sins, which may make me grieve over them as long as I live, and weep for the insults I have offered Thee, the Sovereign Good, Who art worthy of infinite love, and Who hast loved me so much. Sixthly, I pray Thee to give me the spirit of true humility and meekness, that I may accept with peace, and even with joy, all the contempt, ingratitude, and ill-treatment that I may receive. At the same time I also pray Thee to give me perfect charity, which shall make me wish well to those who have done evil to me, and to do what good I can, at least by praying, for those who have in any way injured me. Seventhly, I beg of Thee to give me a love for the virtue of holy mortification, by which I may chastise my rebellious senses, and cross my self-love; at the same time, I beg Thee to give me holy purity of body, and the grace to resist all bad temptations, by ever having recourse to Thee and Thy most holy Mother. Give me grace faithfully to obey my spiritual father and all my superiors in all things. Give me an upright intention, that in all I desire and do I may seek only Thy glory, and to please Thee alone. Give me a great confidence in the Passion of Jesus Christ, and in the intercession of Mary immaculate. Give me a great love towards the most Adorable Sacrament of the Altar, and a tender devotion and love to Thy holy Mother. Give me, I pray Thee above all, holy perseverance, and the grace always to pray for it, especially in time of temptation and at the hour of death.

Lastly, I recommend to Thee the holy souls of Purgatory, my relations and benefactors; and in an especial manner I recommend to Thee all those who hate me or who have in any way offended me; I beg of Thee to render them good for the evil they have done, or may wish to do me. Finally, I recommend to Thee all infidels, heretics, and all poor sinners; give them light and strength to deliver themselves from sin. Oh, most loving

God, make Thyself known and loved by all, but especially by those who have been more ungrateful to Thee than others, so that by Thy goodness I may come one day to sing Thy mercies in paradise; for my hope is in the merits of Thy blood, and in the patronage of Mary. O Mary, Mother of God, pray to Jesus for me! So I hope; so may it be!

PRAYER TO CONSECRATE ONESELF TO THE BLESSED VIRGIN.

Most holy Virgin Mary, Mother of God, I, N. N., although most unworthy of being thy servant, nevertheless, moved by thy wonderful compassion, and by a desire to serve thee, choose thee this day, in presence of my angel guardian, and of all the heavenly court, for my special lady, advocate, and mother; and I firmly resolve to serve thee always, and to do everything in my power to make others serve thee also. I beseech thee, then, most merciful mother, by the blood of thy Son, which was shed for me, to take me into the number of thy clients as thy servant for ever. Protect me in my actions, and obtain for me grace so to measure my thoughts, words, and works, that I may never offend thy most pure eyes, nor those of thy Divine Son Jesus. Remember me, and abandon me not at the hour of my death.

www.ingramcontent.com/pod-product-compliance
Lightning Source LLC
LaVergne TN
LVHW021309110826
845150LV00003B/527
* 9 7 8 1 4 2 5 5 5 8 2 3 9 *